A PICTURESQUE TOUR ALONG THE RIVERS GANGES AND JUMNA, IN INDIA

A PICTURESQUE TOUR ALONG THE RIVERS GANGES AND JUMNA, IN INDIA

Foreword by

Prof. Lokesh Chandra

NIYOGI BOOKS

This book is a collaborative effort between the
NATIONAL ARCHIVES OF INDIA and NIYOGI BOOKS

Published by
NIYOGI BOOKS
D-78, Okhla Industrial Area, Phase-I
New Delhi-110 020, INDIA
Tel: 91-11-26816301, 49327000
Fax: 91-11-26810483, 26813830
email: niyogibooks@gmail.com
website: www.niyogibooksindia.com

ISBN: 978-93-83098-72-9
Publication: 2015

Printed at: Niyogi Offset Pvt. Ltd., New Delhi, India.

Contents

Foreword

A work that reminds of the caravan of wanderings through history's paths, and how the sun of human development over two centuries has driven away the gloom of life, eventually opening up resplendence. This memoir chronicles a sparse population, structures shattered by time, and roving officials of the British Crown trying to comprehend the mysteries of the vast land of India with its divine dignity conversing with ruins of imposing architectural buildings. Lt Col. Forrest made coloured drawings of ancient monuments on the spot to see the beauty of their inner form beyond what is seen by the bodily eye. These twenty-four coloured views are reproduced in the depth of 19th century etchings and give us a glimpse of India as it once was in the mists of time. The author wanted to excite the interest of the British people in the "manners of that wonderful empire" from "its gradual rise to a splendour rarely attained by nations, and thence to its sad and disastrous decline and downfall". The brief survey of the history of India is an inspiration as well as a challenge to introspect and to carve out a glorious destiny. Some facts given by Forrest have become obsolete, but the work as a whole summons us to a journey into creativity and to selfhood. The ancient shores have to scintillate in modern waves.

The splendid plates of Hindu temples and villages on the holy banks of Ganga, Murshidabad the capital of mediaeval Bengal, or mountains of Rajmahal where they descend to the Ganga, or the Fall of Pearls in the Rajmahal hills, are all part of Forrester's "tour of Ganga and Yamuna". Ganga is mentioned in the Rigveda, but she assumes great sanctity in the Purāṇas. She is the daughter of Himavat and Menā and the mother of the Eight Vasus who are personifications of natural phenomena and the elements: *Pratyūsha* "light", *Prabhāsa* "dawn", *Dhruva* "Pole Star", *Soma* "Moon", *Anila* "wind", *Anala* "fire", *Dhava* "earth" and *Āpah* "water". The water of the Ganga is elixir and a bath in it purifies one of sins. The Ganga-Yamuna confluence in the Sangam at Prayaga (Allahabad) is where the relics of every Hindu find their final rest. The account of Forrester subsumes that the control of this basin of the two rivers with its large population enabled the British to contend against the French and raise the Empire. The symbol Ganga-Yamuna appears as an architectural motif in early Gupta temples at Bhumara (4th century AD) and on their coins. Both rivers were enshrined as goddesses by the Rastrakutas, Eastern Chalukyas, Gajapatis of Orissa, in Vijayanagara and Andhra Pradesh. Lt. Col. Forrest has gathered pearls from the shorelines of history in his evocative etchings where we hear a song that transcends the forgotten. In the etchings we refresh the mindscape, the silence of the landscape, to resume our interrupted journey, enlivened by new echos vibrating with life, lightening the shadows and silences, in interaction between technological progress and socio-cultural inheritance.

This book is an engrossing account of the mediaeval period of Indian history and given a racy idea of the storm of attacks, plunders, dreadful massacres, internecine conflicts of the princes to grab power, the magnificent regalia of the Lucknow monarchs, the amazing distances, the daring and active spirit of the English that inspired its merchants to establish direct trade with India leading to the British Raj: an evocative and spell-binding account of the Islamic and East India Company periods. Lt. Col Forrest recounts his picturesque tour in equally striking words and we become his fellow travellers from Calcutta to Agra where he is entranced by the Taj Mahal "this wonder of the world". He left Calcutta on 2 December 1807, and drew his first art work of a Hindu temple below Barrackpore on the expansive bosom of the Ganga. Passed a night on the celebrated battlefield of Plassy where Lord Clive totally defeated the Nawab of Murshidabad. About to enter Bihar, he recalls this wonderfully fertile tract as Prasii (Prāchi in Sanskrit) and Gangaridae of the Greek historians. He is impressed by "the grandeur of the appearance which the city of Benares exhibits as seen from the river in its solemn sanctity". He is on his way to Allahabad, ranked equally with Benares, where mingle the mighty bulk of waters of the great rivers of Ganga and Yamuna and the subterranean Sarasvati. He is in Kannauj whose ancient opulence and splendour has passed away like the traces of a dream. Thence to Kanpur the headquarters of the Field-command in Bengal. At the Surseya bathing ghat on the Ganga River he is bewitched by the dripping garments of the ladies emerging from a sacred bath: "India's daughters, rising thus like Naiads of the flood from the bosom of their adored river, their finely wove simple garb, ... clinging closely to their figure, exhibit a symmetry of form which might fairly vie with the Medicean". At Agra, he looks with wonder "the stupendous and noble fortress" of Akbar, and reminds us that it is mentioned by Ptolemy as *Agara*. He speaks of Akbar's dazzling scenes of martial glory and the magnificence of his palaces. Akbar wanted to change the name of Agra to Akbarabad but that was not to be. The tour of Forrester closes "with the description of this wonder of the world", the Taj. This book is a "must read" to feel the silent footsteps of the British might taking over and their wonderment at the historic splendour of our centuries. Little did they know that the darkness of foreign rule will one day see Light and they would have led us to a world of new concepts of power and polity. In the years to come this creative leap will whisper in our deeds: "I am a drop of nectar with tomorrows inside."

New Delhi
January 2015

Lokesh Chandra

A

PICTURESQUE TOUR

ALONG THE

RIVERS GANGES AND JUMNA,

IN INDIA:

CONSISTING OF

TWENTY-FOUR HIGHLY FINISHED AND COLOURED VIEWS, A MAP, AND VIGNETTES,

FROM ORIGINAL DRAWINGS MADE ON THE SPOT;

WITH

ILLUSTRATIONS, HISTORICAL AND DESCRIPTIVE.

By Lieutenant-Colonel FORREST,

LATE ON THE STAFF OF HIS MAJESTY'S SERVICE IN BENGAL.

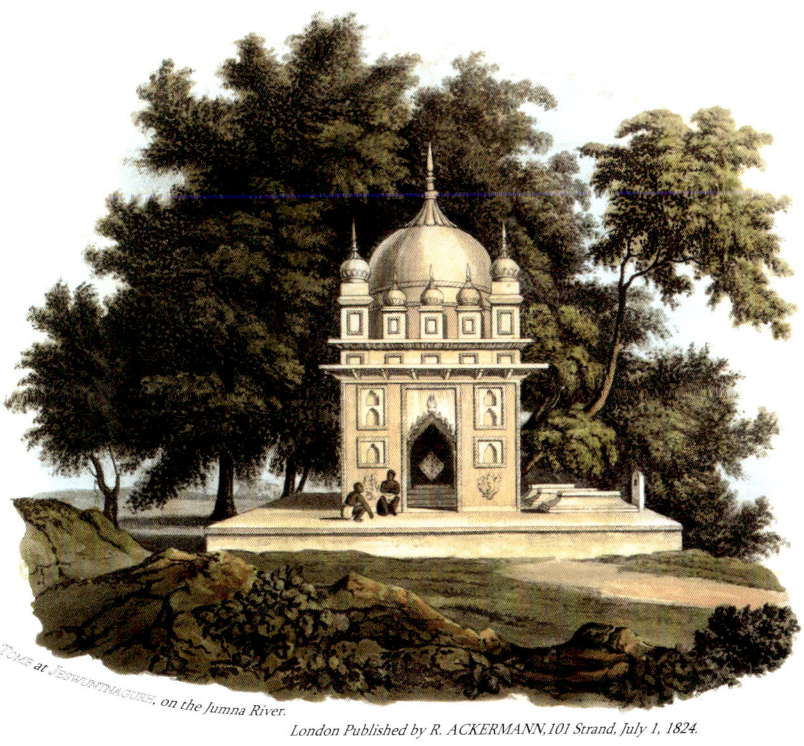

Tomb at Jeswuntnagurh, on the Jumna River.

London Published by R. ACKERMANN, 101 Strand, July 1, 1824.

PREFACE.

IT is with some feeling of diffidence that the author of the following pages ventures to submit to the notice of the British public this his first effort. He trusts, however, to that indulgent consideration and that encouraging approbation which, on all occasions, distinguish his countrymen in their judgment on works of science or of art.

It was thought advisable by the author, with the view to excite the attention and increase the interest of such of his readers as are little acquainted with India, to give a correct but very compressed sketch of the history, customs, and manners of that wonderful empire. In this he has passed over no one event of importance, from its first origin in the gloomy clouds of superstition, through its gradual rise to a splendour rarely attained by nations, and thence to its sad and disastrous decline and downfall. It is therefore hoped that the following pages will be found to comprise a connected and satisfactory detail, extracted with much attention and labour from the best and most esteemed authorities, containing in its essence the matter of many large volumes.

With respect to the picturesque description of the Tour, the author can with perfect confidence appeal to those who have passed through the same scenes.

The drawings were all attentively copied from nature, and in many instances coloured on the spot, and always while the magic effects of the scenes represented were still impressed on his mental vision. The reader will recollect with indulgence, that the colouring of the views, which so far exceeds that of the scenery of Europe, is but a just portrait of the enchanting features of India, eternally glowing in the brilliant glory of the resplendent Asiatic sun.

DIRECTIONS FOR PLACING THE PLATES.

Picturesque Tour

ALONG THE

GANGES AND JUMNA.

BRIEF SURVEY OF THE HISTORY OF INDIA.

THE more closely we pry into, and the more intimate we become with, the wonderful and enchanting country of Hindoostan and India at large, the more we must feel convinced, that in no part of the world have so many and such awful changes occurred, no where have such torrents of human blood been shed, or such great and wonderful revolutions been so frequently experienced. India is a field on which have been accumulated the largest armies, the greatest mass of force the world perhaps has ever witnessed; where the most dreadful and awful struggles have taken place, and the most astonishing results arisen.

The strong and singularly marked features of its soil and surface; the peculiarly striking character of its inhabitants, in manners, customs, and religion; the grand and majestic rivers, which, by their annual inundations, spread fertility through its numerous and rich plains and valleys; the masses of stupendous mountains giving birth to these streams, rearing their summits, clad in everlasting snow, far above the clouds, to an elevation which no other chain on earth attains: these and a thousand other traits, which the eye of the attentive observer will contemplate in this interesting country, excite a deep and intense feeling in the heart. Strengthened by recollection, time effaces not, weakens not its impressions: it serves rather to blend and unite them in the memory; conjuring up, as an ecstatic dream, all of grand, soft, brilliant, and interesting which the eye has wandered over, or the soul felt, in traversing its wonderful and mysterious beauties.

The early ages of Indian history are so obscured by fable, and so involved in superstitious gloom, that no probable conjectures can be formed on this head. The Hindoos, in common with most of the Eastern nations, consider the world as much more ancient than the Mosaic account records; and they cite a long list of sovereigns as having swayed the sceptre of India some thousand years previous to the invasion of the Punjab by Alexander the Great, when he planted his standards within a short distance of the frontiers of India on the banks of the Rauvee river, the Hydraotes of the Greeks, one of the five streams which, uniting their waters, form the Indus or Nilab.

The people of Hindoostan have, as far back as any authentic records exist, been divided into several principal tribes or casts; and these again subdivided into smaller branches, many of which are prohibited to intermingle by marriage; and some of the higher casts would subject themselves, by the mere touch of the inferior, to the severest penalties, and even to the loss of cast altogether, which reduces them to a state resembling that of an outlaw, and to which a Hindoo would far prefer death itself.

The minute and intricate system of this division into casts has never been accurately ascertained, and learning has declined so much amongst the Brahmins, that even they, to whom the treasures of science and literature were alone laid open, appear to have very vague and indistinct ideas of the origin or motives of those ordinances, which their forefathers, many centuries ago, instituted. These, uttered in the spirit, have been received and acted upon in the letter, and in process of time so veiled and obscured by superstition, as to form a strange compound of ignorance and bigotry (the Brahmin of the present day), little calculated to excite any other feeling than contempt for this sect, once the highest and most sacred of their casts. It will here perhaps be satisfactory to the reader, who may possibly not be much acquainted with the ancient history of India, to give a hasty glance at the most remote periods, the events of which have been handed down; without, however, any other authority than that of an ancient Hindoo poem, translated into Persian by the orders of Acber Shah, when he sat upon the throne of Hindoostan.

According to this poem, entitled the ***Maha Barit***, or Great War, India, about five thousand years ago, was united in one empire under ***Krishen***, whose posterity reigned over the Indians for four hundred years; but little is known of this race of monarchs, except that they held their court in the city of Oude.

Maharaja, descended from a female of the royal house of Krishen, and his family, who all bore the same name, enjoyed the throne of India for seven hundred years. Learning flourished under him, and he is said to have been the first who divided the Indians into tribes or casts. At the close of this dynasty, an invasion of Hindoostan by a Persian army took place: the war on this occasion lasted ten years.

B.C.

Kisroo Raja mounted the throne about this period: the island of Ceylon 1429.
was said to have been conquered by him. His posterity reigned over India for two hundred and twenty years, and their capital was Oude.

Ferosera's dynasty comprehended one hundred and thirty-seven years. 1209.
During his reign there was a second invasion by the Persians, who conquered
the country, and placed on the throne of it ***Suraja***, who with his family reigned 1072.
two hundred and eighty-six years. The great city of Cannouge, so long the capital of Hindoostan, was built by one of the Surajas, on the banks of the Ganges: its walls are said to have been nearly one hundred miles in circumference.

Bahrajah reigned thirty-six years, and built the city of Barage.

Keidar, who deposed Bahrajah, was himself deposed in the nineteenth year of his reign, and put to death by

Sinkol, a warlike and magnificent prince. He rebuilt the capital of Bengal, celebrated under the name of Lucknowti and Goura, which is said to have been the chief city of that province for two thousand years.

B.C.
731. In the third Persian invasion of Hindoostan with 100,000 men, Sinkol was defeated and dethroned, and his son

Rohata ascended the throne. From this period, the descendants of Sinkol held the sceptre of India eighty-one years, and his family then became extinct. After violent commotions,

586. ***Mahraja,*** a Rajpoot chief, mounted the throne. He was contemporary with Hystaspes, the father of Darius, and reigned forty years.

546. ***Keda Rajah,*** nephew to the last sovereign, succeeded him, and reigned forty-three years.

503. ***Jei Chund,*** general of the army, mounted the throne, and reigned sixty years. His son succeeded him, but was deposed by

443. ***Delu,*** a prince of great bravery and generosity. He built the city of Dehli, and was afterwards deposed by

Phoor, a prince of his own family, and imprisoned in Rhotasgurh. He was succeeded by his son, named also ***Phoor,*** in whose reign Alexander the Great invaded India, and Phoor was defeated by him or some of his generals near Sirhind.

Sunsarchund and his son successively sat upon the throne of India for seventy years.

The enterprising Alexander is said to have himself advanced in his projected invasion of Hindoostan no farther than the Rauvee river, the ancient Hydraotes of the Greeks, on which the city of Lahore is situated, and which is the centre stream of five, having their sources in the mountains to the north-west of India, and, from various points, flowing through a rich and fine country, called the Punj-ab, or country of the five rivers, at present occupied by the manly and independent nation of the Sickhs. These five streams form, in uniting their waters, the Nilab or Indus.

A spirit of discontent exhibited itself so universally throughout the Grecian army of Alexander, occasioned possibly by the hardships the troops had undergone, and the length of their march, that their commander, at the very moment when India appeared within his grasp, had the mortification to perceive, that his ambitious designs were frustrated, that his gigantic plans of conquest were paralized, and that his safety, and that of his army, depended upon a speedy and immediate retreat across the Indus.

B.C.
This event occurred in the 323d year before the birth of Christ. 323.

The sovereigns of Hindoostan after the invasion of Alexander were,

Jona, who paid tribute to Arsaces king of Persia. He and his posterity 260.
reigned peaceably at Cannouge for ninety years.

Callian Chund was on the throne about this period. He was a tyrannical 170.
and cruel prince, and was at length dethroned. After him there was no regular successor to the crown, every prince and rajah aiming at independence, and nothing worthy of notice is recorded until the time of

A.D.
Bikir Majit, who is represented as one of the greatest characters that ever 89.
filled the throne. He reigned many years, and fell in battle.

Hindoostan again relapsed into confusion and anarchy, but ***Raji Boga*** in a manner held the sovereign power for fifty years.

Basdeo succeeded him, and mounted the throne at Cannouge, and, with his 330.
family, reigned for eighty years.

Ramdeo, a great prince, followed, and reigned fifty-four years.

A. D.
500. ***Pertaub Chund,*** a tyrannical prince, at whose death India declined in power. The name of ***rajah*** became extinct, and that of ***rana*** was substituted.

Annindeo succeeded, and reigned sixteen years. During his reign one ***Maldeo*** raised himself to great power, and took the city of Dehli, and soon afterwards that of Cannouge, and reigned forty years. The name of universal empire fell with him.

977. ***Subáctági,*** who this year mounted the throne of Ghasni, at the close of the first year of his reign invaded and ravaged Cabul and the Punjab. In a great battle between the Ghasnians and Hindoos, the latter were defeated with great loss.

997. Subáctági died, and was buried at Ghasni.

1000. ***Ismael,*** second son of the late king, succeeded; but was soon defeated and put in prison by his elder brother, ***Mahmood.***

About this period, and not long after Mahmood ascended the throne of Ghasni, that enterprising, ambitious, and able commander turned his thoughts to India, to carry into that country the Mahomedan faith, and overthrow and exterminate the idolatrous worship of its inhabitants. Thus urged by what he considered a religious duty, and equally, no doubt, incited by the immense riches which the enterprise promised him, he levied an army of 10,000 cavalry, and commenced his march. Jeipal, prince of Lahore, a country to the eastward of the Indus river, and forming part of the Punjab district, opposed the invader with a force of 12,000 horse, 30,000 foot, and 300 elephants of war. An action took place on 8th Mohurrum, in which the latter was totally defeated and taken prisoner. On his neck were found sixteen rows of precious stones, valued at 22,000*l.* sterling each.

Urged by the most fanatic phrenzy to extend the Mahomedan faith over the rich and fertile plains of India, hitherto undisturbed by foreign aggression, these enterprising warriors, eager for plunder, rushed like an impetuous torrent, carrying slaughter and destruction from the frontier of Thibet (where they made their irruption) into the very heart of the empire.

Mahmood retired with his plunder, but it was only to repeat, in a short time, his first aggression. A third expedition was undertaken by him in the year 1004, in which Mooltan, the capital of the province of Sinde, was taken. In 1008, a fourth invasion of the Punjab took place: the prince of that country appealed to, and was joined by, the principal rajahs of Hindoostan, and an immense but ill-disciplined force was collected. But the discipline of the Mahomedans prevailed; the contest was obstinate and most bloody; and it is stated in the histories of this period, that upwards of twenty thousand Hindoos perished in the pursuit alone. The plunder captured by Mahmood's army was immense, and is said to have loaded above thirty elephants with precious treasures.

In 1009, Gaur, a principality famed for its antiquity, and also for its warlike population of the Afghan tribe, was invaded, and, after a short struggle, submitted likewise to the insatiable Mahmood. In a sixth expedition into Hindoostan, Panniput, a revered and sacred city of the Hindoos, and Dehli, the capital of the Soubah of that name, were taken possession of, sacked and destroyed.

The latter is an ancient city, founded, according to the historian of India, Ferishtah, about 400 years before the birth of Christ, by Delu, who seized upon the throne. It is believed, by the ancient records, to have been built upon the site of a town called Indriput. After Cannouge was destroyed, Dehli became the capital of Hindoostan, and has continued so to the present day, through all the various changes and revolutions it has experienced.

Prompted by his wonderful success, and the immense plunder of which he had possessed himself, Mahmood marched, in 1016, on his eighth expedition to Hindoostan, with an army of 100,000 horse and 30,000 foot. His object on this occasion was Cannouge, then the first in consequence, and the richest city of India.

Sinkol, one of the kings, brought into the field, on one occasion, 4000 war-elephants, 100,000 cavalry, and 400,000 foot. This is not a large force when we reflect on the vast population of Hindoostan. Even Timour Shah had at one time 900,000 men in the field.

Mahmood's route was by the mountains of Thibet to the north of Cashmere. An immense horde of light cavalry preceded his march, ravaging the country as they passed. Merut, a principal city of the Dooab (a district of the two rivers Ganges and Jumna), first fell into his hands. Muttra soon after experienced the like fate; and thence moving on Cannouge, with the sudden and overpowering impetuosity of an angry torrent, he reached this wonderful and rich capital so unexpectedly, that no effectual resistance could be opposed. This city, at that period the capital of Hindoostan, and which is said to have occupied an area one hundred miles in circuit, and whose remnants of shapeless ruins, at this remote period, give a sanction to this assertion, by their vast and almost boundless extent, was overthrown, plundered, and annihilated. Its rich and superb pagodas, or temples of Hindoo worship, containing inestimable wealth, shared the same fate; the most revered images of divinities, venerated from time immemorial, were disgraced and destroyed; and the wretched natives massacred by millions, or forced (it was their only alternative) to embrace the religion of their cruel oppressors.

A tenth invasion, in 1022, was undertaken by this restless marauder, in which an unsuccessful attack upon Cashmere stung him with rage and disappointment; passions which urged him to revenge himself on Lahore, which was given up, undefended, to the merciless plunder of his troops.

Mahmood's eleventh expedition was directed against Gualior, a hill-fort and almost impregnable fortress in the heart of Hindoostan, eighty miles south of Agra, and one hundred and thirty west of the Ganges. The timely submission, and large and splendid presents of the rajah, saved it this time; and Callinger was spared on the same terms.

His twelfth and last invasion of India was in the year 1024, when the magnificent and highly celebrated temple of Sumnaut, in the province of Guzzerat, was sacked and overthrown. It was situated near Diu, lately in the hands of the Portuguese. The plunder here was immense; the opposition obstinate, madly and superstitiously frantic, but unsuccessful.

Mahmood lived not to pursue farther plans of conquest and slaughter. After his return to Ghasni, his health declined, and he died, aged sixty-three, in the 1030th year of the Christian era.

The several successors to the throne of Mahmood were destitute of the vigour and enterprising spirit which he possessed; and we consequently find, in a list of the sovereigns of Ghasni and India, that from the death of Mahmood, fourteen of this dynasty successively filled the throne, few of whom died natural deaths; and there appears, with few exceptions, a series of usurpations, dethronements, and assassinations, highly disgusting, and which present an afflicting picture of the dreadful state to which this portion of India was reduced by its intestine divisions, the weakness of its government, and the folly and imbecility of its rulers.

With the deposition of ***Chusero II.*** driven from his throne by ***Mahommed Gauri,*** ended the dynasty of Ghasni and Dehli. The dynasty of Gauri, in the person of ***Mahommed Gauri,*** succeeded. He reigned thirty-two years, and has been considered one of the wisest and best of its princes that ever ascended the musnud of Hindoostan. But neither his virtues nor his talents could save him from assassination in 1205.

To Mahommed Gauri succeeded a favourite of his, a slave, of the name of ***Cuttub,*** who had held the most important trusts under his late master. These sovereigns assumed the title of kings of Dehli. Cuttub reigned four years, and died A. D. 1210.

Eldoze, another favourite of Mahommed Gauri's, succeeded, reigned nine years, and died in prison, 1219.

A. D.
1220. *Aram*, son of Eldoze, mounted his father's throne; but proved so unfit to rule, that he was deposed by the Omrahs of his kingdom; and *Altumsh*, son-in-law of Cuttub, was called by them to the throne, and reigned one year.

Altumsh was an enterprising, able, and virtuous prince. In the year 1231, he marched with a force to the attack of the fort of Gualior, which he captured; thence he led his army towards Malwa, and took the city of Ougein, where he destroyed a large and celebrated Hindoo temple. He reigned twenty-six years, and died at Dehli, 1235.

Ferose I. son of the late king, succeeded. He was an indolent and voluptuous prince, and gave up the reins of government to his mother, a wicked and cruel woman. He was dethroned, and died in prison, having reigned only six months.

Sultana Rizia, eldest daughter of Altumsh, a woman of considerable political talent, was called to the throne. Her conduct was wise and politic: still disturbances arose in the distant provinces of the empire. She marched at the head of her army, and reduced to obedience the viceroy of Lahore. In a second expedition of the same nature, against the governor of Tiberhind, her army revolted and forced her to return, when she was deposed by the Omrahs, who chose for her successor her brother, a son of Altumsh, named

1239. *Byram II.* By his ill management he disgusted the people, and they rebelled against him. The vizier of the empire headed the insurrection, and besieged Byram in Dehli, of which city he at length got possession, as also of
1242. the person of the king, who was thrown into prison, and there assassinated,

after reigning only two years and a month. In this reign the Moguls, under Gengis Khan, invaded and plundered Lahore.

Massud IV. son of Ferose, the late emperor, who had been some time in confinement, was taken from a prison to be placed on the throne. He soon gave himself up to every excess and extravagance, and became cruel, unjust, and oppressive. His subjects thereupon revolted, and called Mahmood his uncle to their aid: he immediately advanced, and was received as king. Massud
was deposed, and thrown into prison, where he ended his days, after a reign of A.D. 1246.
four years and one month.

Mahmood II. the youngest son of the emperor Altumsh, was a child when his father died. He was kept in confinement by the cruel empress, till Massud bestowed on him the government of Barage. He evinced talent and virtue, and rendered his province happy and flourishing. In 1257, a Mogul army having crossed the Indus, the king took the field; but the enemy, who had some time occupied the country on the opposite side of the Indus, retired at his approach. A.D. 1259, an ambassador from the king of Persia arrived at Dehli. He was met by the vizier with 50,000 horse, 200,000 infantry, 2000 elephants of war, and 3000 carriages of fire-works. These drew up in order of battle, and performed some evolutions, when the vizier conducted the Persian to his emperor. His reception was very magnificent; five princes of Persian Irac, who had fled from Gengis Khan's tyranny, were present, and several Indian tributary princes stood also near the throne of Mahmood. The emperor fell sick, and after a long illness died, A.D. 1265.

Balin, the vizier of the late emperor, ascended the throne by the unanimous desire of the people: he proved a magnificent prince. All the princes of the East whom Gengis Khan had expelled from their dominions, were received and supported in splendour by Balin. He was the great patron of learning, and some

of the most able men, both philosophers, poets, and others in Asia, were invited to Dehli, and entertained by him. In 1279, an insurrection broke out in Bengal: two armies were sent by Balin to check it, but both were defeated. The emperor then marched with a third, and reduced the rebels to obedience. Balin
A.D. 1286. reigned twenty-two years, and died in his eighty-second year.

Kei Kobad, grandson of Balin, who succeeded him, proved a weak, effe-
1289. minate, and luxurious prince, and was assassinated. During this reign the conquest of China was completed by the descendants of Gengis Khan.

Ferose II. an avaricious tyrant, mounted the throne, and changed the imperial umbrella from ***red*** to ***white***. He was assassinated by his general, 1295.

Alla I. proved a valiant and magnificent prince, but ferocious and sanguinary: he extended his conquests into the Deccan. Two years afterwards, one of the Mogul generals, Cutulich, son of the king of Maver-ul-nere, invaded Hindoostan with 200,000 horse, and drove every thing before him towards Dehli. The whole population of the country crowding into the city, in a short time produced a famine. The king therefore led his army forth to meet the Moguls. It consisted of 300,000 horse, 2700 war-elephants, and infantry innumerable. He found the Moguls in position on the plain beyond the suburbs of Dehli, and Alla immediately formed his troops in order of battle. Never since the first invasion of Hindoostan by the Mahomedans had two such mighty armies been opposed. The troops of Punjab, Sind, and Mooltan, under Ziffer (a great general), were on the right. The king had in the centre a corps of 12,000 chosen men. With the finest elephants he formed an imposing line in his front, and a reserve of cavalry under the vizier was in his rear. The corps of Ziffer commenced the attack, and completely routed the Moguls at the first charge; but pursuing too eagerly, and being unsupported, the enemy rallied, and attacking Ziffer in their turn, overwhelmed his force, and nearly annihilated it, himself being killed. The Moguls, however, retired after this, and did not stop till they again reached their own country. In 1303, Alla ordered the fort of Dehli to be pulled down and rebuilt. In the subsequent years of his reign, he invaded the Deccan four different times, purely for the sake of plundering it. Among the treasure and immense wealth brought from thence, were 312 elephants, 20,000 horses, and 96,000 maunds of pure gold, besides chests of jewels and pearls, and other precious things. The gold alone was worth one hundred millions of English money. Alla died in 1316, of vexation at a violent insurrection which arose in the southern provinces. In his reign Hindoostan was in A. D. 1316. the zenith of its glory.

Omar, the youngest son of Alla, was placed on the throne at seven years of age by the intrigues of Cafoor, one of Alla's generals, who hoped to reign in his name. To secure Omar on the musnud, he caused the eyes of his two elder brothers to be put out. The third brother, Mubaric, was brought to Dehli for the same inhuman purpose; but Cafoor's designs being discovered, he was assassinated, and Mubaric raised to the throne.

Mubaric I. This prince deposed his brother Omar, after a reign of three months, deprived him of his sight, and confined him in the fortress of Gualior. His next act was to put to death those who had been instrumental in placing him on the throne. He then, as if to obliterate this cruel deed, released all prisoners in his empire, and plunged into dissipation; and the court too soon followed his example. In the second year of his reign, he marched with a large army towards the Deccan, to punish Ramdeo's son-in-law, who, assisted by other princes of that country, had recovered his states. Arriving at Deogurh, he encountered the Deccan troops, and routed them. Their chief being taken, was brought before Mubaric, who caused him to be flayed alive, and his head placed over the gate of his own capital. His next act of barbarity was, under

some frivolous pretence, to put his brother, in confinement in Gualior, to death. Thus freed from all apprehension, Mubaric gave free scope to the vices of his heart, and became perverse, proud, cruel, bloodthirsty, and capricious. Ferishtah describes him as infamous in every vice which can taint the human mind. Chusero, his general, conspired against him, with other Omrahs of the empire; and entering his room one night, assassinated him, and put his whole family to
A.D. 1321. death, exterminating thus the whole race of Alla. This appears a just judgment upon this wretched family, for the ingratitude of its founder to his uncle Ferose, and the innocent blood he so wantonly shed.

Chusero placed himself on the throne, and attempted to usurp the imperial dignity, but was put to death in a very short time by a general conspiracy of the Omrahs against him, who raised ***Tuglick,*** a Patan prince, and one of the chief conspirators, to the musnud of Dehli.

Tuglick I. proved a great and virtuous prince, calling to his court men of learning and genius. He kept a corps of observation on the frontiers towards Cabul, to watch the motions of the Moguls, and thus experienced no molestation throughout his reign. He sent his son with a large force into the Deccan to chastise the Indian prince of Arinkil and the rajah of Deogurh, who had
1325. swerved from their obedience. Tuglick was killed, some say by lightning, others by a building erected by his son to entertain his father in—an event which does not appear to have been purely accidental. He reigned four years.

Tuglick's son succeeded his father, and took the name of ***Mahmood III.*** He made so great a display of wealth on entering Dehli, that it strengthened the suspicion entertained of his having been concerned in his father's death, the treasury being but scantily furnished. It was supposed, that in his expedition to the Deccan he had amassed a vast sum, and concealed it from his father's knowledge.

At the commencement of this reign, a Mogul chief of great talent, named Siri, invaded the frontier of Hindoostan with a large army. He subdued Limghan and Mooltan, and overran the northern provinces; thence advancing with rapidity on Dehli, he invested that capital. Things were in a state very unfit for an effectual resistance: a bribe was the only resource. An immensely rich present in gold and jewels softened the Mogul chief, and on receiving a sum nearly equal to the price of the whole empire, he retraced his steps. Mahmood now turned his thoughts to the disciplining of his armies, and reduced many distant countries to his authority; but these, in the troubles which assailed the empire soon after, were wrested from him. In 1337, the emperor planned a wild enterprise to conquer China. He moved a large force of 100,000 men towards the frontier for that purpose: the difficulties they had to encounter, however, were so great, and the force of the Chinese opposed to them so superior, that the expedition ended in a shameful retreat. Very few of the whole army returned to Dehli, the greater part having perished by want.

Having, in one of his excursions to the southern provinces, taken a liking to the fort and site of Deogurh, Mahmood gave orders that the grand and beautiful city of Dehli, the envy of the world, should be razed to the ground, and that a general migration of its inhabitants should be made to Deogurh, with all their substance. This produced the most serious consequences: a great famine was the result. He once again returned to Dehli; but a second time relinquished it. His reign appears a succession of the most horrible cruelties. This monster died of a fever, on the banks of the Indus, near Tatta, whither he had gone to punish
some of his subjects who had offended him. He died abhorred and feared by all. 1351.

Ferose III. the cousin of the late king, and nephew of Tuglick, succeeded to the throne. He proved himself a wise and merciful prince, and caused in his reign many very grand and useful public works to be erected. In 1357, he built

the city of Feroseabad, near Dehli; and the year after cut a canal from the Suttluge river to the Jidger: he also caused another canal from the Jumna to be formed, which divided into seven branches, and one of which he brought to Hassi, and thence to Baraisin; another canal from the Caggar, by Sirsuti, to the river Kera. Bengal in this reign became almost independent, and the Deccan
A. D.
1388. was left unmolested. Ferose died at the age of ninety years, in 1388, having reigned thirty years and nine months, and left many memorials of his magnificence in Hindoostan. He built fifty sluices, forty mosques, thirty schools, twenty caravanserais, one hundred palaces, five hospitals, one hundred tombs, ten baths, one hundred and fifty wells, and one hundred bridges.

At this period Timour Shah had carried his victorious arms over all Persia, and was now engaged on the banks of the Euphrates.

Tuglick II. who now seized the throne, was a dissolute and abandoned prince, and the victim of imprudence: he reigned but three months, and was
1389. then assassinated.

Abu Bieker, grandson of the emperor Ferose by his third son, was placed
1390. on the musnud; but deposed in eighteen months by Ferose's son, Mahmood.

Mahmood IV. son of Ferose, succeeded: his reign is barren of events. Mahmood died in 1392. He was followed by his son

Humaioon, who, however, enjoyed his power only forty-nine days, and died.

Mahmood V. an infant son of Mahmood IV. was then placed on the throne. Under this reign the state much declined, and its difficulties and misfortunes increased, divided by factions and torn by internal disputes.

During the last ten years, the enterprising Timour Shah had extended his conquests over all Western Asia; had reduced Northern Tartary, and spread his ravages even into Russia. The events of his renowned invasion of Hindoostan, and the important changes which that measure produced throughout all Asia, and which established that dynasty on the throne of Hindoostan which still holds the regal title, now demands our notice.

Timour, the renowned conqueror of Hindoostan, as celebrated for his military talents, as his cruel, bloodthirsty, and bigoted persecution of the Indians, is said to have been a descendant of Gengis Khan. He was born in the city of Kash, in Transoxiana, or Great Tartary, A. D. 1336, and very early in life exhibited talents of the highest class, both as a general and statesman. By a succession of brilliant exploits, he compelled all the surrounding sovereigns to submit to his power: he mounted the throne of Persia, and the extensive territories of East and West Tartary owned his sway.

The victorious armies of Timour had scarcely reposed from the fatigues of A.D. 1398.
a succession of toilsome and hard-fought campaigns, by which Northern Asia had been annexed to his empire, when that insatiable tyrant cast his longing eyes towards India. A restless ambition, combined with a wild and frantic zeal for the propagation of that religion which had for ages overwhelmed with destruction the most flourishing and fertile provinces of Asia, urged him on. He put his ever-victorious and daring bands in march from Samarcand, his capital, and these hardy and experienced warriors, eager for the conquest and plunder of an empire so rich as India, poured like a furious torrent from the northern Indian Caucasus. Vain was the opposition of the Afghan and Patan tribes, although aided by the intricate and difficult nature of their country. Pir 1399.
Mohammed, a grandson of Timour, was detached with a large force to reduce Mooltan, a city of Guzzerat, of great commercial importance, and which had a strong garrison of the troops of the king of Dehli to defend it. The attacks were repeated and desperate, but the defence was obstinate and gallant, and no serious impression could be made. Timour upon this, relinquishing his intended route direct upon Dehli, turned off towards Mooltan; following the course of

the Cheelum (the ancient Hydaspes) downwards for the sake of the water, he crossed that river and the Jenaub below the confluence of the two.

Subsequently passing the Beyah, he was joined by Pir Mohammed, who had reduced Mooltan, where he had taken an immense treasure. Hence, with a body of 10,000 horse, this intrepid warrior made an incursion to attack the fort of Batnir, a strong fortress, about one hundred and fifty miles to the west of Dehli. The defence was most obstinate, but the infuriated Timour overpowered all resistance, and carrying the works by escalade, an indiscriminate slaughter of the inhabitants took place, in which 10,000 Indians are said to have fallen, amid the burning ruins of this once celebrated fortress.

Timour, concentrating his army at Semana, about one hundred and seventy miles from Dehli, proceeded thence in order of battle; Pir Mohammed and Rustam commanding the right, and Sultan Mahmood, khan of Zagatai, and other Omrahs, the left wing; while Timour himself was in the centre with the *élite* of his troops.

The cities of Togluckpore and Paniput were, on the approach of the enemy, abandoned by their inhabitants and delivered up to destruction, and left heaps of ashes. On the 24th December, Timour encamped his army in sight of the city of Dehli, a torrent of blood and an all-devouring flame having marked the route of the invader from the Indus to the Jumna.

Here Timour addressed his army, and by representing the inferior numbers and discipline of the enemy, the amazing riches of Dehli, and the glory and wealth they would acquire, inspired a feeling of enthusiasm, and a frenzied eagerness for the onset, of which it would be difficult to form a conception.

A few days previously to the awful and tremendous battle which decided the fate of Dehli, the ruthless tyrant, whose legions surrounded the city on all sides,
A.D. 1399. added another to the list of his atrocious crimes, and dyed yet deeper his hands

in human blood. During the advance from the Indus, in the various actions and their subsequent pursuits, nearly 100,000 Indians had been made prisoners, and were distributed as slaves among the leaders and most distinguished persons of the army. Instigated by a suspicion of the treachery of these captives, or by a dark and fatal impression, that being idolaters and worshippers of fire, they fell under the denomination of enemies of his prophet, Timour issued orders for the whole to be put to death, in cold blood, and in sight of the armies of their countrymen.

The two armies at length met; the conflict was dreadful and bloody. The fortune and conduct of Timour at length prevailed, and the weak Mahmood first fled in dismay into Dehli, and then sought refuge in the deserts. The conqueror mounted the musnud, the most glorious of all Asia, and received the homage of his new subjects, who, prostrate, implored his mercy.

A scene of sumptuous banqueting and festivity followed, to celebrate the A.D. 1399.
capture of this rich mine of wealth. The reins of discipline once slackened, the barbarous and rapacious soldiery of Timour by degrees insinuated themselves into the city, and by their barbarity to the natives produced acts of retaliation on the part of the latter, which, increasing the animosity on both sides, led to the greatest excesses on the part of the soldiery, and ended in a free and unlicensed plunder of this rich city, the destruction of its grand and ancient temples, the defacing of its public buildings, and, in short, the reduction of the once proud and magnificent Dehli to a heap of ruins.

Timour, on leaving the ruined capital of Hindoostan, marched towards Merut, a celebrated city of the Doo-ab, and strongly fortified. This place fell before his conquering arms, and the same scenes of cruelty and slaughter were here repeated. The inhabitants were reduced to slavery, and their city razed to the ground.

The victorious Tartar, having no longer any opposition to dread, commenced his retreat towards his Persian dominions, impeded by the spoils with which his army was encumbered, and by the repeated and obstinate attacks of the people of the mountainous ridge of the Caucasus which approaches the northern parts of India. The progress of his army was slow, but he at length reached Samarcand, having completed the conquest of a mighty empire in the short space of ten months, which, on a moderate calculation, would have been supposed to require as many years to achieve.

Timour, to commemorate this wonderful event, caused a grand and spacious mosque to be erected at Samarcand. India remained in nominal dependence on the viceroy whom Timour had appointed.

A.D. 1405. Timour, previously to his death, which occurred in 1405, in the seventy-first year of his age, and thirty-sixth of his reign, had nominated his favourite descendant, ***Pir Mohammed Jehan Ghir***, to succeed him. The Omrahs, however, of the court preferred placing ***Khalil Sultan***, a grandson of Timour's, on the musnud. The rightful heir had recourse to arms, but in vain. An agreement then took place, in which the power was divided, Pir Mohammed retaining his command over Hindoostan. The new monarch soon proved himself unworthy of the high situation in which he was placed, and lavished the treasures amassed by his predecessor on unworthy subjects. ***Sultan Shah Rukh***, fourth
1446. son of Timour, was called to the throne.

To the talents of a warrior, Shah Rukh added those of patron and associate of learned men; he erected many noble mosques, and founded several edifices dedicated to philosophical pursuits. After a reign of glory, he died at Rey, in Persian Irac, in the seventy-first year of his age, and the fortieth of his reign.

Uluk Beg, eldest son of the late king, succeeded his father. His reign was disturbed by the rebellion of his three nephews, who all aspired to the throne.

He foiled them in most of their attempts; but a new opponent springing up in A.D.
the person of his own son, Abdollatiff, Uluk Beg was defeated, taken prisoner, 1450.
and eventually put to death by this unnatural monster. The reign of Uluk Beg was distinguished, like the former, by a liberal patronage of science. He possessed great personal bravery and many very eminent qualities. He fell in 1450, in the fourth year of his reign over the Tartar empire.

Abdollatiff, after the atrocious murder of his father, ascended the throne, and in order to secure himself more firmly in the sovereignty, he put to death his only brother. He reigned, however, little more than six months; for his cruelties so disgusted and exasperated his soldiers, that they shot him to death with arrows.

Abdolla, son of Ibrahim, second son of Shah Rukh, laid claim to the throne, and assumed the imperial titles. He, however, encountered a formidable rival in Abusaid Mirza, grandson of Miran Shah, third son of Timour, who threw off his allegiance, and raised the standard of revolt in Bokhara. Abdolla, collecting an army, marched to crush this rebellion, and drove Abusaid beyond the utmost verge of his dominions. The latter, however, was not to be discouraged by one defeat; returning the year following at the head of a horde of Usbeck Tartars, who, like a mighty torrent, spread terror and desolation to the very walls of Samarcand. A sanguinary and desperately fought general action between the two competitors for the throne, attended with circumstances peculiarly horrible, concluded the struggle. Abdolla fell in this action, and his fortunate rival mounted the throne for which he had so long and so obstinately contended.

Abusaid Mirza's reign was one continued series of war and disturbance, 1451.
occasioned by the jealousy and hatred of the neighbouring princes, and the obstinate perseverance of Abdollatiff's sons, who contended for the empire of their father. He considerably enlarged the territories, which had been encroached upon by his neighbours, and acted with vigour and decision during his reign

of seventeen years. At that period, in an engagement with Hassan the Turkoman, having advanced too far upon the frontiers, he was taken prisoner in his
A.D. 1468. retreat, and ungenerously put to an ignominious death.

With Abusaid declined the splendour of Timour's once mighty empire in Tartary, but the sun of its glory sunk here only to rise more resplendent at Dehli. The talent, the genius of Timour, still lived in one branch of that intrepid warrior's posterity; and in the farthest provinces of his empire, a new government arose as it were from the ashes of the old, destined to equal the latter, if not in extent, at least in renown and splendour.

1469. ***Ahmed,*** the eldest of eleven sons of Abusaid, unopposed, mounted his father's throne. He was destitute of that vigour and those military talents so essential in these turbulent times; and the daring and successful incursions of the neighbouring powers in a few years robbed him of nearly the whole of his dominions. His life, undistinguished by any brilliant event, terminated in
1493. 1493, when he died at Samarcand, in the twenty-fifth year of his reign.

Baber, son of Omar, fourth son of Abusaid, succeeded to the throne: he found his dominions in a most disorganized, defenceless state, of which an enterprising enemy, Shah Bakht, khan or chief of the Usbeck Tartars, took advantage and invaded Great Bokhara, the only remnant of the empire of Timour which now remained to his family. Baber, unable to cope with the immense force brought against him, was compelled to abdicate his throne, to which he never returned. Sultan Baber soon saw that no hopes remained of reconquering the territory of his ancestors; instead therefore of vain and fruitless attempts to regain it, he turned his eyes eastward, and conceived the possibility of establishing a new empire, and renovating the fallen splendour of his family. For this purpose he retired to Gazna, there to mature his plans of future conquest.

During the inactive reign of Ahmed Shah, the several provinces of Hindoostan had almost all shaken off the yoke of the Tartar race, which was odious to both the Mahomedan and Hindoo princes. This offered a wide field for the prudent and aspiring Baber. Collecting a small but highly disciplined and effective army, devoted to his interests, he entered upon his hazardous expedition.

So odious, however, had the Tartar dynasty become, that the most obstinate and determined resistance of both the Afghan and Indian tribes rendered his progress very slow and tedious, and exposed him to great difficulties. Often repulsed in his attempts, sometimes totally defeated, Fortune did not smile upon him till his fifth invasion, when, by the total defeat of his opponent, Sultan Ibrahim Lodi, he may be said to have gained a footing in India. This action A.D.
occurred in 1526, and evinced in the strongest manner the military talents of 1526.
Baber, and the excellence and intrepidity of the troops he commanded; since, with a force of only 12,000 men, he overthrew and put to flight the Afghan army of 100,000, accompanied by a great number of elephants regularly trained to war. Thus a remote, though a lineal descendant of the great Timour, a fugitive from his own kingdom, ascended the throne of Dehli, one hundred and thirty years after its conquest by that great warrior. Some disturbances in Bahar and Mooltan alone disturbed the reign of Baber, which were speedily quelled. Being taken ill, and finding his end approaching, he recalled his son Humaioon, who was engaged in the siege of the strong fortress of Callinger, and nominated him his successor. He died in the year 1530, and his body was interred by his desire in a mosque at Cabul. Baber was an accomplished and learned prince, excelling in poetry, writing, and music. His own commentaries in the Mogul language are universally admired, and he established his reputation for justice and honour.

Humaioon immediately mounted the throne of India. He was devoted to the sciences. Several rebellions in the remoter parts of his empire occasionally disturbed his reign. In A.D. 1535, he besieged and carried the strong fortress of 1535.

Chunar, and, having thus made himself master of the passes, entered Bengal, and marching to Gour, then the capital of that province, took it. He was speedily recalled, however, by the rebellion of his two brothers, Hindal and Camiran, and the aggression of Shere Khan the Afghan, who, finding the army of the king much reduced, advanced from Rhotas in great force. A sort of agreement or treaty of peace was drawn up between this treacherous adventurer and Humaioon, in which the latter agreed to give up Bengal and Bahar to Shere, who was to hold them in the king's name, paying a small tribute annually.

The wily Shere made this treaty a pretence to cover his treacherous designs; for during the truce he suddenly attacked Humaioon's army, routed it, and forced it across the river, in which numbers perished. Humaioon himself nar-
A.D. 1539. rowly escaped, and, with a few of his people who survived, fled to Agra. The successes of Shere and his Afghans at length roused the feelings of the Moguls, and laying aside their animosity, they united in one common cause—the repulse of the invaders. A second serious defeat, however, reduced the unfortunate Humaioon to the verge of ruin, and he was compelled to retire, first to Agra, then to Lahore, and ultimately towards Tatta and Bicker on the Indus. In passing the sandy desert from the last-named place to Amercot, thousands of his men, after the most dreadful sufferings, perished from want of water; and Humaioon, after unheard-of sufferings, reached Amercot, where he was received and kindly treated, with the few who had accompanied him.

1541. At the town of Amercot, in the year of the Hegira 949, the immortal Acber was born; and the unfortunate Humaioon, after a variety of ineffectual struggles, retired towards Persia, where he was received with the greatest respect by Tahmasp, its sovereign.

On the flight of Humaioon, the enterprising *Shere* seized upon the sovereign power. He was the son of Hussein, of the Afghans of Roh, a moun-

A.D.

tainous country on the confines of India and Persia. Shere's name was origi- 1541.
nally Ferid; and being on a hunting party with the king of Bahar, an enormous tiger was suddenly started, which Ferid slew with one stroke of his sabre. For this bold deed, performed in the king's presence, he was honoured with the sir-
name of Shere Khan. The king of Bahar dying shortly after, his son, yet a 1542.
minor, succeeded; and his widow, the Sultana Dudu, who acted as regent, placed in the hands of Shere the most weighty affairs of the state. The sultana dying, all the authority remained with Shere, who soon after invaded Bengal, and possessed himself of Malwa, Rantampore, and Chittore. At the siege of
Calliager, soon after, he was killed by the bursting of a shell in one of the bat- 1545.
teries. He reigned five years.

The character of Shere is a strange compound of the most distinguished virtues and most degrading vices: he was rigid in administering justice; in private, often guilty of the basest perfidy. It seemed as though he had fixed his heart on the empire, and cared not how he attained it. Shere left many splendid monuments of his magnificence behind him. From the kingdom of Bengal to the Nilab or Indus river, a distance of 3000 miles, he built caravanserais at every stage, and dug a well every two miles. Several mosques were also erected by him on the highways. He ordered that all travellers, without distinction of country or religion, should be entertained at the public expense; and he planted rows of fruit-trees along the road-side, to shade the traveller and gratify his taste.

Shere was buried in a magnificent mausoleum at Sasseram, which he had caused to be built in the centre of a lake nearly a mile in length. This grand edifice still remains entire.

Tahmasp meanwhile sat upon the throne of Persia in peace during the usurpation of Shere, and protecting Humaioon.

A.D.
1545. ***Selim,*** the second son of Shere, was raised to the throne by the Omrahs of the empire, in opposition to the just claim of Adil, the eldest. In consequence of this infringement of his brother's right, his reign was distracted by commotions and rebellion, and several attempts were made to assassinate him, which,
1552. however, he was fortunate enough to escape. Selim died after a reign of seven years. He possessed not the talents of his father, though he followed his example in magnificence.

Ferose, the son of Selim, at twelve years of age succeeded his father. He had reigned but three days when Mubaric, his uncle, basely assassinated the young prince.

Mohammed Adil, the title by which Mubaric ascended the musnud, gave himself up entirely to pleasure and dissipation, despised learning, and associated only with the most illiterate and lowest of his subjects. He became in a short time contemptible in the eyes of his people, and all order and government totally declined. Owing to a harsh act in depriving Sermalli of the province of Cannouge, and bestowing it upon another, in a full audience Secunder, son of Sermalli, strongly remonstrated, and upbraided the king for his conduct. The Omrah, to whom Cannouge was promised, interfering, was stabbed to the heart by the impetuous Secunder, who subsequently slew some other nobles then present, wounded many more, and finally rushed at the king, who was compelled to leap from his throne and retire to his palace, followed by the infuriated Secunder. This desperate youth, foiled in his pursuit of Mohammed, returned with tenfold rage, and rushing back into the chamber of audience, dealt death to all around. Ibrahim, a cousin of the king's, and some others attacking Secunder, cut him in pieces.

1553. Although deeply indebted to Ibrahim on this occasion, Mohammed grew very jealous of him, and meditated his destruction. Warned of his danger, however, Ibrahim escaped to Ghazi, his father, at Biana.

A.D.

He soon raised a large army, and possessed himself of the city of Dehli, where he mounted the throne, assumed the ensigns of royalty, and marching thence to Agra, reduced the neighbouring provinces under his subjection. Mohammed moved immediately from Chunar to oppose Ibrahim; but abandoned by his Omrahs, whom he had sent to negociate with the latter, he had no resource but to seek his safety by flight to the eastern provinces. 1553. 1554.

Ibrahim III. had scarcely mounted the throne when a new competitor sprang up in the province of Punjab. This was Ahmed, nephew of the emperor Shere, and brother-in-law of the expelled Mohammed. This prince, assuming the title of ***Secunder Shah,*** and collecting a force of about 10,000 cavalry, marched towards Agra, within four miles of which he pitched his camp. Ibrahim came out to meet the invader with 70,000 horse, having two hundred Omrahs in his army, who pitched velvet tents. Secunder, alarmed at this mass of force, sought to accommodate matters, requiring only the Punjab. Ibrahim, puffed up with pride, rejected all terms, and the two armies approached to combat. Secunder, feeling his inferiority, had recourse to stratagem: investing an Omrah with all the insignia of royalty, he himself with a chosen body of cavalry occupied an ambush on one flank. The action commenced; numbers prevailed, and the forces of Ibrahim carried all before them, and feeling secure of victory, commenced as usual a scene of plunder. Occupied in this manner, they were surprised by Secunder, who, rushing out from his ambush, attacked them with vigour, entirely routed them, and pursued them till they were dispersed, and no longer existed as an army. Ibrahim after this defeat abandoned his capital, and fell back to Simbol. Secunder took possession of Agra and Dehli, but did not long enjoy his fortune; advice being received that the emperor Humaioon, having left the court of Persia, was advancing with an army to recover his possessions.

A.D.
1554. Humaioon had been treated at the court of Tahmasp, king of Persia, as his misfortunes, his rank, and virtues deserved. After an exile of five years and a half at that court, having been furnished by its sovereign with 10,000 horse, he commenced his march towards Hindoostan. On the 1st September, A.D. 1545, he took Candahar; and on the 16th November, conquered Cabul. In the spring of the following year, he got possession of Badakshan. By the conquest of rebellious chiefs, and the power of the Afghan emperors' adherents, Humaioon was detained, and could only commence his vigorous efforts to regain his throne in the year 1554.

Humaioon now received addresses from both Dehli and Agra, pressing his return, to quell the disorders which prevailed throughout the empire. Struck with the important consequences of acting with vigour, although he could muster no more than 15,000 horse, he decided to march towards India. At Peshawir Humaioon was joined by Byram, whom he appointed his captain-general, and sent him forward with the van of his army.

The emperor Secunder had meanwhile sent from Dehli a force of 40,000 horse to oppose Humaioon. This superior force Byram boldly attacked and defeated, taking many elephants, and a vast spoil in baggage and horses. The king hearing of this great victory, conferred on Byram the title of ***Khan Khanan*** (or lord of lords).

Secunder Shah, mustering a force of 80,000 horse, a train of elephants, and a vast artillery, moved towards the Indus. Byram on his approach shut himself up in Sirhind, and prepared the place for a siege. Secunder sat down before the city. Humaioon hastened from Lahore to succour Byram, and finally joined him. Thus united they made repeated sallies, and much annoyed the investing army of the enemy.

At length the latter one day drew out their forces and offered battle. Hu-

A.D. 1555.

maioon, with his son Acber, now only thirteen years of age, advanced to attack the enemy, who intrepidly awaited him; a desperate conflict ensued, which ended in the total defeat of Secunder, who fled with precipitation to the mountains.

This victory decided the fate of the empire, which, from this moment, fell for ever from the hands of the Patans. Humaioon entered Dehli in triumph, and became a second time emperor of Hindoostan. Byram, to whose conduct so much was owing, was invested by his master with the first offices of the state, and large estates were assigned to him. But the glory and the reign of Humaioon were now approaching their fall. By accident, whilst walking on one of the terraces of his palace, in descending a flight of marble stairs, and resting on his staff, it slipped, and the emperor was precipitated from top to bottom. When taken up he was insensible, and being placed on a bed, recovered his speech; but all the endeavours and skill of the physicians were in vain exerted. On the fourth day he expired, having attained the age of fifty-one years, of which he reigned, with some interruptions, twenty-five years over Cabul and India. He was buried in the new city, and a magnificent tomb was erected to his memory some years after by his son Acber.

The character of Humaioon is thus portrayed by the celebrated historian Ferishta: "The mildness and benevolence of this prince were excessive, if there can be excess in virtues so noble and elevated as these. His affection for his brothers proved the source of all his misfortunes, while they rewarded him with ingratitude and contempt. He was learned himself, and a lover of literature, as well as a generous patron of the men of genius who flourished in his time. In battle he was valiant and enterprising; but the clemency of his disposition prevented him from using his victories in a manner suitable to the vices of the times. Had he been less mild and religious, he would have been a more successful prince; had he been a worse man, he would have been a greater monarch."

During the last three reigns, the Portuguese had been gradually establishing themselves in India, and at length consolidated a vast empire on its coasts.

A.D. 1556. On the death of Humaioon his son ***Acber*** was declared emperor by the generals of the imperial army. Although not yet fourteen years of age, this young prince had distinguished himself in several actions by deeds of dauntless valour. Byram Khan, his guardian, undertook the management of public affairs, being invested with the whole military and civil power of the empire.

A competitor for the throne now started forth in the person of Mohammed Adil Shah, nephew to the usurper Shere Khan, in Bengal. This prince dispatched his vizir, named Himu, with 30,000 horse and 2000 elephants, to seize the two cities of Agra and Dehli. The former was not prepared to resist so formidable a force, and the viceroy therefore retreated from it. Overcoming all opposition, Himu entered Dehli in triumph. The viceroy took the route towards Sirhind, where he met Acber on his march to assert his title to the throne. Acber immediately issued orders for collecting the forces, and found himself, on arriving at the plains of Panniput, at the head of 20,000 men. The rebels, to nearly five times that amount, advanced from Dehli, to crush at once the small army of their opponents. Himu commenced the attack with his elephants, on which he placed great dependence; but these unwieldy animals were so warmly received by the troops of Acber, so galled with arrows, and so pierced with spears, that they became furious even to madness, and rushing back upon their own ranks, spread havoc and disorder through the whole army of the rebels. Himu performed prodigies of valour, and wading through seas of blood on an enormous elephant, and followed by 4000 chosen horse, penetrated into the heart of the Mogul army, when an arrow piercing his eye, lodged in that tender

A.D.
organ. Regardless of the excruciating pain, he tore out the barbed shaft, and 1567.
with it the eye from the socket. Thus he continued fighting, until nearly all his troops being cut to pieces, he was himself taken prisoner, and brought into the presence of Acber, who, it has been said, fired with the ardour of a youthful warrior, smote off the head of the rebel with his own hand, and ordered it to be affixed to the gate of Dehli.

Acber marched with a large force to Chitore, a strong fortress of Malwa, and after a long siege gained possession of it. The revolt of his brother, Mohammed 1570.
Hakim, who held the government of Cabul, compelled Acber to march in that direction, which he did with such wonderful rapidity, that the rebel army, alarmed at his decision and promptness, dispersed, leaving behind their camp, baggage, and spoil.

Soon after, two of his Omrahs in Bengal having erected the standard of revolt at Lucnow, carried their incursions even as far as the gates of Agra. With his accustomed celerity, the emperor soon arrived on the Jumna river, and falling suddenly upon the revolters, drove them from their encampment, and pursued them with great slaughter. The two Omrahs were taken, and immediately punished, one being trampled to death by the horses of the pursuers, and the other strangled upon the spot.

A peace, which succeeded these events, lasted nearly two years. During its continuance Acber removed the seat of government from Dehli to Agra, where he commenced building a magnificent palace and fort, superior in point of extent and strength to any previously constructed in India. A more detailed description of this splendid undertaking, and various other grand and bold designs of this wonderful character, will be given when our tour shall conduct us to the vicinity of these ancient and grand remains of the former splendour of India, which was at its height under the immortal Acber.

A.D.
1572. This year another rebellion burst out in the province of Guzzerat. This province being overrun with robbers and pirates, especially on its coasts, Acber determined to penetrate as far as possible into that country, and carry his arms to the very gates of Surat, of which, together with Baroach, the rebels had gained possession. He accordingly collected a number of dromedaries of the greatest swiftness, and taking with him his most resolute and esteemed generals, and a small chosen body of horse, he travelled the amazing distance of 400 kos, or 800 miles, in seven days, and pitched his tents under the walls of Ahmedabad. Being here joined by Azim Khan and all the troops which could be collected, Acber advanced; and the rebels, taken by surprise and unprepared to resist such a force, retired rapidly before him. The emperor, however, pressing them very closely, at length brought them to action. The struggle was obstinate; Acber found enemies worthy of his sword; but at length, their commander being slain, the rebels gave way, and were routed with great slaughter. The fortress of Baroach, at that period one of the strongest in India, was taken after a short siege; and Surat, opening its gates, received a Mogul garrison, to keep in awe the hordes of lawless robbers that infested its vicinity. Shah Selim, Acber's eldest son, accompanied his father in this expedition, and exhibited the greatest bravery and spirit in the several actions in which he was engaged.

1576. Bengal again in this year struggled for independence. Acber with 50,000 horse and 600 elephants passed the Ganges, and laid siege to Patna, then the capital, where Shah Daood, an indolent prince, had shut himself up. For six months Acber in vain tried to bring his enemy to action; in the seventh month it was therefore attacked and carried by storm, when a dreadful massacre ensued, unlimited like the anger of the incensed monarch. The plunder was immense.

Acber next marched on Allahabad, then called Priag, a principal bulwark of the kingdom of the Patans. Having invested and taken it, he was so struck with the beauty of its situation, that he at once determined to make it an impregnable fortress by vast labour and great expense.

Elated with his success against the Patans, the emperor next turned his arms A.D. 1581.
against the declining power of the independent rajahs, and took from them successively their strongest fortresses of Rantempore in Malwa, Rhotas in Bahar, and Jalour in the sandy deserts of Agimere.

Acber now turned his eyes to the country which gave birth to the renowned 1585.
Timour, and thought upon the bright series of conquests that distinguished its ancient sovereigns. The ignominious expulsion of Sultan Baber, his immediate progenitor, then occurred to his mind. These sensations in turn fired him with the ardour of the most exalted ambition, and depressed him with a generous shame. He would instantly have made arrangements and plans for an attempt to regain these extensive and remote countries, but he held it in the first place necessary to obtain, if possible, possession of the valley and kingdom of Cashmere.
Acber was too much aware of the extremely difficult nature of that country, 1590.
however, to attempt its reduction by open force; he had recourse to treaties, and supported these by an army ready to take advantage of any opportunity of success which force could secure. By bribes to an enormous amount, industriously distributed amongst the nobles and generals of the Cashmerian forces, who were charged with the defence of the principal passes into this country, so singularly protected by nature, he paved the way towards its future conquest, and finally entering it, marched almost unopposed to its capital, made the sovereign and his son, the gallant Yacoub, prisoners; but allowed them, on his retiring from the country, a magnificent and princely stipend.

The enterprising and indefatigable Acber next turned his arms against the kingdom of Sinde. Embarking a numerous army on the river Rauvee, one of the five branches of the Indus, he committed this force to Khan Khanan, before noticed as a distinguished general, who, sailing down the river, reached Tatta, the capital of Sinde, invested it, and took it after a tedious siege. Its sovereign was sent prisoner to Lahore, while his kingdom was reduced into a province of the empire.

A.D. 1595. The emperor next employed his thoughts on a project long a favourite with him. This was no less an exploit than the entire conquest and subjugation of the whole peninsula of India within the Ganges, comprising many great and powerful kingdoms, of which those subjected afterwards to the Mogul arms were included under the general denomination of the Deccan (or the South). The kingdoms of Balagat, Viziapore, Golconda, the Carnatic, anciently called Bisnagurh, with all their other conquests in the southern extremities of India, amounted nearly to one third part of the empire.

1597. Acber had with his usual policy sent four ambassadors to the four courts of the sovereigns of the Deccan, proposing terms of alliance with them, but in fact to obtain accurate accounts of the power and resources of those kingdoms preparatory to his attack. His viceroys of the provinces bordering on the Deccan had also orders to keep a strict watch upon these princes, and take every advantage and opportunity of extending the limits of his dominions on that side. Many forts were in consequence taken possession of on the part of Acber.

But the sovereigns of the Deccan paid no respect either to the secret or open attacks of the Mogul emperor; they rejected his proffered alliance with indignant contempt, and dismissed his ambassadors. Acber instantly resolved to commence hostilities, and in the first instance sent Khan Khanan and the most celebrated of his generals in that direction, with a force not numerous, but skilful and well disciplined. These, on reaching Brampore, the capital of Candeish, the southernmost province of his dominions, were joined by the forces of Ali Khan, the governor: they were opposed by the armies of the Begum Chaund Bebee, great-

A.D.
aunt of Secunder Shah, which were led on by Soheil Khan, a general of great skill and intrepidity; and the sovereigns of Visiapore and Golconda, considering the Begum's as a common cause, contributed each a proportion of troops towards the defence of her kingdom. At the head of these forces, which united amounted to 40,000 horse, Soheil boldly advanced to give battle to the invading army, which scarcely equalled half this number. Khan Khanan and his generals, however, were not dispirited, but urged on by the importance of the duty intrusted to them, and aware of the sanguine expectations entertained by their emperor from their exertions and bravery, as well as excited by devotion to his cause, rushed with a dreadful impetuosity and inconceivable fury upon the Deccan troops. An awful struggle commenced, and lasted no less than twenty-four hours, during which victory was doubtful; but the spirit and discipline of the Moguls were at length successful. The brave Soheil Khan and nearly half his army fell, and the remainder were driven from the field, and saved themselves by a precipitate flight. 1597.

This victory, however, did not prove by any means decisive in its effects: both sides increased their forces, and the contest was renewed with obstinacy, and with various success.

Acber at length marched to join his army in the south, taking with him vast 1598.
reinforcements. A few miles north of Brampore was situated the fortress of Hassera, one of the strongest in that part of India. Its works consisted of three castles, one rising above the other, the highest being visible at twelve miles distance, on the summit of a mountain extremely lofty, steep, and craggy. It was surrounded besides by three walls, so disposed that the upper commanded and completely protected the lower; it was also well provisioned, and complete in ordnance, troops, and stores, proportioned to its importance. His army of the south here joined the emperor, who invested the fortress with the whole of

his forces, amounting to 200,000 men, and pointed against it the whole force of his numerous artillery. Bahadur, the resolute rajah who commanded Hassera, defied their utmost efforts. Acber, however, had too much policy to attempt an open attack, when the more certain and easy method of bribery and flattery was in his power. Presents to an immense amount, and flattering promises of preferment at the emperor's court, prevailed on the rajah not only to yield up his fort, but to enter with all his family and followers into Acber's service. This
A.D. 1601. successful and consummate stroke of deep policy opened the road to the Deccan, and rendered the vast designs of Acber against that country easy and sure. He accordingly made every disposition to carry into execution his favourite and long-contemplated design of completely subjugating the southern provinces.

A dark and stormy cloud, however, was now gathering over the hitherto bright and serene sunshine of this hero's destiny, which involved his latter days in the gloom of domestic affliction.

On leaving Agra, Acber had sent his eldest son Selim on an expedition against Rajah Ranna, the most powerful of all the Indian rajahs. This prince, however, finding himself at the head of so fine and numerous an army, and his father so far distant, returned suddenly to Agra, and having amassed a large sum by the plunder of the royal treasury, openly avowed his intention of dethroning him. The castle of Agra was too strong and its governor too faithful to submit; but other places soon yielded to his authority. Among these was Allahabad, where he fixed his head-quarters.

Acber, overwhelmed with affliction at the news of this revolt, hastened instantly his return to his capital, leaving his third son, Shah Daniel, to carry on the Deccan war, assisted by Abul Fazil, Khan Khanan, and his ablest generals. Acber sent, on his reaching Agra, the most soothing letters to his son Selim, to induce him to submit and return to his duty: all were haughtily rejected, and this refusal was accompanied by insolence and expressions of direct defiance. Acber then determined to have recourse to force, and summoned his confidant and faithful counsellor, Abul Fazil, from the Deccan, to assist him in reducing his rebellious son to a sense of duty: but on his journey he was waylaid and inhumanly assassinated by the orders of prince Selim, who bore a deep and ancient hatred to him. Thus perished the most elegant and learned writer Asia could at that time boast. This cruel act overwhelmed Acber with affliction, and only urged him to the severest measures against his son. A.D. 1601.

The arms of Acber meanwhile prospered in the Deccan. The army under Shah Daniel had approached and invested Ahmednaghur, in which the intrepid queen Bebee had shut herself up, determining to defend it to the last extremity. The siege was long, the assault violent, and it required the united efforts of the whole army, which at this period amounted to between 4 and 500,000 men, to reduce it. Considerable treasures were the reward of this conquest; but the indignant queen would not survive it, and had previously rushed upon voluntary destruction. The entire subjugation of the Deccan followed, and the ambassadors of the kings of Visiapore and Golconda soon after met the triumphant generals at Brampore, bringing presents of great magnificence, and letters couched in humble and submissive terms.

Thus was the grand scheme of Acber for the reduction of the Deccan in part effected, and he derived much satisfaction from the prospect which opened on his view. Nothing was wanting to complete his happiness but the return of his son Selim to his obedience, and he was on the point of setting forth on an expedition for this purpose, when news arrived of the death of Shah Daniel, his third son, who lost his life by his excesses, and fell a victim to the grossest intemperance at Brampore.

Again urgent letters were sent to Selim, now his only son, and the heir to

his empire, severely upbraiding him, yet still holding out the promise of pardon. These letters, aided by the counsel and advice of an aged Omrah, had at length
A.D. 1605. the desired effect, and Selim, hastening to Agra, threw himself repentant at the feet of his father. After severe upbraidings, a full and perfect reconciliation took place; the emperor completely restored him to favour; taking precautions, however, to remove any possibility of his son engaging in any future schemes of the same nature.

The reign of the illustrious Acber now hastened rapidly towards its close. The cause of his death has been variously stated. Some writers contend that he died in consequence of taking poison by mistake, intended by him for an Omrah of his court, who had rendered himself obnoxious. Others ascribe his death to a violent fever. The latter would appear the more probable, and will better accord with the former long, brilliant, and successful career of this monarch, who may be justly ranked with the greatest statesmen and heroes of antiquity. His personal valour and presence of mind upon all occasions were astonishing: with one vigorous arm he repelled the barbarians of the north, and with the other spread his conquests through the southern regions of India. The prince of the Usbecks trembled on his throne at the name of Acber; the intrepid race of Rajepoots bowed before him; and the kings of Visiapore and Golconda poured out their exhaustless treasures to appease his anger. His generosity and clemency were alike unbounded. He deserves the glory of establishing on a firm basis the mighty empire, the foundation of which was laid by Baber, which was extended by Humaioon, but which it was reserved for himself to bring to perfection.

Instead of persecuting and exterminating with the remorseless bigotry of his predecessors the race of patient and timid Hindoos, overthrowing their beloved idols, and plundering and burning their venerable shrines, Acber nobly

A.D.
and wisely extended to them the tolerating system of their own creed, and gave them protection and security. 1605.

In fine, the history of Asia exhibits not a character parallel to that of Acber in the extent and grandeur of his designs, the wisdom and vigour of his counsels, his moderation in peace, or his success and renown in war.

The illustrious Acber, a short time previous to his death, which took place on the 13th October, 1605, in the sixty-third year of his age, and fiftieth of his reign, finding his end approaching, sent for his son, and placing on his head his own rich turban, he girded him with the victorious sword of his grandfather Humaioon.

During the reign of Acber, a number of Portuguese merchants had established themselves at Agra; and the emperor, who ardently encouraged commerce both domestic and foreign, granted them most extensive immunities.

Acber died and was buried at Secundra. The empire at this period comprehended a vast extent of territory, which was divided into twenty-one provinces, as follows: Khandahar, Ghizni, Cabul, Cashmere, Lahore, Mooltan, Sindc, Agimcrc, Sirhind, Dchli, Dooab, Agra, Allahabad, Oude, Bahar, Bengal, Orissa, Malwa, Berar, Candeish, and Guzzerat.

The revenues amounted to thirty-two millions sterling, exclusive of the customary presents and the estates which reverted to the crown, which amounted at an average to twenty millions more. These immense sums, forming a total of 52 millions sterling, or 2080 millions, or 4160 lacs, of rupees, were expended in maintaining an army of 300,000 horse and 300,000 foot, in supporting the splendour of the court, and in the salaries of civil officers.

After the decline and final overthrow of the Portuguese power in India, 1595.
occasioned chiefly by the fatal tyranny of Philip of Spain, the Dutch, who had hitherto been the chief carriers of the Indian treasures poured into that country

from Lisbon to the different marts of Europe, finding themselves excluded, now decided to explore those regions whence this vast wealth was drawn, and boldly passed the Cape of Good Hope for that purpose. This occurred in 1595, when Cornelius Houtman, an able and intrepid mariner, sailed with four ships for this purpose. That enterprising seaman, having been a prisoner in Portugal, strove to obtain from the Portuguese the best possible description of the route to be pursued, and the species of commerce carried on with the Eastern nations. This first voyage being one of discovery, little wealth was acquired by it; but a vast mass of information was obtained of high interest respecting the coasts he had visited, especially that of the Island of Java, with whose king an alliance
A.D. 1597. was formed, which promised much future advantage. On the return of Houtman, therefore, eight ships were immediately equipped, and placed under the command of Admiral van Neck, who sailed from Holland in 1597. Opposed in vain by the Portuguese and Spaniards, he formed a settlement both at Java and on the Molucca Islands, and eventually returned home loaded with the rich produce of those countries. This success spread the thirst of Indian wealth throughout the United Provinces; ships in vast numbers were built, and sums subscribed by the merchants to prosecute this enterprise.

The Portuguese traders had appeared on the coasts of India as conquerors as well as merchants: the Dutch more wisely adhered to the latter character alone, and were proportionably successful. Their after plans of conquest were deeply and carefully concealed.

One serious obstacle, however, tended materially to prevent their arrival at the pinnacle of opulence and prosperity. So many trading companies and societies every where appeared, that by underselling each other at the different trading ports of the East, they materially lessened their respective profits. To remedy this evil, the directors of all the principal companies were convened in

A.D.

one general assembly at the Hague; and the result was, the union of the whole of their several stocks into one common fund; thus forming themselves into one corporate body, whose acts the government of the country authorized. 1602.

The Spanish and Portuguese nations in vain threw obstacles in the way of these enterprising people, obstacles which tended rather to excite them to more strenuous exertion, than in any way to lessen their efforts; and after a long series of successes over their implacable rivals, the Dutch finally succeeded in making themselves masters of the vast Indian Archipelago, and founded a city in Java, which, in a short period, became equal in wealth and splendour to the proudest capitals of India.

But a more formidable rival than those they had hitherto contended with was soon to appear, to oppose the growing power of the Dutch in their Eastern empire: this formidable opponent was the English, who, with their characteristic daring and active spirit, now displayed their flags in the Eastern ocean.

England had up to this period been supplied with the costly manufactures of India, its rich silks, and its aromatic spices, by the route of the Arabian gulf, Cairo, and thence by the Nile to Alexandria, whence the Venetians were the carriers to the various ports of the Mediterranean and of Europe. But as the naval power and wealth of Britain increased, she was no longer contented to receive through other hands those valuable and esteemed productions of India, that enriched the nations which trafficked in them. The Levant was the first scene of the enterprise of the merchants of England: a fleet was fitted out for this destination, and recommendatory letters were granted to them by Queen Elizabeth to the emperor of the Turks, which ended in a treaty between the two nations, highly advantageous to the British. A considerable and lucrative trade was for some time carried on with Candia, Chios, Cyprus, and the Mediterranean ports on the Syrian coast. Their imports were silks and camlets, malmsey,

A.D.
1602. muscadel, and several Greek wines; sweet oil, carpets, pepper, cinnamon, and other spices. The exports from England consisted mostly of woollen cloths, leather, tin, and lead.

The perfect and full success of the two celebrated circumnavigators, Sir Francis Drake and Cavendish, who, about this period, returned from their voyage round the world, greatly contributed to rouse the attention and curiosity of the nation at large, and incite its merchants to endeavour to establish a direct trade to India. On their application to the princess who then wore the crown of England, a charter was granted on the 31st December, A.D. 1600, insuring to them an exclusive right of trade to the East Indies, free of all duties, together with various other privileges. Sir T. Smith of London was appointed their first governor, with a court of twenty-four directors, who were annually chosen. This charter was to remain in force during the space of fifteen years.

The original shares were only fifty pounds, and their total capital amounted to no more than 72,000*l.* Of this sum 45,000*l.* was instantly appropriated to the fitting out of five ships, under the command of Captain James Lancaster; and the remaining sum of 27,000*l.* was employed in the purchase of their cargoes. This fleet, manned by 480 able mariners, sailed from Torbay on the 5th June, 1602; and with few accidents (considering the length of the voyage, so totally new to an English squadron,) reached Acheen, in the island of Sumatra; by the sovereign of which they were, after delivering the letters of their queen, and presents which accompanied them, kindly and honourably received, and a treaty concluded with them. They then sailed to the Molucca Isles, where a similar reception awaited them; and loaded with the precious and spicy products of these Eastern shores, they arrived safe in the Downs, after a prosperous voyage, in the month of September 1603.

1604. The second fleet left England under Sir H. Middleton in the following year,

1604, with only three ships. These pursued the same route, traded to the same points, and with similar success; returning with a far more valuable cargo than their predecessors, and charged with letters and valuable presents to their sovereign, James I. from the kings of Bantam and Tidore.

The third expedition, under Captain Keeling, carried out Captain Hawkins in quality of ambassador to the court of the Mogul emperor, where he was received with great respect, and had the success to procure considerable commercial advantages for his country.

The minds and views of these enterprising managers of this great national concern expanded with the enlargement of their commerce. Their charter was renewed with additional immunities, and they now applied themselves to the construction of their own vessels; those hitherto employed having been hired from the Hanseatic towns. Amongst the ships built at this period was one of 1200 tons, the largest trading vessel ever launched at that time in England. This ship cost the sum (at that period considered immense) of 80,000*l.* sterling.

The family of Timour, who still sat upon the throne of Dehli, were ever the liberal and distinguished promoters of commerce; and the English Company obtained leave from Jehanguire, then emperor of Hindoostan, to form settlements on the coast of Cambay. The Dutch, jealous of this proceeding, violently opposed it; and they having now the exclusive possession of the Spice Islands, where they used every species of force and fraud to obstruct the views of the British, a plan was formed to secure a settlement on the coast of Cambay, and
Surat was the point selected for the first display of our military and commercial A. D. 1611.
exertions.

Four ships of a large class were accordingly sent under Captain Best, an enterprising and gallant officer. The Portuguese, long settled on this coast, guarded the entrance of their port with watchful vigilance. Captain Best, however, with his small force, boldly entered the road of Surat, and, with the consent of the Mogul governor, established a factory in that city. The viceroy of Goa, with a powerful fleet, consisting of four great galleons and twenty-six gallies, having 5000 men on board, and 130 pieces of cannon, arrived to attack and destroy the British; but the latter, not waiting the onset, dashed forward to meet the enemy, and poured their broadsides with such destructive effect into the Portuguese squadron, as to make them decline any further contest. Three times did these baffled and enraged foes return to the assault, but with the like result; and in a fourth attack they were completely defeated, with the loss of 1200 men.

The distinguished reception of Captain Hawkins at the court of Jehanguire encouraged Sir T. Smith, the president of the India Board at home, to solicit his sovereign to send to the Mogul court, as public ambassador, some person of distinction, with full powers to conclude a treaty, and arrange other affairs of commerce with that monarch. Sir Thomas Roe, an accomplished gentleman and scholar, was soon after chosen for this distinguished office; and a squadron of ships, fitted out with great expense, under Captain Keeling, conveyed the British ambassador to the shores of India, where, by the able execution of the duties intrusted to him, and his conciliating manners, he raised the name and character of England at that magnificent court, and obtained many important privileges for the Company.

A.D. 1619. The British fleets, calculated equally by their build for traffic or for war, now poured into the Indian seas in great numbers, and spread rapidly and widely over its shores. They had already established settlements at Bantam, Surat, Agra, Agimere, Brampore, Calicut, Masulipatam, Siam, Banda, and Amboyna. The principal imports from these places were cloves, mace, nutmegs, and pepper; cinnamon, indigo, silks, calicoes, and precious stones.

The Dutch meanwhile had fortified themselves so effectually at Batavia, and rendered its port so impregnable, that after several severe and bloody conflicts with both the Portuguese and English fleets, the contest was relinquished by the latter, and a treaty entered into, which provided that all parties should have a free and open trade in the Indian seas. This treaty was, however, violated by the Dutch almost as soon as made, and the most horrible cruelties were committed by them upon our countrymen at Banda and Amboyna. The result of these proceedings was the total expulsion of the English from the Spice Islands. The government of England took little interest in these events, and merely sent a remonstrance to the States General, which produced no effect; and the matter soon after altogether dropped, to the great injury of the India Company.

The active spirit of the English, however, was not to be depressed. Deprived of the spice trade, they now sought other markets for their enterprise, and having gained a footing in Japan, attempted to establish a trade from thence with China. Urged on and assisted by Shah Abbas, sovereign of Persia, they forced the Portuguese from Ormuz on the Persian gulf, and thus opened a new channel, by which their commerce much increased. They also about this period obtained permission from the sovereign of Golconda to found a settlement at Madraspatam, on the Coromandel coast, from which they supplied the greater part of the peninsula with European goods; and received in exchange diamonds, muslins, chintzes, and other rich articles of Indian manufacture.

No public act took place in aid of the India Company during the remaining years of the reign of James I. Neither in that which followed did any better encouragement dawn upon them. Cromwell indeed, soon after his assumption of the protectorate, declared war against the Dutch, whose main aim appeared to be at this moment the total overthrow of Britain as a maritime power. A long and hard-fought struggle taught them at length that we were too strong, and they were compelled to sue for peace, which was granted; and in a treaty

A.D.
1654. set on foot some time after, their conduct to the English at Bantam and Java did not fail to be noticed. The demand of the Company against the Dutch exceeded two millions; yet the latter bringing in like manner a claim on their behalf, a compromise took place, in consequence of which they paid to England the sum of 85,000*l*.

After this mark of patronage in the government, the Company's affairs became far more prosperous; and a subscription, to the amount of 800,000*l*. sterling, was raised for the more vigorous prosecution of their commercial projects.

In 1655, the Dutch gained possession of Calicut, where the Portuguese had held triumphant sway from the year 1500. Soon after they also tore from their
1655. grasp Colombo, their principal settlement in Ceylon; and to their monopoly of the various other spices now added that of cinnamon. They had, moreover, entered into treaties with the vast empires of China and Japan, and carried on an extensive commerce with them. A Dutch colony was also established at the Cape of Good Hope, which succeeded admirably. Thus, although their naval power declined in Europe, they were rising to eminence and splendour on the ruins, as it were, of the Portuguese empire in India.

If the India Company prospered under the patronage of Cromwell, they were not less indebted to King Charles II. who renewed their charter, and granted them fresh privileges; in addition to which, the port, town, and island of Bombay, on the coast of Guzzerat, ceded by Portugal to Charles on his marriage with the Infanta as part of her portion, was by his majesty made over to the Company for ever. A strong fortress was constructed on the island, and no expense was spared to render its defences impregnable. The harbour of Bombay was very spacious, and capable of sheltering a large fleet in perfect security.

1682. The affairs of the Company continued to prosper in this new acquisition to their possessions until the year 1682, when, to the great detriment of the merchants and factors, Sir John Child was appointed governor. He was a man of an imperious and tyrannical disposition, who ill treated and oppressed all under his authority, and even insulted the officers of the Mogul emperor, the great Aurungzebe. On the ground of pretended injuries received from the governor of Surat, he gave orders to seize all vessels and cargoes of the subjects of the Mogul empire. He went so far at last as to capture a number of vessels loaded with corn for the use of the imperial army, then encamped about fourteen leagues to the southward. Representations in a mild strain had no effect; an insolent reply was sent back to the Mogul general: nor did he feel at all aware of his folly, until informed that the Mogul had landed on his island, and possessed himself of a position only four miles from his principal fortress. Mazagan, a fort near the castle, was taken by the Moguls with little opposition; and gaining an eminence which completely commanded the castle, they erected their batteries, which, but for want of skill alone in the attack, would have carried death and destruction through the ranks of the garrison, who, had the Moguls succeeded, would to a man have been massacred. A submissive embassy to Dehli, soliciting forgiveness, and promising restitution of the plundered property, was the only alternative: this, in respect to the high naval consequence of the English, the emperor accepted, and his army was withdrawn from Bombay, on condition that Child should in nine months quit India for ever. That event, however, never occurred; he died within that period, and in a country where he had caused so much blood to be spilt. This affair cost the Company 400,000*l.* and much injured their credit with the Mogul and his subjects. The settlement at A.D. 1691. Madras had in the mean time made great and rapid advances of importance, and had become in fact the emporium of the commerce of the Coromandel coast, which had heretofore centred at Masulipatam. In Bengal also Mr. Charnock had commenced the establishment of a factory a few miles below Hoogly, on an arm of the Ganges, to which it gives its name. Fort William was likewise constructed with great strength and solidity, and a settlement formed in its immediate vicinity, which rapidly rose in wealth and splendour, and is at present named Calcutta. The exports consisted chiefly of raw silks, muslins, cottons, saltpetre, and opium; for which they received in return the woollen manufactures and ores of Britain, and other productions of Europe.

We shall not enter into the disputes and differences which existed for a long time in the Company, and which caused a separation, one party calling itself the Old, and the other the New Company. Suffice it to say, they were both,
A.D. 1702. with some difficulty, united in the year 1702, under the style and title of "The United Company of Merchants of England trading to the East Indies." This had not only the royal approval, but also the solemn sanction of parliament. With increased funds, and the firm support of the nation, their commercial and military efforts were alike crowned with success.

The situation of the various powers who had succeeded in gaining a permanent footing in India, was at this period nearly as follows: The Dutch had mostly retained the possessions of the islands; the English, the continent. To the Portuguese nothing remained but Goa, Diu, and a few small settlements on that coast. France, whose proceedings we shall frequently have occasion to notice, and to whose history we must advert, was, however, soon to rise with rapid strides to eminence in this quarter of the globe.

In the early part of the seventeenth century, the example and great success of the neighbouring nations had roused a kindred feeling in the French, which the politic Cardinal Richelieu encouraged to the utmost of his power. This was productive, however, of little effect, and the arrangement of a plan for settling a small colony on the island of Madagascar closed the affair. At the instigation and by the talents of the great Colbert, the establishment of an East India Company on a permanent basis took place in 1664. The term of their charter was fixed at fifty years. This society had the support of the government, and such pecuniary assistance as the finances of the court of Louis XIV. could afford. The most alluring prospects were held out for those Frenchmen and foreigners who would embark in this lucrative scheme: in consequence fifteen millions of livres, or about 656,000*l.* sterling, was in a very short period raised, and four ships equipped, which sailed from Brest in the spring following for the island of Madagascar. Here, however, they did not long remain; for in 1668 we find them occupying Surat and other points on the coast of Malabar. They soon succeeded in obtaining a footing at Masulipatam on the Coromandel coast, and a settlement at Bantam in the island of Java. They had also factories at Balasore and Hoogley in Bengal, as also at St. Thomas; and ultimately, after several severe contests with the Dutch, they fixed themselves firmly and in great splendour at Pondicherry. A.D. 1668.

But the most persevering assiduity and the best political talents could not overcome the serious obstacles of want of funds, and an inferiority of naval force, compared with their more fortunate rivals, who had been so long established. The affairs of the French East India Company then began rapidly to decline, before even their charter had expired. On the Malabar coast their influence was extinguished, and Pondicherry and a few of their smaller factories alone remained. Both the founder of their charter and the monarch who patronised it were now no more, and their funds nearly exhausted; while the French nation at large were weighed down with taxes, caused by the boundless expenses of the last reign. A few years passed in this desponding state until 1719, when a union was effected between the French East and West India Companies, under one general title, "the Company of the Indies," with a capital of fifty millions 1715.

of livres, with confirmation and wide extension of all grants and privileges before given. This measure, enabling the India Company to disembarrass themselves from the difficulties under which they had long been labouring, gave a new spur to their exertions; and three ships, richly loaded with European goods and with a large quantity of silver, both in specie and bullion, arrived to their relief about the close of the following year.

The French, thus again in a condition to display their banners on the continent of Asia, speedily regained and fortified several of the forts and stations which they had formerly abandoned. Soon afterwards they had established a trade with China for teas, with Mocha for coffee and Arabian drugs, and with Bassora for pearls and the rich produce of the Persian looms. Mauritius and the Isle of Bourbon were about this time also subjected to the French East India Company; and at Chandenagurh, above Calcutta, on the Ganges, a strong fort was erected.

A certain degree of power must be possessed by a company of merchants to protect their commerce in all despotic Eastern countries. This was evident at this period at Calcutta, which town had now risen to a great pitch of splendour, being the emporium of the British East India Company's traffic in Bengal. At the same time it was subject to continual extortions, from the rapacity of the ruling viceroy and his officers. An embassy, accompanied by a rich present, was therefore sent by the merchants of Calcutta, complaining of this oppression, to the court of the emperor. They were favourably received; their grievances were redressed; they were exempted from all duties, and permission was given to them to extend the limits of their authority, to construct fortifications, and to coin money. Intercession was also made in favour of the other two principal settlements; and they likewise received redress and several indulgences.

We are now called to return to the contests of imperial ambition, for which the reigns of the successors of the emperor Jehanguire were highly conspicuous.

On the death of this monarch, his ambitious and intriguing queen, who for several years had held unlimited sway over both her husband and the empire, Shah Jehan, the rightful heir, being absent in the Deccan, exerted her utmost influence to place her son-in-law, Sultan Shehriar, on the throne; and a large sum of money was consequently expended in raising a mercenary army of 20,000 men. Azoph Khan, however, faithful to Shah Jehan, as a momentary curb to the usurper, placed on the musnud Sultan Bolaki, son of Khusro, eldest son of Shah Jehan; writing at the same time to the latter, to urge his immediate advance to Dehli to decide matters. The unfortunate Shehriar meanwhile, hurried onwards by his ambition to ruin, and deserted by the greater part of his troops, endeavoured to fortify himself in Lahore against the imperial troops. Azoph Khan, however, with superior forces, stormed that fortress, and taking prisoner Shehriar, caused him to be deprived of sight by a hot iron, which, according to the law throughout Asia, for ever excludes the sufferer from the regal dignity.

Shah Jehan in his advance from the Deccan was joined by the principal rajahs of the country through which he passed with their forces, and soon collected an army sufficiently formidable to support his pretensions; but, skilled in the perfidious practices of Eastern courts, he could not feel satisfied, or secure on his throne, while Shehriar, Bolaki, and the three sons of Sultan Daniel, the deceased brother of Jehanguire, and who were all prisoners in Lahore, continued to exist: an order was therefore immediately sent by a confidential officer for the murder of these unhappy princes. This inhuman order was too faithfully obeyed. The two former were executed as rebels, and for aspiring to the crown. The three younger were strangled in their beds, and the bodies buried secretly by night in the gardens of the palace. Thus Shah Jehan with his sons alone remained of the illustrious house of Timour. These sons, however, were destined at a future period to be the scourge of their father, and to avenge the blood he had so inhumanly shed. The sons of Shah Jehan were, Dara, the eldest, at the period of his father's accession to the throne thirteen years of age. As far as his character had yet dawned, he was of an open, noble, and generous disposition. Sujah, the second son, was in his twelfth year, a youth of shrewd, penetrating, and brave character. Aurungzebe, the third, in his tenth year, had all that cautious reserve and deep dissimulation which marked his career through life. Murad, the fourth son, being only four years old, no idea could at that time be formed of his character. Shah Jehan had also three daughters, Jehanara Begum, Roxhanara Begum, and Banu Begum, all highly accomplished and beautiful.

A.D. 1628. The obstacles to his accession now removed, and profound peace prevailing throughout the empire, the coronation of Shah Jehan took place with much pomp and splendour at Agra, on the 1st February, 1628, in the thirty-seventh year of his age. Azoph Khan was appointed vizir, and the celebrated Mohabet Khan general of his armies. Could Shah Jehan have obliterated the bloody tragedy which preceded his ascent to the throne, no prince would have appeared more worthy of the imperial dignity. He opened the gates of the state prisons in Gualior to all the captives confined there. He intently applied himself to correct those abuses which, in the weak and imbecile close of his father's reign, had crept into almost every department of the state. He established an active and vigorous police throughout his extensive dominions. He promoted agriculture and encouraged commerce. Midnight robberies and assassinations, hitherto so frequent, ceased to be heard of; and by compelling the viceroys of his several provinces to make good the amount of any robbery committed within their respective limits, they became vigilant in the extreme, so that passengers through even the most unfrequented parts travelled in perfect safety.

The emperor's attention was for a time diverted by an insurrection in the south, where Lodi, an Omrah of distinction, had formerly not only espoused the cause of Shehriar, but opposed the march of the emperor through the province. Aware of the power and talents of this chief, Shah Jehan sent a force to reduce him, at the same time offering conditions in case he quietly submitted. Lodi chose the latter as the wiser part, and consented to resign his station in the Deccan, and to be made governor of Malwa. He was next called to court, where a continued succession of insults assured him that Shah Jehan was not sincere in his professions. Dreading assassination, he therefore fled, accompanied by his two sons, and pursued by the king's troops. The elder was killed, bravely fighting for his father: the younger and Lodi reached Malwa, where they endeavoured to raise an army; but the pursuit was so vigorous, that he could make no effectual stand. He thence retired with a few followers into Bundela, where the army gave up the pursuit. From thence traversing Berar and Oudipore towards Golconda, he stopped not till he reached Dowlatabad, where the nizam received him with open arms, and vowed to defend him, even should it cost him his kingdom.

A.D. 1631.

Shah Jehan, partaking of that strongly rooted desire to quarrel with, and finally to conquer, the Deccan, manifested by Acber and Jehanguire, lost no time in marching towards the south with 100,000 horse. Arriving at Brampore, the capital of Candeish, he sent Eradit Khan, governor of Candeish, with 25,000, and two other Omrahs with 14,000 horse each, making a total of 53,000, to combat the enemy. This force was directed against the territories of the nizam, with orders to ravage them as his oldest foe. Lodi by his military talents, however, occupying all the passes and strong holds, and declining an engagement, effectually prevented Eradit Khan from penetrating. The emperor, seeing the latter general's inability to cope with Lodi, recalled him, and sent Azoph Khan in his place, with 10,000 additional horse. Lodi, after the greatest exertions, was defeated, his allies dispersed, and himself compelled to fly. Fortune, however,

failed him in this last extremity; for, being overtaken by a body of horse sent in pursuit of him, he fell covered with wounds, after a gallant resistance, and having slain numbers of the enemy. A desultory species of war succeeded this battle: the allied rajahs solicited for peace, but Shah Jehan's demands were far too exorbitant to be complied with. A variety of sieges rapidly followed each other,
A.D. 1633. till at length in 1633 the fortress of Dowlatabad, hitherto deemed impregnable, was taken by Mohabet, and it is said by bribery. The aged nizam had died; the young nizam, his successor, was sent prisoner to Gualior, and his territories annexed to the empire. During this year the Portuguese settlement at Hoogley was attacked and plundered by order of Shah Jehan, who had taken a dislike to that people, from their refusing him assistance when in distress in his earlier career. This is the first instance of hostility against Europeans recorded in the Eastern annals.

A revolt of the rajah of Bundela (now Bundelcund) called for chastisement; and Aurungzebe, then only thirteen years of age, was sent under Nusirit,
1636. governor of Malwa, to reduce him to obedience. The youthful prince displayed great bravery in this expedition, being ever foremost at the post of danger, and exhibiting strong traits of those abilities which afterwards so much distinguished him. The refractory rajah was defeated, slain, and his head sent to Agra, where soon afterwards the young conqueror appeared, and laid above three millions in gold, jewels, and silver, at the foot of his father's throne.

It was not until near the end of 1636 that Shah Jehan commenced his long-projected expedition to reduce the different governments in the Deccan not yet conquered: Mohabet Khan having died, the success of his armies in that quarter had ceased. The kings of Visiapore and Golconda defied, in their strongly fortified castles, the efforts of the Mogul commanders; and although their country was overrun and devastated, still they remained unconquered. Their total reduction was left for the emperor and his son Aurungzebe to complete. In this expedition avaricious motives it is probable actuated Shah Jehan equally with those of ambition: the enormous sums he had lavished on his new palaces and buildings at Dehli and Agra, and the splendour of his luxurious court, rendered large supplies necessary; and the riches of the princes of the Deccan, both in hoarded money and great quantities of the finest jewels of Golconda, excited the avarice of the emperor, and spurred him on to appropriate these immense treasures to schemes of still greater magnificence. The kingdom of Golconda was a mine of jewels in itself, and rich in the great wealth of its dependent kingdom of Bisnagurh. The tiara worn by the sovereign of Golconda is thus described by Thevenot, a traveller of great veracity, whose statement will convey an idea of the riches and magnificence of this court and kingdom:

" This prince wears on the crown of his head a jewel almost a foot long, said to be of inestimable value. It is a rose of great diamonds, from three to four inches in diameter. On the top of this rose there is a little crown, out of which rises a branch resembling a palm-tree, and that palm-tree is a good inch in diameter, and six inches long; it is made of several sprigs or leaves, each having at its extremity a lovely long pearl, in shape like a pear. At the foot of this posy are two bands of gold, in which are set large diamonds, set round with rubies, which, with great pearls hanging down, dangling on all sides, makes an exceeding great show. These bands are fastened round the head by clasps of diamonds."

Shah Jehan, having given orders to the several Omrahs to join him, and some of these having long distances to march, was much delayed in his progress in this expedition. Aurungzebe accompanied his father, and the army at his request passed through Bundelcund, where the young prince exultingly pointed out the spots where in his first campaign he had so distinguished himself. In

A.D.
1637. hunting parties and other delays nearly a year elapsed before the emperor reached the borders of the Deccan. Arriving at length at Dowlatabad, and being joined by all his forces, his army was so prodigious, as to be almost beyond calculation. Twelve different corps were formed out of this mass, and sent under the most experienced generals by different routes into the territories of his enemies. War and destruction were thus let loose: attacked in all directions, the amazed inhabitants knew not whither to fly; no quarter was given to any who resisted. Towns were seen in flames on every side; the mountains were shaken with the continued roar of artillery; and the tigers of the desert fled from the more savage fury of the invaders. One hundred and fifteen towns or fortresses were overthrown in the course of the first campaign. The kings of these countries, unable to assist their unfortunate subjects, and seeing no end to the destructive and depopulating fury of their relentless foes, humbly sued for peace to Shah Jehan, who, taking advantage of their necessities, imposed upon them terms so severe, as amounted almost to the loss of their kingdoms. Deprived of their crowns, they still retained the authority of governors in their dominions, acknowledging the emperor and his successors lords paramount of the Deccan, and paying a large annual tribute. His grand project thus fully attained, Shah Jehan commenced his march for Agimere, leaving the command of the conquered
1638. provinces and a large army to Aurungzebe, under the tuition of Khan Zeman. That prince, now twenty years of age, was married soon afterwards to a granddaughter of the vizir Azoph Khan. The nuptials took place at Agimere, and were celebrated with the greatest pomp and splendour. Khan Zeman dying soon after, the sole command devolved upon Aurungzebe.

The emperor continued his route from Agimere to Lahore, hearing complaints and correcting abuses. His sons Dara and Sujah obtained at this period higher rank in the army: the former being promoted to command 10,000 horse and as many foot; the latter, 7000 horse and as many infantry. The youngest, Murad, now seventeen years of age, was, under proper tuition, invested with the government of Mooltan.

A.D.
Azoph Jah, brother of Noor Mahal, and father of the favourite sultana, died 1641.
in his seventy-second year. He appointed Dara his heir, leaving to him, in plate,
jewels, and money, nearly three millions sterling. Ruling with justice and cle-
mency, the emperor's will was received as a law throughout the vast empire
subject to him; an immense revenue, the result of commerce duly encouraged,
poured into the royal coffers from all quarters. The new capital, to which he
had given his name, was now also nearly finished: residing sometimes at one
capital, and sometimes at another, as his caprice or the season changed; now
engaged in hunting, and then in the delights of an overflowing harem, his
days passed prosperously, flattering him with every appearance of a tranquil
enjoyment of his riches and power, and a bright sunset to his reign. But the
domestic incertitude of this monarch cast a gloom, notwithstanding his flattering
prospects, over the closing years of his life, and involved him in difficulty and
misfortune. Shah Sefi, emperor of Persia, having by his cruelties inundated
his dominions with the blood of his subjects, advanced about this period with a 1642.
large force, to retake Candahar. Shah Jehan immediately dispatched Dara at
the head of 50,000 men, to be joined at Cabul by 30,000 more, to repel the
invasion. The armies, however, never met, Shah Sefi dying, some say by
poison, when his army returned to Persia, and the prince likewise retired with
his forces to his father at Lahore.

The emperor about this period publicly acknowledged his eldest son Dara as 1643.
his successor to the empire, and permitted that prince to enjoy a large portion
of imperial power, giving him a signet equal to his own, and settling on him
an allowance of near two millions sterling for his household. He shortly after

gave up to Dara and the vizir the toils and management of the state, and plunged into dissipation and sensual pleasures, unworthy of so great a monarch and of his former actions.

A.D. 1656. No event of national importance occurred until the year 1656, when new tumults broke out in the Deccan, caused, as Aurungzebe alleged, by the tardiness of Cuttub Shah in paying the annual tribute. He confessed that he had put his troops in motion, and that he required a reinforcement, which he requested the emperor would send him. His request was granted, in direct opposition to the advice of Dara, who was apprehensive of the growing power of his brother, and dreaded its increase, if an army capable of conquering the Deccan should be sent to him from Agra. But Aurungzebe had dispatched a trusty messenger with strong and irresistible arguments, to convince Shah Jehan that the renewal of the war in Golconda was requisite. This messenger was Emir Jemla, a Persian, a native of Ispahan, of low extraction, but good education. He was employed at first by a merchant, who traded to Golconda for diamonds. After some time he settled there, and pursuing the same trade on his own account, soon became wealthy, and purchased a high situation about the court: here his abilities rendering him conspicuous, he attracted the notice of Cuttub Shah, sovereign of that country, who assigned him a post of consequence in his army, and raised him ultimately to the command of the army of Tellingana, or Golconda. He carried on the war in Carnata, or the Carnatic, for that prince, and by his conduct and talents brought it to a favourable termination. His conquests enabled him to transmit immense treasures to the king, but he kept larger heaps for his own coffers, which, when called on, he refused to divide with his sovereign. Being compelled to fly from Golconda, he sought and found a ready asylum with Aurungzebe, who promised to support his cause, and procure the restoration of his family and treasures. Aurungzebe saw in Emir

A.D.
Jemla a man every way qualified to assist him materially in his ambitious pro- 1656.
jects; and of these projects he gradually made Jemla his confidant, explaining to him their depth and extent. Thus fully acquainted with all his views, and firmly resolving to uphold him in them, no better or more faithful ambassador could have been selected for the important mission to Shah Jehan, to impress him with the necessity of immediately renewing the war with the sovereign of Golconda. To ensure success, he delivered, as a present from Aurungzebe to his father, a purse of the most exquisite diamonds, one of which was quite unparalleled for size and brilliancy. The avaricious monarch, delighted with the sight, hesitated no longer: 20,000 horse were instantly ordered to march; and to avoid exciting the envy of Dara, Aurungzebe had appointed his eldest son, Mahommed, to command. The king of Golconda, unable to resist, at once submitted, promising to restore all the riches of Emir Jemla, and endeavoured farther to sooth Mahommed by valuable presents: but the latter sternly rejected his offers; and, in fact, his object being plunder, and not the restitution pretended, a dreadful scene of slaughter and desolation commenced. The horrors attending the sacking of this large and rich city, from the fury and avarice of the assailants, is without parallel: the streets and squares were dyed with the blood of the inhabitants; and the plunder was enormous, there being some streets entirely occupied by goldsmiths, jewellers, and bankers; and the very floors in the palace of the king being covered with plates of gold. This sovereign escaped in the confusion, and sought refuge in the castle of Golconda, standing on a pyramidal hill, and strongly fortified, the city and palace being situated around its base. Mahommed invested this powerful work, while its monarch in despair sallied out at the head of 6000 horse and 12,000 foot, and gave battle to the imperial army. He was, however, defeated with dreadful slaughter, and Ma- 1657.
hommed and his troops entered the castle with the retiring enemy. Here Cuttub

A.D. 1657. threw himself at the feet of his conqueror, and implored mercy and peace. The victor was inexorable, until Rizia, the beautiful daughter of that monarch, appeared to supplicate for her father. Struck, vanquished by her charms, Mahommed sheathed his sword. A treaty favourable to the king of Golconda was concluded. Rizia was given to him in marriage, with a kingdom in reversion for her dowry.

The joy of Aurungzebe in welcoming his son thus successful and triumphant in the field of war and love, may be conceived. He immediately sent a pompous account to the emperor, who raised Mahommed to the rank of 11,000 horse. Emir Jemla was charged with these dispatches to Shah Jehan, and so much ingratiated himself with the emperor, that the vizir of the empire being lately dead, he was appointed to that high and important office. A present of six lacs of rupees, presented by Jemla, is said to have had much influence in his advancement on this occasion.

Whilst Jemla remained at Agra, intelligence arrived of the death of Adil, king of Visiapore; and that, without consulting the emperor, his son had been raised to the throne. Shah Jehan, fired with this neglect, sent the vizir with 20,000 men into that kingdom, to depose the son of Adil, until he should swear fealty to the emperor. At Brampore the vizir joined Aurungzebe, and their united forces pressed forward. The vizir of Visiapore collected an army in haste, but these were too inexperienced to stand before the highly disciplined army of the invaders. The fortress of Beder, deemed impregnable, was taken after a siege of twenty-seven days, and the garrison put to the sword. Here was deposited the treasure of the crown, which became the prize of the victors. Kilburga, a large fort and stronger garrison, was, after an obstinate resistance, also reduced, 11th June, 1657; and Callian, near the coast, soon after shared the same fate. Utterly hopeless of retrieving matters, the unhappy prince threw himself on the mercy of his conquerors, who pardoned him on condition of paying a large sum, besides the expenses of the war, putting his strongest fortresses into the possession of Aurungzebe, and remitting to court, as the annual tribute of the kingdom of Visiapore, a sum equal to 1,875,000*l.* sterling.

A.D. 1658.

These events united more closely the friendship of Aurungzebe and the vizir, and increased their hopes of ultimately succeeding in their ambitious designs. The hour was now fast approaching when these projects were to be executed; for in September this year the emperor was seized with a serious illness, caused by intemperance in his seraglio. This was a signal for his four sons to rush to war and devastate the empire by their sanguinary contests.

The crafty Aurungzebe, the better to conceal the ambitious schemes which filled his soul, and lull the jealousy of his brothers, at all times affected the rigid austerity of a Fakeer, or Mahometan devotee. Constantly occupied in the strict and severe practices prescribed by the Koran in fasting, prayer, and ablutions, he shewed a total contempt for the splendour and pageantry of courts. Being by nature of a reserved and saturnine temperament, he was well suited to the character he assumed. His exterior appearance through life accorded with his professions. Even as a monarch he was rarely clothed in sumptuous apparel of cloth of gold, except on festival days. Still Aurungzebe never could conceal his real character either from his father or his elder brothers. Murad, his younger brother, an open, generous, and unsuspecting character, was more easily his dupe.

But to return to affairs of a more general nature. The illness of the emperor was of an alarming nature; he continued a long time insensible, and by copious bleeding alone his life was saved. Still he remained in so weak a state as to be utterly incapable of attending to public business, and doubts were entertained of his ever being competent to resume the cares of state. Dara, of his own accord, instantly mounted the throne: his first acts were those of violence

A.D. 1658. against his brothers, which clearly indicated his hatred and suspicion. This conduct hurried on the catastrophe which a more moderate course might have delayed. The known agents and partisans of his brothers were seized, with their papers, and placed in confinement, and the money in their hands confiscated. In an assembly of his Omrahs, he explained his conviction of the ambitious designs of his brothers, and called on his friends for their active support. An army, proportioned to the great exigency of the moment, was ordered to be immediately collected, and it appeared as though the event of a single battle was to decide the fate of Dara.

Dara's next act was to cause his father to be removed from Dehli to Agra, down the Jumna river. The recovery of Shah Jehan was very tardy, and he suffered several relapses, which gave rise to a variety of rumours: it was even positively asserted, that he was dead; that he was in confinement; that he had been poisoned by Dara. Sultan Sujah, second son of Shah Jehan, who had long governed Bengal as viceroy, and had amassed considerable wealth, was the first who appeared in the field with a formidable army, and asserted that he was marching to revenge the death of his father, and dethrone the parricide. Letters from the emperor himself were sent to undeceive him; but Sujah treated these as forgeries, and still advanced with his troops, till he arrived at Benares.

The politic Aurungzebe meanwhile determined to oppose the claims both of Dara and Sujah to the empire on the field of battle. With respect to Murad, he hoped to persuade him to unite his army, valour, and resources to his own. He wrote accordingly strong and pressing letters to that young prince in Guzzerat, stating, that as he, from religious motives, declined being a candidate for the imperial titles and honours, and as he objected to the accession of either of their elder brothers to the throne of India—Dara, on account of his incapacity, and total indifference on the subject of religion; and Sujah, because little

A.D.
superior in abilities to Dara, and from his being a heretic (this prince being of 1658. the sect of Ali), he, Aurungzebe, had resolved to throw all his influence and authority into the scale of Murad, who, from his bravery, ability, and principles, was alone worthy to sit on the throne of Timour. For himself he solicited only, that when Murad should be firmly seated, by their united exertions, on the musnud of the empire, a retreat might be assigned to him in some retired spot, where he might pass the remainder of his days in acts of piety and devotion. He farther urged Murad to lose no time in making his claims known, and uniting the army of Guzzerat with the troops he himself commanded in the Deccan, to march with rapidity on Agra. He sent the prince 100,000 rupees, and advised him to seize the castle of Surat, where the imperial treasure was deposited; to employ that treasure in raising troops, and to meet him with the largest possible force he could muster at Ujein, on their road to the capital.

Murad, dazzled by the splendid prospect which opened upon him, and unsuspicious of the artifices of the writer of these letters, implicitly followed the directions they conveyed, and causing himself to be proclaimed emperor of Hindoostan, hastened to meet his brother Aurungzebe at the appointed place. The two armies effected their junction on the Nerbudda river, Ujein having previously been occupied by the troops sent by Dara to oppose their progress.

The imperial army (for this denomination must be conferred on the troops of Dara) was commanded by Kossim Khan, a general of great talents and reputation, and Jeswunt Singh at the head of the Rajpoots of Marwar. These, by the orders of Shah Jehan, refrained from hostilities as long as possible, and attempted by remonstrance to prevail on the princes to return to their soubahs. These offers were received with contempt and as the forgeries of Dara.

The result was a sanguinary battle on the banks of the Nerbudda river, in which the imperial army was totally defeated, and the victorious columns of

A.D. 1658. Aurungzebe and Murad entered Ujein in triumph. In Bengal the imperial arms had been more successful, Sujah having in a position on the bank of the Ganges been surprised in his camp by a night attack of Soliman Shekoh, Dara's eldest son, who, crossing by a ford some distance from the enemy with a large body of cavalry, fell upon and totally routed them. Sujah escaped with extreme difficulty from the field, and took refuge in the fort of Monghir, where he was invested by Soliman. The latter was soon compelled to return to Agra, where circumstances required his presence. A treaty was entered into with Sujah, in which he engaged not to oppose the right of Dara to the throne.

The intelligence of the defeat of the imperial army on the Nerbudda spread consternation at Agra. Shah Jehan recovered from his illness, and apparently at liberty, though really a prisoner at the disposal of his eldest son, saw himself virtually dethroned, without a chance of ever again wielding the sceptre of India; and felt sensibly, that whoever was the victor in the struggle now pending, little good could accrue to him. Dara treated him with great external respect, and consulted him on all public affairs. Fearing a change of masters might be for the worse, the emperor endeavoured to reconcile himself to the necessity of his situation; he espoused warmly the cause of Dara, called round him his oldest and ablest generals, opened his immense treasures, and even wished in person to take the field with his son. From this Dara, however, imprudently dissuaded him, wishing to have no one to participate in the glorious results of that day, which, by a general battle, should fix him firmly on the throne, and for ever annihilate the opposers of his rights. He burned to meet his brothers in the field, and although warmly urged by his experienced father to await the arrival of his son Soliman, already on his march from Bengal, he resolved to strike the decisive blow on the instant. He therefore, collecting an army fully equal to that with which Shah Jehan undertook his famed expedition for the

A.D.
conquest of the Deccan, took leave of the emperor, promising to bring his 1658.
rebel brothers, Aurungzebe and Murad, bound in chains before him. The emperor's last words at this parting were, "Go, my son; but beware of returning to my presence unadorned by the palms of victory." The force Dara had assembled amounted to 100,000 horse, with 1000 guns. He rapidly advanced to the banks of the Chumbul river, about twenty miles south of Agra, where he took up a strong position, which he fortified, and awaited the approach of the enemy. Aurungzebe and Murad, after a few days repose at Ujein, had advanced on their route towards Agra, and on the 1st June gained the banks of the Chumbul. Aurungzebe, on reconnoitring the force and position of the enemy, thought the latter far too formidable to be carried with his inferior numbers, which did not exceed 40,000. A neighbouring rajah, prevailed on by large bribes, agreed to conduct the army by secret paths through the mountains which are situated between the river Chumbul and Agra. Leaving his tents, baggage, and a small guard as a blind, he moved his whole force during the night, and was discovered in full march on the following morning by the army of Dara towards the capital. Dara, astonishcd, brokc up his camp with prccipitation, and retired with all expedition to Agra, placing himself between that capital and the approaching enemy, where he drew out his troops in order of battle. A sanguinary contest, commenced by Dara, was continued with varied success through the day. Prodigies of valour were performed on either side; but Dara having descended from his elephant, his troops conceiving him killed, and struck by a sudden panic, betook themselves to flight. It should be observed, that in the Indian armies all eyes are fixed on the commander, and all movements regulated by his. Dara had left his elephant to mount his horse, to put himself at the head of a corps of cavalry, and strike a decisive blow. All, however, now was lost: he was compelled to fall back upon Agra; but ashamed

A.D. 1658. to see the emperor, pursued his route to Dehli by night, where he hoped, by augmenting his force, to be enabled to make yet one struggle more for the crown. Aurungzebe did not pursue the defeated army, but encamped on the field of action. Soliman, the son of Dara, now on his march to join his father, was too formidable to be neglected altogether by Aurungzebe, who sent a letter to that prince by two generals, Rajah Jeysingh and Delil Khan, to say that Dara was totally defeated; that the great Omrahs had deserted his cause, and joined the victorious army; that Shah Jehan, being from his infirmities no longer fit to reign, a successor ought to be appointed, and that Murad appeared the fittest to govern the empire. He added, that if they would seize Soliman, and join his and Murad's army, they should be rewarded with the highest honours. These tempting offers prevailed with these faithless officers; but they durst not attempt the seizure of the gallant and noble leader: they, however, waited upon him, and represented in the strongest manner the desperate state of his father's affairs, and prevailed upon him for the present to take refuge in the mountainous tracts towards Serinagurh, the rajah of which was his friend, and where he would be secure for the present from the storms which agitated the state.

Four days after their victory, Aurungzebe and Murad advanced towards Agra. The gates of this city were thrown open, the emperor and his family having retired into the citadel. Aurungzebe, through affected respect to the emperor, would not enter the city, but encamped in a garden outside. Here, as he could not with common decency force his way into the asylum which his father had chosen, he had recourse to his old weapons, treachery and deceit, to gain his purpose. His hoary sire, however, was well versed in that science of stratagem which his son practised so generally, and he was fully prepared to repel art by art. Aurungzebe, to follow up the line of conduct he had decided on, sent to the emperor a messenger, who was desired to touch in his name the

A.D. 1658.

ground with his forehead, express his delight at his father's recovery, assure him that his past conduct had been influenced by the inordinate ambition of Dara, and that he was respectfully awaiting the commands of his sovereign outside the walls of the city. Jehanara Begum, the favourite daughter of Shah Jehan, was the bearer of his answer to his rebellious son, which stated that he was convinced of his loyalty and zeal; that he supposed him misled by designing villains; and as he doubted not his sincere contrition, he freely pardoned him. But Murad the emperor considered an obstinate rebel, inasmuch as he had proclaimed himself emperor in Guzzerat; adding, that if Aurungzebe would desert his brother, he should be received with open arms, and whatever he could desire in the empire below the throne of his father should be bestowed upon him. The artful Fakeer affected to be won by these words, and asserted, that he had no ambition beyond the retirement of a derveish, separated from the society of men, and devoted to God; that he had taken Murad's part against Dara from principle, as he thought the former more worthy to rule than his brother; and he concluded by a solemn promise to wait on the emperor in two days in person, to discuss this important point.

Shah Jehan, however, too well knew his son to trust one moment to his professions: never was a deeper game of duplicity acted, or by such able and experienced masters, as by Shah Jehan and Aurungzebe on this occasion. While Aurungzebe was determined that neither Dara nor Murad should sway the sceptre of Hindoostan, Shah Jehan was fully resolved, that Aurungzebe, if he entered the gates of his palace, should never quit it alive. The latter had not the slightest intention of visiting his father: his sister Roxhanara, who was devoted to him, cautioned him against trusting one moment to the emperor, who had formed a plan to have him seized by some Tartar women attached to the seraglio, who, armed with daggers, were fit for any desperate act. Message

A.D.
1658. after message was sent to entice Aurungzebe to an interview, and to draw him to the castle. He sent letters, however, to Dara of a very different purport, which, falling into the hands of Aurungzebe, convinced him of his father's true sentiments, and that no time was to be lost. He at length fixed a day for going to meet the emperor: on this occasion he solicited permission to take a small guard with him; which was readily permitted, and the command was intrusted to his son Mahommed. The royal Fakeer advanced, and his near approach was even announced, when, pretending to be seized with a sudden fit of devotion, he changed his route towards the tomb of the great Acber, there to offer up his prayers. This was the concerted signal for action. Mahommed's party, though small, was composed of men inured to danger, and whom nothing dismayed. These rushed with fury on the imperial troops who guarded the gates, overpowered them, and then admitted a large body of their comrades, who waited in readiness outside. These soon rendered themselves masters of the walls and ramparts, while Mahommed secured the whole of the interior of the castle. The keys of this fortress were demanded from the emperor: he was put in confinement, with the Begum and all his women, and a guard placed over them, with orders that he was not to write or speak to any one, nor without permission to quit his apartment.

This artful hypocrite continued meanwhile to treat Murad with all the servile flattery and attention due to a sovereign. He addressed him on all occasions as emperor, and obliged his Omrahs to do the same. Some of these hinted to Murad their suspicions of his brother's sincerity; but the infatuated youth was not to be awakened from his dream of splendour. The confederate princes now set forward for Dehli with their numerous forces, leaving Shah Hest Khan governor of Agra. On arriving at Muttra, a most sumptuous banquet was prepared by Aurungzebe, to which Murad was pressingly invited; and though strongly

A.D. 1658.

urged by several of his friends to refuse, as the plans of his brother were to them evident, he rejected their friendly counsel, and about the close of evening repaired to his brother's tent. Murad was a luxurious prince, fond of the pleasures of the table, and he was furnished with all the delicacies which could provoke or gratify the appetite; and at the close of the repast some exquisite wine of Shiraz was produced, and Murad invited freely to partake of the sparkling beverage, while the same potent liquor was profusely allowed to the attendant Omrahs. Aurungzebe, feigning business, left the tent, and the prince, overpowered with wine, soon sunk into a profound sleep. In this state he was deprived of his sabre and poniard. Every precaution had been taken: a band of hardy ruffians waited without. At this moment his treacherous, cruel, and ungrateful brother, he in whose breast were mingled the basest cruelties, the blackest ingratitude, entered, and spurning with his foot his victim, his professed prince, friend, and brother, exclaimed aloud, "Is this conduct worthy a great emperor? Murad, thy throne, thy claim to imperial dignity, are for ever forfeited. Here, take this infamous besotted man away; bind him hand and foot, and throw him into yonder room, there to sleep out his wine." The prince in vain sought for his sword and poniard; several persons rushed in, and, in spite of his outcries and opposition, fettered his hands and feet. An elephant and a body of horse were in readiness; he was shut up in a covered amari or castle, and before morning was far on his way to Agra, thence to be conveyed to Gualior, the fatal prison of the unfortunate princes of the house of Timour. This remarkable event occurred on the 6th July, 1658.

Aurungzebe gained over by presents and promises the leading men of Murad's army, with which, united to his own, he marched towards Dehli; but hearing on the road that Dara had gone to Lahore, and resolved not to leave another rival in the field, he pressed with ardour his pursuit under a ver-

A.D. 1658. tical sun, subsisting on the coarsest food, drinking unwholesome water, and sleeping on the bare ground, like the meanest soldier. Dara, dreading his inveterate foe, left Lahore, and moved towards Mooltan. Had he more judiciously taken the route of Cabul, he would have met with a powerful army, commanded by Mohabet, an old enemy of Aurungzebe, who would most warmly have espoused his cause. The latter, dispatching Khan Jehan, his favourite Omrah, at the head of 8000 horse, to follow up Dara, returned himself to Dehli. Here contemplating his success in the ambitious career he had marked out, he determined to secure the diadem of the empire of India. His religious professions, however, as a Fakeer being an objection, he once more employed deceit: he procured some of those Omrahs most attached to his interests to call a council or assembly of the nobles, in which it was proposed that the crown should be offered to him, no other branch of the family being adequate to support its burthen, or to uphold the glory and splendour of the empire. The result was a deputation to request his acceptance of the throne. The crafty and hypocritic Aurungzebe for a long time obstinately resisted, hesitated, and affected even displeasure at the request; but when they urged his compliance as a point of duty, and represented that his devotion could be as freely exercised on the splendid throne as in a retired cell, he yielded; and without any of the pomp and pageantry usual on such occasions, Aurungzebe, the humble Fakeer, on the 2d of August, 1658, publicly ascended the imperial throne at Azabad, near Dehli, assuming on the memorable occasion the title of *Alum Gir,* or Conqueror of the World.

The news of Aurungzebe having ascended the throne was celebrated at Agra, by order of the governor, with every demonstration of joy. The noise of the artillery and the shouts of the populace penetrated even to the ears of Shah Jehan, who, informed of the cause, and forgetting that his own conduct as a son was to the full as wicked as that which he now experienced, burst into a violent paroxysm of rage. Dara, still supposing Aurungzebe to be in pursuit of him, marched towards Sindi: taking the fort of Bicker, he added to its garrison a strong reinforcement of Patan troops; and engaging some Portuguese, Dutch, and French artillerymen, to manage the artillery of the place, he deposited within it his treasure, which was very considerable. He then crossed the Indus by a bridge of boats, and took possession of Sicar; but remained there only a few days, when he proceeded down the western shore of the Indus to Tatta. Khan Jehan still pursuing him, he recrossed the river with his harassed troops, and, undaunted amid all his difficulties, commenced his march across the dreadful desert which stretches between that country and Guzzerat. At Ahmedabad, the capital of that province, he arrived with an army famished by hunger and worn down by fatigue. The governor, Shahnavaz, was the father-in-law of Aurungzebe, and also of Murad, and received him with apparent kindness: but it is strange that Dara should thus have trusted himself in the hands of the father of his bitterest enemy. 1658.

During this period Sultan Sujah, in his great and wealthy government of Bengal, had retrieved his affairs, and repaired those losses he had suffered in the contest with Soliman. This prince it will be remembered vigorously opposed the pretensions of his eldest brother Dara to the throne; but he was far more indignant to learn, that the younger had not only aspired to, but actually occupied that seat, to which he felt he had at least a prior right. He instantly therefore raised a large army, and advancing by rapid marches, fully convinced that it was better to be the aggressor, than to await in his government the bursting of the storm, which must speedily gather over that province, Sujah reached Allahabad.

The emperor, as we must now style Aurungzebe, undismayed by the nu-

A.D. 1658. merous adversaries who sprang up around him, prepared to take the field. He called his son Mahommed from Mooltan, to join him with all his forces, and ordered Emir Jemla, on whom he much relied, to hasten with the best troops of the Deccan towards Bengal. A strong force under Shaista Khan was left in Agra, and the emperor began his march leisurely down the bank of the Jumna.

Sujah meanwhile had advanced from Allahabad, and was encamped in a strong position near Kidjwa, about thirty miles from that fortress, and near a large tank of water: here, feeling his troops to be inferior to those of his opponent, he threw up intrenchments, and awaited the attack of the imperial army. Having collected his detached corps, Aurungzebe pushed on with vigour to meet his brother. Mahommed, his son, commanded the vanguard of 5000 horse. Arrived within one mile and a half of Sujah's position, he halted and encamped; an extensive plain stretching between them, well calculated for a general action. Sujah, however, whose artillery was fine, and defended the front of his camp, issued not from his lines. The following morning at daybreak, the imperial troops advanced to the attack, but found it impossible to force the line, the artillery from which scattered destruction among the assailants. These attacks, several times repeated, all equally failed. Aurungzebe was perplexed. To add to his distress, accounts were brought that Rajah Jeswunt, with a body of Rajpoots, who had accompanied him to the field, had suddenly fallen on the baggage in the rear, seized and were carrying it off. This report, rapidly spread, created the greatest confusion in the imperial ranks: all, anxious to save their property, left the field. Sujah's army, taking advantage of this confusion among the enemy, rushed with impetuosity from their lines, and fell upon their opponents with inconceivable fury: a horrible carnage ensued, and the troops of Aurungzebe appeared on the verge of defeat. But that cool and intrepid warrior, urging on his elephant into the thickest ranks of the enemy, exposed to a heavy shower of missiles, which a complete suit of armour scarcely guarded him against, encouraged, exhorted, and rallied his troops by his animating voice and gesture. Sujah, on an enormous elephant, descried him at a distance, and strove repeatedly, with the most eager anxiety, to meet his brother hand to hand; but the crowds of elephants, horses, and combatants, prevented this rencounter. At this time the leader of the elephant on which Aurungzebe was mounted, was pierced to the heart by an arrow: the elephant, now unmanageable, was about to retreat, and the emperor to abandon his seat, when Emir Jemla, fortunately observing this movement of his master, cried to him, "If you descend from that elephant, you descend from your throne." The emperor paused, and calling for a chain, ordered the feet of his elephant to be fastened together: thus immoveable, he stood upright in the amari, every eye fixed upon him, and every arm of the enemy pointed against him; yet he braved it all, though the shot and arrows fell like hail around him. A.D. 1658.

In this extremity Bernier relates, that he was saved by the very same stratagem that lost Dara the field in the moment of victory. One of Sujah's captains, bribed it is said by Aurungzebe, rode up to his prince, and besought him not to expose himself needlessly: "Come down," he cried, "in the name of God! The Moguls are flying; God has made you sovereign of Hindoostan; let us pursue the fugitives; let not even Aurungzebe escape us!" Sujah descended from his amari, and his army, no longer beholding him in his place, became terrified, supposing him killed or taken prisoner: all immediately dispersed and fled in confusion. So general was the defeat, that it was with the greatest difficulty Sujah escaped from the field, when, with the remnant of his army, he pushed his march for Allahabad. The victor was not in a state to follow; he returned to Agra, sending Emir Jemla, whom he appointed governor of the soubah of Allahabad, and his son Mahommed, to oppose Sujah. Dara had meanwhile

A.D.
1658. left the southern provinces, with the intention of moving on Agra. His force was considerable, but he placed his chief reliance on Maha Rajah Jeswunt, an independent and powerful Mahratta prince, who had long been the inveterate foe of Aurungzebe, and had closely allied himself with Dara. The latter, however, on reaching the borders of Jeswunt's country, learned, with astonishment and dismay, that, by the intrigues of the emperor, he had been induced to abandon his cause. Dara still moved towards Agra, and arrived at Agimere, about eight marches from the capital. Here he took up a strong position, and awaited the attack. The emperor meanwhile rapidly advanced, and a severely contested action took place. It has been said that Shanovas, a general, and high in the confidence of Dara, betrayed his plans and intentions to the emperor. Bernier indeed goes so far as to state, that the guns were fired without balls. Certain it is, that Aurungzebe gained a complete victory; and although his army was occupied in pillaging the rich effects in the camp of the conquered, yet Dara was compelled to an immediate and rapid retreat, in the most sultry season, across that arid and desert tract of country situated between Agimere and Ahmedabad, to which latter city he directed his march. Arriving there, he found a new governor lately appointed by the emperor, who refused him admittance. This ill-fated prince then moved to Cutch, where its rajah at first received him kindly, but, gained over by the emissaries of Aurungzebe, obliged him once more to depart, to encounter new perils. Dara next took refuge with a Patan chief, named Jihon, a man of ferocious character, at the head of a tribe of savage robbers, but whose life the prince had twice saved: to him therefore he might look for protection. Jihon received and treated him with distinction, and a short repose was allowed this persecuted prince; but news was soon brought, that a large force of the imperial army, under Khan Jehan, was approaching, and was in fact close at hand. The road of the desert was again

pursued by the prince and his followers, who had not proceeded far when they A.D. 1658.
perceived Jihon at the head of a thousand horse coming after them at full speed. Dara, supposing this chief had some important communication to make, turned back to meet him; but judge of his astonishment when the Patans suddenly surrounded and disarmed him! The prince, resigned to his fate, kept an indignant silence: after plundering his benefactor of all he had of value, the perfidious chief sent him to Khan Jehan, who immediately forwarded Dara and his betrayer, under a strong escort, to Dehli, where the emperor then held his court. Aurungzebe had already decided on his brother's fate, but he thought it politic to assemble the nobles, to demand their opinion as to what punishment should be inflicted. Confinement for life and instant death were severally sentenced; but all concurred in a public exposure of the prince in bonds. Dara accordingly, mounted on a lean elephant, meanly caparisoned, and with his son seated by his side, was led in melancholy procession through that great and populous city. The concourse of people was immense; all of them shed tears and bewailed his fate.

After this cruel exhibition, the prince and his son were closely confined in a strong fort near Dehli. Jihon, his betrayer, received a title and magnificent presents; but on his return home he fell a sacrifice to the just indignation of the people. This feeling at length became so strong, that the emperor, alarmed at its consequences, issued his order for completing the fatal tragedy, by the immediate execution of Dara. Nazir, an Afghan chief, known to bear a strong hatred to Dara, being selected for this bloody office, he, with three others, entering the prince's chamber by night, quickly dispatched him, and bore his head reeking with blood to Aurungzebe, who anxiously awaited its arrival. It was so disfigured, that he ordered it to be thrown into a vessel of water and cleansed. He then gazed some time intently on the features, and exclaiming,

A.D.
1658. "Ah! unfortunate man!" burst into tears. Dara's body was interred in the tomb of Humaioon. The youthful companion of his afflictions was, on the following morning, sent under a strong guard to the fortress of Gualior.

1659. Sultan Sujah, whom we left at Allahabad, with prince Mahommed and Emir Jemla, now governor of Bengal, in full march to attack him, feeling apprehensive that his retreat upon his capital, Rajmahal, might be cut off, fell back upon Monghir, which commands the pass into Bengal. Emir Jemla, however, by his superior skill turned this position by a mountain circuit, and appearing in Sujah's rear, compelled him again to retire. Another position was taken at Rajmahal, and intrenched, not wishing with his enervate troops of Bengal to meet in the open field the hardy veterans of the north. He was attacked in this position for six successive days, but his works being much injured, he retired on the seventh at night, and crossing the Ganges, marched for Tanda. The rainy season now coming on suspended all further operations.

Prince Mahommed, disgusted at the authoritative manner of Emir Jemla, and the occasional severe reproofs of his father Aurungzebe, felt his proud spirit rise to oppose this treatment. He had long been passionately attached to a daughter of Sujah's, and was even betrothed to her before the commotions in the empire had taken place. He therefore, at a time when Jemla was absent from the camp, took the opportunity, with a large party of his adherents, to go over to Sujah, by whom he was received with every demonstration of joy and respect. The marriage soon took place with great pomp and magnificence, and Mahommed was appointed commander-in-chief of the army. Jemla, as the season for military operations again approached, moved forward to attack Sujah at Tanda. Mahommed persuaded him, that his usual system of waiting for the enemy was bad; that he ought to meet them boldly in the field, and victory would surely favour him. Sujah, though averse to the experiment, submitted;

A.D.
and in the battle which took place a short time after, repented that he had done 1660. so, for the impetuous attack of the disciplined troops of the north overwhelmed and carried all before it. Sujah and Mahommed escaped with the greatest difficulty from the field, and with the shattered remnant of their army reached Dacca. The victor entered Tanda, and halted there some time, to regulate the affairs of that province.

Aurungzebe, though highly incensed at the defection of his son, stifled his resentment, and had recourse to that fraud and stratagem by which he had so often succeeded, to entice Mahommed by kindness and entreaty to return to his duty. By means which it would be tedious to enumerate, the wily emperor so far succeeded, that the prince arrived, all penitence and contrition, at Agra. His unrelenting father, however, immediately sent him a prisoner for life to Gualior. The unfortunate Sujah, harassed and constantly pursued by Jemla, sought refuge at length in Arracan. Here he was at first well received; but the king of that country, frightened by the menaces of Aurungzebe, or tempted by the great wealth of his guest, either effected himself, or was privy to, the destruction of the fugitive prince and his whole family.

Soliman Shekoh, the only remaining branch of this unfortunate race, still at liberty, was left at Sirinagurh, meditating the delivery of his country, and vengeance for his murdered father. The deep-designing and insatiate emperor could not rest whilst one relative existed. By his bribes and flatteries, he persuaded the rajah of Sirinagurh to give up Soliman; but this prince having timely notice, effected his escape, and being pursued, fled till he reached the borders of Thibet.
He, however, was so closely followed, that he was taken at length, and being 1662.
bound in golden fetters, was conducted to Dehli. This unfortunate prince soon took the same road as the other members of his family, being doomed to imprisonment for life in the same fortress.

Aurungzebe held the throne, thus iniquitously gained by the murder or imprisonment of all his family, for a period of fifty years; his fame, his valour, and his wisdom spread far and wide over all Asia, and brought the ambassadors of the several sovereigns with the richest presents to the foot of his throne. Jemla for his services was created vizir, and his son commander of the troops.

A.D. 1664. During this year, the emperor was seized with a violent fit of illness: this circumstance produced some commotions in the empire; but to put an end at once to all doubts respecting the succession to the throne, Sultan Mauzim was publicly proclaimed heir apparent, by the title of ***Shah Alum,*** or King of the Universe. This prince, however, was not devoid of that feeling inherent in his family, of aspiring to the throne before his father or nature intended; and this conduct was not unnoticed by the penetrating eye of Aurungzebe, whose affection for Mauzim rapidly cooled, and his second son Acber became his favourite and
1665. intended successor. This year, the emperor finding his health far from established, undertook, by the advice of his physicians, a journey to Cashmere, accompanied by his favourite sister Roxhanara, who had ever faithfully attached herself to him and his fortunes, as Jehanara had to those of Dara. But although so remote from the seat of government, the affairs of the state suffered no interruption. The great Omrahs attended the presence regularly as at Dehli, and constant messengers passed and repassed, bearing orders or reports, on the fleetest horses. Stern in manner, inflexible in justice, every passion, save that of ambition, subdued in his breast, Aurungzebe made few allowances for the passions or frailties of others. The governors of the distant provinces trembled at his frown, and the smallest deviation from his commands was followed by degradation or chains.

1666. This year Mahommed, son of Aurungzebe, died at Gualior, carried off it is supposed by a slow poison, usually administered to the state prisoners. Murad, brother of the emperor, perished soon after, and by the same means. In this year also, in the month of February, the aged Shah Jehan died in the castle of Agra, after an imprisonment of seven years, and was interred in the same tomb with his favourite and beautiful wife, Moomtaz ul Zemani.

Aurungzebe, only recently returned from Cashmere, proceeded to Agra, but did not enter the castle till he had written a letter of condolence to Jehanara, Shah Jehan's favourite daughter, requesting permission to enter. He was received by this Begum with extreme magnificence, and a large golden ewer, filled with the jewels of her deceased father, was presented to the emperor. The princess was apparently received into high favour; but she did not live long after this event, and the general opinion was, that her death was the effect of poison.

Some disturbances having occurred in the Deccan, and the king of Visiapore, A.D. 1668.
assisted by the sovereign of Golconda, refusing the annual tribute, prince Mauzim, governor of the Deccan, not being equal to subdue to the full extent these strongly situated and almost impenetrable countries, Aurungzebe marched with the whole power of his empire, and completely and effectually reduced them to obedience. He obliged them, as well as several other rajahs and princes bordering on Guzzerat, to pay all arrears, and large offerings for peace. One country in particular is said to have sent nearly two millions sterling to the royal treasury.

A rupture was at this period on the eve of breaking out with Shah Abbas, 1669.
emperor of Persia. Candahar, that so often disputed spot, was the chief subject of this war; and an insult unintentional, but not less felt, to the Persian monarch, urged matters to a crisis. Sultan Mauzim was ordered to move with 20,000 horse on Candahar, and Aurungzebe prepared to follow with the whole army of the north. Shah Abbas had advanced also with 80,000 horse and an immense train

A.D.
1669. of artillery, and every thing foreboded a desperate struggle. Fate, however, decided otherwise. Aurungzebe's progress was delayed by an imagined conspiracy among the Persian nobility, who had certainly no desire for a war with their own country. This soon passed, but before the armies met, death seized the Persian monarch; and his successor having no motive to continue hostilities, the two armies retrograded to their respective countries. An incursion of the Patans from the mountainous regions of Gazna, Cabul, and Candahar, occurred this year. Rushing like a torrent from the sources of the Attock and Nilab rivers, they overspread and devastated the fertile plains of the Punjab. Several hard-fought actions took place between these daring adventurers and the Mogul troops sent by Aurungzebe to expel them. The latter in the end succeeded, and the invaders were driven back with great loss. A second attempt was made
1673. by the same people some years afterwards. On this occasion they produced a person whom they asserted to be the Sultan Sujah, who, as we have already noticed, had perished with his family in Arracan. That this person had a likeness to Sujah is strongly credited, but no proofs are adduced that he was that identical prince. This man was placed at their head, and they marched in a mass, countless in numbers, towards Dehli, to establish their champion on the throne of Hindoostan. Aurungzebe, on advice of this attempt, assembled the whole mass of his force, and marching forward from Dehli, reached the Indus with
1674. his vast army at the close of the year 1674. A conflict, one of the most sanguinary that had for a long period occurred in India, here took place. The invaders were, however, finally and effectually repulsed, and betook themselves to the mountainous defiles and frontiers of their country, occupying the whole chain nearly of the Paropanisan range: here they carried on a desultory kind of war, which was protracted for near fifteen months. Despairing then of suc-
1676. cess, they severally dispersed; and their fictitious emperor, Sujah, fled into

Persia. The war being now considered as finished, Aurungzebe returned to Dehli, having been two years and three months absent.

A new species of warfare was soon after entered upon by the emperor, partaking somewhat of the nature of a crusade. Not satisfied with having carried destruction into the mountains of Afghanistan, he now turned his fury upon the superstitions of the Hindoos. He every where persecuted their priests, defaced their pagodas, and destroyed their images. At Muttra and Benares, two of the most sacred and venerated sites of Hindoo worship, the temples were levelled, and mosques built upon their ruins. Goaded to desperation by these oppressive measures, the whole body of Rajpoots, with the three great rajahs of Chitore, Agimere, and Joudpore at their head, rushed to arms, vowing war and revenge. These rajahs uniting their forces could bring into the field 200,000 men. Against A.D.
these the emperor, collecting all his disposable force, marched in 1678 with two 1678.
separate armies, one under Azem and Acber, his sons, the other commanded by himself in person. Aurungzebe entered the Rana's dominions with the intent to attack the ancient city of Chitore, but the difficulties of the country were so great, that he became entangled in its intricate mazes, and reduced to much embarrassment. After persevering for a year, he therefore resigned the command
to his sons, and having directed the same plan to be persisted in, returned him- 1679.
self to Agra.

Early in 1680 died the renowned Sevajee, the Mahratta chief, who had been so long a thorn in the side of Aurungzebe. Chitore fell into the power of the emperor also this year; but the Rana and the Rajpoots still opposed with success all attempts to penetrate their mountainous territories. Acber, son of Aurung-
zebe, this year threw off his allegiance, and being joined by 30,000 Rajpoots, 1681.
he sent a resolute Patan, his general, to murder his father at midnight in his camp. This villain nearly accomplished his purpose, having reached the tent of Au-

rungzebe; but being discovered, he was cut down by the guard. Sultan Mauzim was sent in pursuit of his rebellious brother, with orders not to give it up until he had secured his person. Acber, however, with 500 chosen horse, escaped, and took refuge with Sambajee, the son and successor of Sevajee, who publicly declared, that he would march immediately with 50,000 horse to Brampore, and declare Acber emperor of Hindoostan. In order to enable him to direct the whole force of the empire against this formidable rebellion, Aurungzebe patched up a peace with the Rajpoots, and sent three large armies into the field; the
A.D. 1683. united efforts of which, however, for three years, could not make any serious impression upon the strong country and warlike force of Sambajee. But Acber, seeing no likelihood of his ally placing him on the throne of India, soon retired into Persia, where he married the sister of the reigning monarch, and whence neither the threats nor promises of Aurungzebe could ever draw him. The king of Visiapore died this year. Azem was sent immediately at the head of a large force to seize that kingdom, which, with Golconda, he determined to annex to the empire; but Azem was defeated in two battles, which caused a sus-
1684. pension of hostilities in that quarter. The year after, however, Aurungzebe, collecting a force triple that which his enemies could bring into the field, marched with it into Visiapore, and encamped near the capital of that kingdom. By means of vast bribes and promises to the generals and nobles of the court of Visiapore, the insidious Aurungzebe felt so convinced of success, that he sent Sultan Mauzim to attack Golconda, being well informed that that kingdom had strongly supported and acted in concert with Sambajee and the sovereign of Visiapore. The king of Golconda, being weak and voluptuous, the weapons used against him were not those of war, but the bribery and corruption of his courtiers and his army: by these means he was left nearly alone in his palace, and having no alternative but to submit, he pacified the conqueror by a vast

A.D.
quantity of gold and several jewels of great value from his mines. After a 1686.
variety of attacks, Visiapore was stormed and taken about the middle of June 1686. The unfortunate sovereign appeared before Aurungzebe in fetters of silver, and humbled himself in the dust before the haughty conqueror.

This year, notwithstanding the treaty entered into, and the tribute imposed 1687.
on, the king of Golconda, the insatiate emperor once more directed his course against that city, which he closely invested. The wall and ramparts of Golconda are six miles in circumference, and above them is another tier of works of less extent. The siege was long and arduous, and it was not until September, that, in a night attack, possession of it was gained by the Mogul army. Thus were the two mighty and rich kingdoms of Visiapore and Golconda torn for ever from their rightful sovereigns, and added to the vast empire of Hindoostan. Other provinces in the south subsequently followed their fate, and there remained scarcely an enemy to struggle against, with the exception of the Mahrattas, who, daily becoming more formidable, made repeated and harassing attacks on the flanks and rear of the Mogul army.

Beholding the complete realization of all his plans of conquest, Aurungzebe, a few weeks previously to his death, took up his winter quarters at Ahmednagurh. There finding his dissolution rapidly approaching, at the advanced age of ninety years, some symptoms of remorse appear to have oppressed his mind, long hardened by crimes and blood. On this occasion he wrote two letters to his sons Azem and Kambuksh, which displayed strong evidence of a perturbed mind, and may be considered the dying declaration of this emperor. On Friday,
21st February, 1707, after performing his morning devotions, in company with 1707.
his attendants, he suddenly exclaimed, "Oh! that my death may happen on a Friday! Blessed is he who dieth on that day!" Returning towards his bed to perform his ablutions, he sank down suddenly, and yielded up his breath. His

A.D. 1707. hands remained clasped and in a tremulous motion some time after he ceased to breathe. Thus at an age to which few of the human race attain died the merciless destroyer of his family, the scourge of the persecuted Hindoos. No excuse can be made for his atrocious conduct to his father, his brothers, and their children. He lived almost entirely on herbs and pulse. No fermented liquor ever passed his lips; and in the pleasures of his seraglio he was at least more temperate than his predecessors. He allotted but little time to sleep or to his meals; and that part of the day in which he was not employed in hearing petitions, or attending to other affairs in the hall of audience, he passed in prayer, ablution, and reading the Koran. Except on public festivals, the vest he wore was seldom worth above eight rupees; nor were his sash and tiara loaded with jewels. In camp he was the most active of his whole army, rising early, and retiring late to rest; and in his younger days he generally slept on the bare ground, wrapped up in the skin of a tiger.

In his more public character, Aurungzebe as a sovereign, though deeply stained with blood, possessed many eminent qualities. He was versed in literature beyond most of the princes of the dynasty of Timour. He spoke correctly the Arabic and Persian languages, and also that of his ancestors, the Moguls. He patronised learning, and corresponded with learned men throughout the empire. He built many schools, and endowed them, storing them with books in all branches of learning, and placing able masters at their head. Naturally of an austere and unsocial temper, superstitious by habit, if not by principle, he discouraged gaming and intrigue among the nobles of his court. His administration of justice was inflexible: the highest rank could not avert, nor the greatest wealth arrest, its sword, when raised to strike the guilty; and the princes, his sons, were equally liable to punishment with the meanest of his subjects; he himself appearing to be the only one privileged to commit crimes with impunity.

He was intimately acquainted with the characters and talents of all the governors of his provinces, as also the generals and officers of his armies. Of the revenues of the empire, amounting to the enormous sum of thirty-two millions sterling, he knew the precise expenditure. These were not idly dissipated, or avariciously hoarded; all appear to have been faithfully applied to the exigences of the state. To prove this, only about 7000*l.* sterling was found in his private treasury at his death. Aurungzebe was buried at Hydrabad, in the Deccan. A.D. 1707.

On the death of Aurungzebe, Azem immediately marched from the south towards Agra and Dehli, where he hoped to seize the imperial treasure; nor did he attend to the generous offers made to him by his elder brother for an accommodation. Mauzim also without delay moved from Cabul to the same destination, and by the aid and exertions of his faithful vizir, Monauim Khan, fortunately secured the treasure which had been constantly accumulating from the time of Acber, to which, as eldest son of Aurungzebe, he had certainly a prior right, and which was sufficient to pay and support, if necessary, all the troops that could be levied in the empire. The rival princes met at the river Chumbul, which Mauzim placed in his rear. Seldom had India witnessed two such masses as here appeared in arms: that of Mauzim consisted of 170,000 horse, 150,000 foot, 3000 elephants, and 3000 pieces of cannon; that of Azem was little inferior. These two princes it must be remembered shared the empire between them, and with followers, &c. their armies must, united, have amounted fully to one million. This great battle was fought on the 9th of June, 1707: they contended for an empire at that time unrivalled in wealth and extent. Most of the great Omrahs who had served under Aurungzebe joined Mahommed Azem, and the greater part of them, with the two sons of Azem, fell in the action. Azem, however, stood his ground, though his force was reduced to 6000 horse only; and these being surrounded by a host of enemies, several times their own

A.D.
1707. number, the prince, seeing all lost, stabbed himself to the heart. No victory could be more decisive. Mauzim immediately mounted the throne, under the assumed name of ***Behaudur Shah.***

1708. Vengeance still cried, however, for the accumulated murders of Aurungzebe; another victim was yet demanded from his family to appease Omnipotent Justice. Kambuksh, the son nearest to his heart, had been sent by the late emperor a few days before his death to Visiapore. But this rash youth, inflamed with more ardent desire for independence than his brother Azem had shewn, on arriving in the province he had been appointed to govern, assumed the imperial titles, and caused coin to be struck in his name. Hurried away by the headstrong passions of youth, his conduct at times bordered on insanity, on the slightest suspicion devoting to tortures and death the most beautiful women of his harem, his most tried friends, and most faithful servants. This violent conduct soon deprived him of the affection of the great Omrahs of the Deccan, Mahomedans as well as Hindoos, who, disgusted, retired from his banners to their respective castles, where they determined to await the result of the contest.

Behaudur marched with an immense force, exceeding by 100,000 men the army with which Aurungzebe had invaded the same country. Kambuksh had meanwhile advanced to Hydrabad. The emperor, willing to settle the dispute amicably, wrote the most pressing letters to his brother, offering him, in addition to the two provinces he had hitherto governed, the nizamut of the Deccan, with unlimited authority in the south. The infatuated youth, callous to kindness, and deaf to the remonstrances of his brother, madly prepared for battle. Behaudur then moved to within twelve koss of Hydrabad, and there sought by secret emissaries to detach the few chiefs who still adhered to his cause. Rustum Dil Khan, Syef Khan, and his brother-in-law, Meer Mulling, determined to accept the protection thus offered; but intimation of their intention having

reached Kambuksh, he ordered them all to be put to death, and their estates A.D. 1708.
confiscated. This act detached almost all his army from his interests, so that not 10,000 remained under his banners. With these he advanced to attack the formidable masses opposed to him. A detachment sent forward to reconnoitre, headed by Zoolfeckar, an enemy of Kambuksh, resolved if possible to seize him; but before the adverse parties met, the troops of the prince turned their backs and fled, leaving with him only a few attendants. Even in this desperate situation he contrived with his arrows to scatter death among the surrounding foe, who, irritated by his wanton and frantic defence, shot several arrows in return, which soon piercing him, he fell from loss of blood, and was taken prisoner and carried before the emperor, when a most affecting scene took place. The prince, however, did not appear to lament what had occurred; but bequeathing some valuable jewels which he had on the elephant with him to his brother, the emperor, he soon after expired.

Having completed the war in this part, Behaudur had a plan in view of reducing to more complete submission the Rajpoots, who appeared disposed, and nearly ready, to burst out. He was, however, compelled to postpone this object for the present, a more pressing motive calling him in another direction without delay: this was the account that the Seikhs had risen in the north, and overrun and destroyed all the country between the rivers Jumna and Indus.

The Seikhs are a tribe of Hindoos, who profess to worship one invisible Being, omnipotent and omnipresent, and whom they consider as degraded by any similitude or images. In short, in theory and practice they are pure theists. They owe their origin to one Naneek, of the Kuttery or war tribe, who flourished in Lahore towards the end of the fifteenth century, and who, from his piety and talents, was revered as a sort of prophet among them. They are tolerant in matters of faith, and admit proselytes. This sect had, long after their founda-

A.D.
1708. tion, behaved with moderation and temperance; but with their number their power proportionably increased, and towards the close of Aurungzebe's reign they had become really formidable. Hardy from their climate, mounted on fleet horses, and panting for independence, it was necessary to adopt some strong measure to reduce them to order.

Behaudur, leaving a force in the Deccan, marched rapidly to the north, and passing Agra and Dehli, reached the vicinity of Sirhind, where the Seikhs were assembled in great numbers. The approach of the imperial army, however, caused their retreat to Daber, the original residence of their chief, where they strongly fortified themselves. Daber is situated on the summit of a rocky mountain; and round it, at different elevations, the greater part of the Seikh force had encamped, secure, as they thought, from the vast chasms and abysses interspersed throughout its slopes. An attack was made upon the enemy thus
1709. posted by the vizir of the empire, contrary to the advice of Behaudur. The contest was obstinate and bloody, and ceased only from darkness: it was renewed with the morning, and the Mogul troops being considerably reinforced, a dreadful and general slaughter commenced, no mercy being shewn to wretches who had themselves evinced none; they were cut off to a man. The fort was afterwards taken by storm, and all within it put to the sword; the chief, called the Ghooroo, alone making his escape during the night, and following by-paths well known to him, had fled to the Snowy Mountains.

The vizir, who had vowed to bring this man dead or alive, returned much mortified by his disappointment, and was received very coldly by the emperor. This had so great an effect upon him, that he fell ill soon after, and is supposed to have died of a broken heart. This severe check did not by any means destroy the active spirit of the Seikhs, and Behaudur was compelled to take up his residence at Lahore, to be on the spot for any decisive measures which might be

A.D.
necessary: here the emperor continued until 1712, when he died suddenly, as 1712.
some have reported, by poison.

Behaudur left behind him four sons, who all aspired to the sovereign power; a severe but short struggle, in which the second and fourth sons perished; and, in an after-fought battle between the remaining two, ***Jehandar***, eldest son of the late emperor, was conqueror, and now, without any competitor, mounted the throne. He proved, however, a weak and dissolute prince, and relinquished all the power and business of the state to Zoolfeckar, his vizir, a base and aspiring Omrah, who had been his chief assistant in gaining the sceptre of the empire. This favourite's conduct soon became so overbearing, that he disgusted the whole of the court, and even put some of the highest of the nobility to death: this conduct excited the feelings of the whole body of the nation against him, and a conspiracy was formed among the chief nobles and Omrahs to drive him from his place. At the head of this party were two brothers of high birth, possessing great wealth and influence; the one named Seyd Abdoolah Khan, the other Seyd Hossain Khan; both much attached to the late emperor, who had appointed the former to the government of Allahabad, and the latter to that of the province of Bahar. These, raising a very considerable body of troops, advanced from the former fortress towards Agra. The emperor's army assembled at Agra moved thence to meet them; the two met near Kudjwa, where the general action formerly described between Aurungzebe and Sujah took
place. A sharply contested action was the result, which ended with the total 1713.
overthrow and dispersion of the royal army, its commander, Dowran Khan, having shamefully abandoned it. Jehandar advanced with a force to retrieve his affairs, but his troops and their leaders, little attached to him, and disgusted with the conduct and manners of the court, made but a slight resistance; the

vigorous attack of the Seyds bore down all opposition. The emperor, quitting his elephant, fled in dismay, and an entire rout of his troops was the immediate consequence: the unfortunate Jehandar was taken soon after, and strangled in prison. Thus perished these four brothers, victims of that ambition which had so profusely shed the blood of the race of Timour.

Furrukseer, grandson of Behaudur, and great-grandson of Aurungzebe, was seated on the throne of Hindoostan by the Seyds, but they in fact exercised the sovereign power. The emperor, weary of these haughty and aspiring ministers, Abdoolah being vizir, and Hossain Seyd emir ul Omrah, sent the latter with a large force to quell an insurrection in Marwar, where the Maharajah, or chief of the Rajpoots, had invaded the country, carrying fire and sword through it, and overthrowing the Mahomedan mosques, erected Hindoo pagodas. Hossain soon reduced these rebels to obedience, and returning to the court, found affairs in a state of the utmost confusion; Meer Jumla, a new favourite of the weak emperor, ruling all with despotic sway, his brother Abdoolah being a mere cipher. The Seyds withdrew to their palace, and armed their followers, pretending that designs were forming against their safety. At length an accommodation was
A.D. 1715. brought about by means of the mother of Furrukseer, and Meer Jumla was invested with the government of Bahar, while Hossain Seyd was promoted to the richer soubahship of the Deccan. Soon after this event, the marriage of the emperor took place with the daughter of the Maharajah, a union which promised important results. The magnificence of this ceremony far exceeded any thing of the kind hitherto seen in India, ostentation being the characteristic of this vain prince.

About this period, ambassadors sent by the East India Company from Calcutta arrived at the court of Dehli. The great success they met with is said to have been due to Mr. Hamilton, a medical gentleman who accompanied the embassy, who, by an operation skilfully performed, restored the emperor to health, when given over by his native physicians.

The Seikhs were now again in the field, carrying on their usual warfare of devastation and blood. The governors of Lahore and Cabul marched against them, but the former was totally defeated, and the latter basely assassinated by a Seikh sent by Bundah, the chief of that tribe, and the same person who escaped from the storm of Dabur. The governor of Cashmere now advanced, and soon defeated the enemy, exterminating them without mercy. Bundah, their chief, being taken, was put to death with horrible tortures.

The Mahrattas, a nation now rising into power, here demand attention, as A.D. 1716. they were destined to act a very important part in the history of future years. Aurungzebe, who foresaw the turbulent and restless character of this enterprising people, was deeply engaged in a war with them during the latter years of his reign: he found them, however, too formidable to make any serious impression on them. During the struggles which had convulsed the empire in the contests between the successors of that monarch, the Mahrattas had wonderfully increased in power and extent of territory: they harassed on all occasions the rear of the royal armies on their line of march; and on the plea of being lords of the soil, exacted the tribute called the ***chout***, which amounted to one-fourth part of the revenues. Hossain's first efforts to subdue these freebooters were unsuccessful. A larger army being sent, the wary Mahratta chief declined a contest in the open field, and retired to Sattara. Here Hossain would have besieged him, but the violent dissensions raging at Dehli were at the moment reported to him; and also that the emperor had sent privately to Sahojee, chief of the Mahrattas, to harass and distress the army of his own general. Enraged and indignant at this base and treacherous conduct, Hossain sought to make friends with Sahojee, and to bind him by strong ties to his own interest and that of his brother; and for this purpose he so far degraded the imperial dignity as to permit that chief to have an agent at Aurungabad to receive the *chout*. This impolitic measure placed at once the crown of Timour at the feet of its most inveterate enemy, and most rapidly increased the power of the latter, whose bold aggression and shameful extortions will be noticed in future pages.

A.D. 1719. The Seyd brothers at length decided on the deposing of Furrukseer, and for this purpose Hossain rapidly pushed on with 30,000 horse, 10,000 of whom were Mahrattas. These poured in one irresistible torrent into all the streets and avenues of the capital, filled the great squares, and pressed on to the very palace. Furrukseer, in a delirium of fear and wild with terror, took refuge in the harem; but the doors were soon forced, and he was torn from the arms of his shrieking women. He was not at the instant put to death, but being thrown into a dark chamber, his eyes were put out by means of a hot iron. A few days after, in an attempt to escape from his gloomy prison, he was assassinated, on the 16th February, 1719.

The Seyds, thus succeeding to full power, still thought it politic to have a nominal sovereign of the house of Timour; and therefore took from the castle of Selimgurh, in which the royal princes were confined, ***Raffeh ul Dirjat***, a mere child, who had neither voice nor power. To conciliate the Nizam, the soubahdary of Malwa was bestowed on him, whence he soon appointed himself to his former government of the Deccan. This able man and enterprising warrior was long an important actor in the eventful and sanguinary scenes about to be presented in rapid succession to the reader.

The young prince died in four months after his accession; it is said by some historians that he was murdered: there appears not any sufficient cause, however, to have urged the Seyds to so wantonly cruel an act. A brother of the

A.D.
deceased prince was next raised to the precarious rank he had held, and died in 1720.
three months: the same suspicion of violence being the cause was again excited. A son of Jehandar, so celebrated for his valour and talents, and who has been noticed above, and now aged seventeen, was yet in the fortress of Selimgurh. He was named Sultan Rooshum Acber; and under the title of ***Mahommed Shah*** he succeeded to that throne for which his father died contending.

Hossain Seyd was assassinated this year by a noble of high rank, one of a band of conspirators: the assassin fell an instant sacrifice to the victim's guard. On this news reaching Dehli, the brother of Hossain, in the first burst of his resentment, forced open the royal treasury, and plundered the famous peacock throne of some of its richest jewels. By this means he collected a mixed force of 80,000 men, and publicly proclaiming Ibrahim, the infant son of Raffeh Ooshaun, emperor, marched forward from Dehli, to meet and give battle to the enemy. The contest took place on the 2d November, 1720, at Sirkad, twelve kos from Muttra; it was long and severely disputed, but at length Abdoolah was totally defeated, himself wounded and taken prisoner. The emperor Mahommed's conduct to his fallen foe was generous and noble, no punishment beyond
confinement being inflicted on him. He died, however, of his wounds a short 1721.
time after. Mahommed's vigour and decision on this occasion awed the governors of the distant provinces; tranquillity was restored to the distracted empire, and hopes were entertained that his reign would be as glorious as any of the distinguished sovereigns of the family of Timour.

But Mahommed, once firmly seated on his throne, having got rid of his foes, and 1722.
being no longer excited by events which called his talents into action, became voluptuous and indolent. As the danger ceased to exist, the sword returned to its scabbard, merit was unnoticed, and valour unrewarded. The Rajpoots, active and restless, seized this moment to enter Agimere, where they spread desolation

A.D.
1722. and death; while the Mahrattas extended their fast-growing empire, unresisted, through Guzzerat and all the western coasts.

The Nizam defended the Deccan from these marauders, but not for the emperor; that subtle and able general had long sought independence, and was deeply planning to gain this portion of the empire for himself and descendants. Mahommed, plunged in voluptuous excesses, took no measures to check the torrent of invasion that threatened to overthrow his empire. Negociations alone were employed to stop the Rajpoots and Mahrattas; and the Nizam was solicited to accept the office of vizir, in order to decoy him to court, and keep a watchful eye upon him. After a long resistance he consented, and marched with 10,000 troops as his escort: he was met by the emperor, who received him most graciously, and appointed him absolute agent, a rank above that of vizir; he was also dignified by the title of Azoph Jah. The crafty Nizam soon urged his sovereign to apply himself seriously to the restoration of order in the various parts of his empire. His admonitions were listened to with respect by Mahommed, but nothing was done; the dissolute and depraved nobles derided the old vizir, who soon quitted a court where he had met with nothing but insult. The emperor's party were delighted to get rid of him.

1730. The Nizam, after his return home, entered into an agreement with the chief of the Mahrattas, that a large force of that nation should invade and ravage the country as far as Agra and Dehli. He trusted that this would rouse the indolent Mahommed and his ministers, and shew them the necessity of protecting themselves and the crown before they attempted to move an army towards the Deccan. The Mahrattas, under Badjerow, commenced that invasion which for ever lowered the dignity of the empire. Malwa and Guzzerat first fell under the yoke; and though the troops of the government long defended themselves most gallantly, yet, unsupported from Dehli, and not receiving any reinforcements, they were repulsed, and finally driven from these provinces, which the enemy occupied, and have ever since retained.

A.D.

Thus in two years the Mahrattas had extended their incursions into the immediate vicinity of Agra and Dehli. Armies were sent to expel them, but the crafty foe avoided any general action, and wholly confined themselves to a harassing and desultory warfare. 1732.

After a second unsuccessful campaign, the Mahrattas this year made an attempt to plunder the rich province of Oude; but Saadut Khan, an able commander, having a well-disciplined force, attacked and totally routed them, with the loss of 5000 of their number. 1734.

Badjerow next made a dash at Dehli with a well-mounted body of his best cavalry; he seized upon and plundered Feridabad, and arrived under the walls of the capital before any news of his approach had reached it. The confusion was extreme; three days the plunder of the suburbs was continued, till Saadut Khan arrived, and attacking the enemy, routed them. The vizir and the royal army followed the retiring foe, and came up with them about seven kos beyond Dehli; an action here took place, which was so obstinately contested, that the Mogul ministers agreed to the inglorious compromise of their own honour and that of the empire, by consenting to pay the disgraceful tax of the ***chout*** for Agra and Dehli, on condition that the Mahrattas should withdraw from those provinces.

The Nizam meanwhile extended his influence and conquests in the Deccan, and under pretence of the great expense necessary to support the force to oppose the Mahrattas, remitted no revenue to the treasury of Dehli. He was again enticed to that court, but his reception was more galling than on the former occasion, and he again left it, breathing vengeance. This deep and able politician and commander had endeavoured to form a party to overthrow the existing government, and had attempted, but in vain, to draw the vizir over to his scheme. 1735.

He next applied to Saadut Khan, who still felt sore from his late disappointment, and was ill affected to the emperor and his party. These two consummate statesmen and generals, after a mature consultation, decided that Nadir Shah, sovereign of Persia, should be the instrument to distress the emperor, and remove his
A.D. 1737. favourite, Dowran, for ever from his councils. Thus was the foundation laid for the total subversion of a mighty though declining empire, and the irretrievable ruin of an ancient dynasty. The annals of Asia record no event more momentous in its consequences than this invasion of Nadir Shah.

That conqueror, newly seated on the usurped throne of Persia, harboured a secret hatred and enmity to the court of Dehli; but no serious idea had ever been entertained of any hostile attempt, until the proposition made by the Nizam and Saadut Khan. Having completed the subjugation of the provinces of
1738. Persia, and taken Candahar, Nadir Shah moved with an army of 80,000 horse, of various nations and tribes, all highly disciplined and inured to service. The Mogul governor in vain solicited a supply of troops from Dehli, none were sent; he therefore fell back upon Peishore. Shirzeh Khan, the more resolute commander of the castle, held out bravely for six weeks, when the place was taken by storm, and the brave officer and his son put to death. Nadir Shah here found treasures, arms, and jewels to an immense amount.

Nadir tarried at Cabul until the middle of June; he then moved on, and crossed his army over the five branches of the Indus, although at that season each stream was a furious torrent.

1739. Mahommed meanwhile advanced and encamped on the plains of Karnaul, with an army of 30,000 Indians and 2000 armed elephants, while the rest of his forces were hastening to join him. Nadir, informed of this position of his adversary, sent 6000 Persians to reconnoitre, and following them up, reached Amballa on the 10th January. He advanced the following day, and encamped

A.D. 1739.

within six miles of the Mogul line. The latter, depending on their vast numbers and their formidable batteries of artillery, drew out their lines in order of battle, and shewed a great extent of front. Nadir, however, not at all intimidated, rushed with wild impetuosity upon the Indians. The shock was violent on both sides, the contest continuing five hours, when the rout of the Indians became general: ten princes of high rank, 100 officers, nobles of distinction, and 30,000 soldiers, fell in this action.

Nadir then advanced to storm the camp, but it was so formidably retrenched, that it could not then be attempted; it was consequently blockaded, and all supplies being cut off, the Moguls saw no hopes but in speedy surrender. The nobles counselled and besought Mahommed to go at once and throw himself on the mercy of his conqueror: the wretched prince, seeing no alternative, submitted, and proceeded on horseback, attended by several great Omrahs of his court, to the camp of the enemy. Nadir Shah, apprised of his approach, received him at the door of his tent, and taking him by the hand, led him to the throne, and seated him beside himself. For two days Mahommed was entertained as his guest by the Persian monarch, and was treated with the utmost respect.

On the 1st February, Nadir advanced towards Dehli, and encamped in the gardens of Shalimar, where Mahommed obtained permission to enter the city, and prepare his palace for the reception of his conqueror, who, on the 9th, entered the beautiful palace built by Shah Jehan. The unfortunate prince, his captive, was prepared to attend his victor with marks of the lowest submission: Nadir, however, raised him from this state of abject dejection, declaring he would reinstate him on his throne, would repair the breach in their friendship, and maintain a perpetual alliance with the Indian empire. Mahommed, penetrated by this generosity and clemency, brought forth and presented to the

A.D.
1739. Persian monarch some of the richest and rarest jewels of the crown, consisting of rich vases inlaid with gems, vast heaps of gold and silver in coin and ingots, sumptuous furniture, thrones and diadems, among which was the celebrated peacock throne, worth, it has been said, two millions sterling. Nadir Shah, after reproaching Mahommed with obstinacy, and with degrading the throne by paying the *chout* to the infidel Mahrattas, proceeded to fix the amount of the sum to be paid as a ransom of the empire. This, after various conferences, was finally decided, under the name of *peishcush* (or present), at the enormous total of 25,000,000*l.* sterling. The sums exacted from the various Omrahs and nobles of the Indian court amounted to an equal sum. Eight millions were levied on the citizens and merchants of the city of Dehli; and this was exacted from the wretched inhabitants by the most cruel tortures, under which numbers expired. The Nizam and Saadut Khan, who had invited Nadir to India, and brought such evils on their country, were amerced in large sums; from the former a million and a half, and from the latter one million, was exacted. The oppression on all classes of the people was excessive; murmurs were heard on all sides, and partial insurrections and resistance to the exorbitant and cruel exactions imposed occasionally shewed themselves. To add to these evils, a famine threatened this unfortunate city, from the immense multitude of men and horses which inundated the province of Dehli. An attempt to regulate the price of wheat in the public granaries by the Persian commander caused the spark already kindled to burst out into a flame. This commotion began about noon, and increased very much towards evening. After dark, a report was spread that Nadir Shah was a prisoner; others said that he was poisoned. The mob and tumult now exceeded all bounds. The idle and the disaffected from that vast city rushed towards the castle, armed with any weapon they could at the moment snatch, devoting to death every foreigner they met, and vowing vengeance against the invaders: of the guard

on the outside of the gates a vast number were sacrificed; the remainder sought safety in flight. A.D. 1739.

Nadir Shah, on the first intelligence of these disturbances, ordered his general, Thamas Khan, to commence his march from the camp without the city with 30,000 horse direct to the capital. The advanced guard of these troops soon arrived, and routed with dreadful slaughter the infuriated populace: soon after the rest of this force entered and occupied the city. At midnight Nadir led forth the whole of the troops in Dehli, and advancing to the mosque of Roshun ul Dowlah, in the very centre of the city, there took his stand. All was raging tumult and confusion around him; while he, calm and firm, acting solely on the defensive, awaited the dawn of day to let loose his vengeance on the devoted city.

The morning, big with the fate of Dehli, at length dawned, and shewed him heaps of his Persian soldiers weltering in their blood. A momentary, awful pause ensued, during which a pistol, discharged at him from a neighbouring terrace, killed an officer close to his side. He instantly ordered a general massacre to commence from that very spot. His squadrons of horse, pouring through the streets, put to death every one without distinction, aged and young, women and children. His infantry, mounting at the same time the walls and terraces, consigned to the same fate every soul they found upon them. The love of spoil and thirst of blood acting equally on these barbarians, all the bazaars of the jewellers and houses of the rich citizens were plundered and then set on fire. Fearful of the violation of their women, many of the Indians of higher rank, collecting their females and their treasures, and setting fire to their apartments, consumed them, with themselves, in one common conflagration. From a similar dread, thousands of women plunged headlong into tanks and wells.

A.D. 1739. During this dreadful carnage, this scene of desolation and death, the king of Persia continued in the mosque of Roshun ul Dowlah. His countenance was dark and terrible, and during his paroxysm of rage, none but slaves durst approach him. At length Mahommed, the wretched emperor of India, attended by his principal Omrahs, their eyes fixed upon the ground, ventured to draw near, and intercede for the half-ruined and depopulated city and the surviving inhabitants. For a time he was obdurate; at length the sternness of his countenance relaxed, and sheathing his sword, he said, "For the sake of the prince Mahommed, I forgive." The tidings of the king's wrath thus appeased were rapidly spread throughout the city; the work of destruction was instantly stayed. Between issuing the bloody mandate, however, at sunrise and two o'clock in the afternoon, 100,000 Dehlians had been inhumanly butchered. The tyrant then retired into the citadel, and inquiry being instituted into the cause of the tumult, several Indians of distinguished rank were seized, and their execution closed the scene of carnage.

The sudden transition from rioting in blood to rioting in intemperance is a practice congenial to the soul of a tyrant. On the 26th of this same month, while the sabres of his soldiers were yet warm with Indian blood, the Persian monarch solemnized the marriage of his son, prince Nasr Allah, with a grand-daughter of the great Aurungzebe. Presents of the most costly and sumptuous kind were made on this occasion to the bride by Nadir Shah, Mahommed, and his Omrahs. The *peishcush* was, however, rigorously exacted from the miserable citizens of Dehli, and then Nadir Shah began to think of returning to Persia. He first, however, crowned Mahommed with his own hands, with a diadem of the most exquisite workmanship, and set with the most costly jewels; giving him the best advice as to his future conduct, and telling him to beware of that hoary

A.D.
traitor, the Nizam; and, lastly, if Mahommed should ever require his assistance, 1739.
he could be with him at any time in forty days from Candahar. He then commenced his march homewards: the same scenes of plunder and desolation marked his return as his approach. Loaded with the immense wealth he had amassed in this expedition, he was still unsatiated, and at the passage of the Indus he plundered his very soldiers of all their jewels and precious stones, being compelled to render them up on pain of instant death.

With these treasures Nadir Shah, some time after his return to Persia, caused a tent to be constructed, the vast splendour of which far surpassed every thing of the kind before seen. It was of scarlet cloth lined with violet-coloured satin, which was covered with the richest embroidery, in patterns of the nobler beasts, the most beautiful birds, flowers, trees, &c. all formed of precious stones, as pearls, diamonds, rubies, emeralds, amethysts, and others. The tent-poles were similarly decorated; and in the centre stood the peacock throne of Shah Jehan, with a screen on each side, having an angel embroidered in precious jewels, and the tent-pins were of solid gold. This pavilion required seven elephants to carry it, and it was always pitched on state occasions in the capital during the reign of Nadir Shah: his successors, with more limited territories and great expenses, took to pieces this splendid tent, and its valuable materials were disposed of and dissipated.

After the departure of Nadir Shah, Mahommed and his ministers relapsed 1743.
into their former apathy. The Nizam made use of this opportunity to strengthen his interests, which his close alliance with the vizir of the empire much favoured. He soon after returned to the Deccan, where he now possessed nearly one-fourth of the empire; his revenues were immense, and he wanted only the name to be indeed a sovereign.

Little occurred to disturb the tranquillity of India until 1748, when Abdalla,

A.D.
1748. a general of Nadir Shah, who was treasurer to that monarch at his death by assassination, secured a portion of his master's wealth, and retiring to the mountains of Afghanistan, his native country, raised a strong body of hardy and daring soldiery, with the idea of playing the same game as Nadir had done before. He accordingly, having seized upon Candahar, and expelled the Mogul troops from the country west of the Attock, having now the road to Dehli perfectly open, approached the frontier with a body of 50,000 horse. Ahmed, Mahommed's son, a prince of great promise, assembling an army of 80,000 men, advanced to meet the invader. The hostile armies met at Sirhind, and after a pause of a few days, the attack was made by Ahmed, who, with an impetuosity that was gallantly resisted for three hours, at length burst into the enemy's fortified camp, and totally routed them. Abdalla was forced to retire across the Indus, and a force being left to watch him, Ahmed returned triumphant towards Dehli. On his way he received intelligence of the sudden death of his father Mahommed, who had long been declining, and who expired while sitting on his throne and administering justice. ***Ahmed*** hastened his return, and reaching the capital, was immediately proclaimed emperor. Ahmed by degrees relaxed from his active and ardent relish for military achievements, and became
1750. indolent and voluptuous. The Rohilla and Afghan tribes made many incursions into the province of Oude at this period. Sufdar Jung, vizir and soubah of that province, led an army against them, but was unsuccessful, until he obtained leave to call in 40,000 Mahrattas to his aid, when the business was soon settled. Sufdar then returned to Dehli, followed by the hordes of his mercenaries, clamorous for their arrears, and ready to plunder the city if refused. The sum due to them was fifty lacs of rupees, which the vizir, Ghazi ul Deen, son of the old Nizam, advanced to the government, on condition of being appointed soubah of the Deccan: this was caught at with avidity, and he immediately marched at

the head of these very Mahrattas, ever ready to move where there is a chance, however distant, of plunder, to his new government.

A.D. 1753.

The empire was about this time torn by intestine troubles, caused by the inroads and depredations of various tribes of freebooters, the Jauts, Rajpoots, Rohillas, Seikhs, and still more formidable barbarians of Afghanistan. In this latter direction the brave Munnoo Khan, son of the late vizir, ably and successfully combated the Abdallies, a name given at this period generally to the different portions of Abdalla's force; but supplies, both of money and troops, not arriving, the Mogul general was compelled slowly to fall back: he was killed soon after in a skirmish. Abdalla now advanced and seized on the capital of the province, of which he made his son governor, under an able and experienced general, and then formed his plan for the invasion of Hindoostan in the following year.

The Jauts meanwhile had gained the greater part of the country round Agra, and the royal army being all engaged in watching the Abdallies, the old remedy of calling in the Mahrattas was resorted to. Mulhar and Roganaut Row, with 40,000 horse, entered that beautiful country, and carricd fire and sword through its whole extent. Ghazi, son of Ghazi ul Deen, commanded in chief this force as captain-general of the empire, and the Jauts were driven into their forts and strong villages. Artillery being required to reduce these, Ghazi wrote to Dehli for the royal train, but to his surprise he was refused. This was the work of the young vizir, who had vilified the character of Ghazi in his absence, and had persuaded the emperor, that he wanted the guns only to besiege Dehli and raise himself to the throne. Ghazi, inflamed at intelligence to this effect, resolved instantly to turn his large force against the imperial army. The two adverse corps met near Secundra: Ghazi here declared his intention to dethrone a king so unfit to reign. The royal army, being unequal to cope with him, fell rapidly back upon Dehli; but they were so closely pursued, that Ghazi gained one of the gates, closely invested the castle, and at length compelled the emperor to give himself up to his mercy. The unfortunate prince was put into the custody of a person to be relied on, and on the day following was deprived of sight by the usual method, which barbarous act naturally closed his reign of seven years, the commencement of which only was at all brilliant or successful.

A.D. 1755. Ghazi ul Deen raised to the throne a grandson of Behaudur Shah, by the title of ***Alumgire II.*** He was immediately appointed vizir, and reigned over the monarch and the empire with the most despotic sway. The court party, disgusted, succeeded in thwarting several of his plans; and party spirit was fast rising to an alarming height, when the intelligence of Abdalla's mighty preparation for the invasion of India was brought to Dehli. The emperor having neither talent nor spirit for military affairs, his eldest son, Ali Gohar, afterwards Shah Alum, headed a force of 80,000 men, and advanced beyond Sirhind; but here they found Abdalla so strongly posted, that it was not thought prudent to attack him. A negociation took place; but though the Persians withdrew, it only delayed the fatal day. On the return to Dehli, the conduct of the vizir became so haughty and overbearing as to disgust the emperor, who sent to invite Abdalla to invade the country, and rid him of his cruel tormentor. Nujib ul Dowlah, a Rohilla chief, was to command that part of the army which was to meet the enemy; the vizir was in charge of the remainder. A sort of mock fight succeeded, in which Ghazi was deserted by the Rohillas, and the greater part of his army and himself fell into the hands of the enemy: he was deprived of the vizirat, but he afterwards found means to propitiate Abdalla.

The irruption of the Afghan troops, far more ferocious than the Persians under Nadir Shah, was attended by circumstances more disgusting and barbarous. Twenty years had accumulated a considerable mass of wealth in the

A.D.

capital in specie and rich merchandises, though it had lost all its jewels; and 1757.
these the ruthless and cruel soldiery exacted from the wretched inhabitants by every mode of torture that ingenuity could devise; palaces and rich mosques were plundered, and even the tombs of former emperors and of many pious and revered saints, held sacred for ages, were robbed of their gold and silver ornaments. This continued for two months. Abdalla next marched towards Agra, but here he was repulsed by the Mogul governor; in revenge for which he turned his steps towards Muttra, that venerable and ancient seat of Hindoo learning, upon which he wreaked his indignation, sacking it, and leaving it a heap of ruins. Abdalla was recalled this year by a threat of invasion from Western Asia: he had reinstated Ghazi in the vizirat, and as a check upon him, he made Nujib ul Dowlah emir ul Omrah, with orders to protect the emperor against the intrigues of the former. Then having celebrated his nuptials with a daughter of Mahommed Shah, he commenced his retreat; and on his route left his son, Timour Shah, with a large force at Lahore.

The following year Abdalla, unsatiated with the spoil of India, again moved 1758.
towards its plains; but his present object was rather to check the Mahrattas, who were making encroachments on the eastern frontier of his dominions. Their armies indeed at this period were seen in motion in all quarters, their aim appearing to be the extermination of all the Mahommedan princes, and erecting a sovereignty of their own on the ruins. To oppose a power so formidable, and to settle once more the distracted affairs of Dehli, which he had been regularly apprised of from Lahore, Abdalla accelerated his march with the whole force of his empire, and with an energy equal to the interests at stake. We must leave him pursuing his victorious career, to turn for a moment to the usurper Ghazi and the unfortunate monarch his prisoner. The state in which that minister now found himself was indeed desperate: having violated all confidence, and

A.D.
1758. trampled gratitude under foot, he could entertain no hope of appeasing Abdalla. We have noticed the large force of the Mahrattas which he was compelled to keep in pay to maintain his usurped authority. These were the decided enemies both of Abdalla and the Mogul dynasty. With these barbarous hordes he had inundated the whole neighbourhood of Dehli, had driven Nujib from its walls, and held the soubahs of Oude and Bengal at defiance. He suspected the Abdallies were now, as formerly, invited by Alumgire; he knew attempts had been made to detach the troops he had raised from their allegiance, and felt too that that army could not for a moment stand before the myriads of Abdalla. His vision of greatness had passed away, but he determined to close his sanguinary career by a blow that should make Hindoostan totter to its centre, and remind ungrateful monarchs of their doom. He, in short, resolved to murder the sovereign he had created, and disappoint Abdalla of the half of his spoil, by permitting his own ferocious Mahrattas to plunder the capital.

1759. Alumgire was much addicted to superstition, and it added greatly to the atrocity of the murder, that it was perpetrated during an act which strongly marked the piety of the victim. Being told that a Fakeer, or Mahommedan saint, highly venerated, had arrived at Dehli, the emperor expressed an anxious wish to visit this holy man; for saints in India disdain to visit even the palaces of kings. Every thing being prepared in the apartment of the pretended saint, as the emperor slowly approached the reverend impostor, two assassins rushed from behind a screen, and with their scymitars divided his head from his body. The headless trunk was exposed for two days on the sands of the Jumna, and then interred without regal honours. The regicide then proceeded to the state-prison of the princes of the house of Timour, and thence selected a grandson of Kambuksh, the youngest son of Aurungzebe, and placed him on the throne, by the title of ***Jehaun II***. He is, however, not reckoned among the number

A.D. 1759.

of emperors. The city-gates were then thrown open to the Mahrattas, who renewed for several days the dreadful scenes of desolation and death, until the near approach of the Abdallies forced them to decamp. Ghazi retired to a strong fort belonging to Suraje Mull, and there, whatever atrocities he may subsequently have committed in a less public character, history loses sight of him.

Abdalla found Dehli in a deplorable state; his own exactions added not a little to its misfortunes, which were so great, that, in a paroxysm of despair, the populace flew to arms. More stern than Nadir Shah, because more in danger, Abdalla gave orders for a general massacre, which continued unceasingly for seven days, when nearly one-fourth of the inhabitants had perished, and the chief public edifices were in flames. To add to the horrors of the moment, the approach of the Mahratta force, under Mulhar Row, was announced: these came to share in the spoils of Dehli. Abdalla instantly marched to give them battle, and bringing them to action about four miles from that city, he totally defeated them, and pursued them for some distance with great slaughter. This partial defeat, however, was the grand tocsin for the united exertions of the entire Mahratta nation to crush the invader. This would probably have been the case, as they could have cut off his supplies, constantly harassed his rear and his flanks, diminishing his army, now far too remote from all its resources, had not all the great Mahommedan powers of India taken the alarm, and, however various their interests, seen the imperious necessity of joining Abdalla, or being crushed themselves. The Mahommedan religion and government, established for eight centuries in India, at an enormous expenditure of blood and treasure, must be subverted, or the vast power of the Mahrattas annihilated by one decisive blow.

Meanwhile Ali Gohar, whom we have seen lately cutting his way through

A.D.
1758. the besieging troops of Ghazi, and retiring to the estate of Nujib ul Dowlah for protection from the bloody foe of his family, finding his protector unable or unwilling effectually to aid his cause, pursued his way with a few firmly attached and faithful followers to Oude, where Sujah ul Dowlah received him with every mark of respect, and with even royal honours; though he declined at present to take an active public part in his affairs.

The prince next repaired to Allahabad, where in Mohammed Kuli Khan, the viceroy, he found an ardent and strenuous supporter. This enterprising chief, however, recommended him in the first instance to seize the rich provinces of Bahar and Bengal, with the tributary wealth of which they might be enabled to raise an army fully adequate to attain the great object in view. This project being communicated to Sujah ul Dowlah, received his assent, and he in addition made an offer of a considerable body of troops. Towards the close of this year the expedition commenced; but, unfortunately for the prince, at this period the English army, under Colonel Clive, closely connected in alliance with the government of Bengal, which had assumed independence, presented too powerful a front, even with all his high and imperial claims, for him to hope to overcome. This caused the failure of the entire plan. The prince, throwing himself upon the mercy of the British force, solicited their military aid in his favour: this, however, for the present they declined, not deeming it prudent to interfere at that period in his concerns. The prince therefore returned to Oude, where intelligence of the death of Alumgire having arrived, he caused a throne to be erected, which he publicly ascended, and was proclaimed emperor at Patna; and he ever after acted and was addressed in that capacity.

1759. One of his first acts was the appointment of Sujah ul Dowlah to be perpetual vizir of the empire; a situation gratifying to the ambition of the one, and beneficial to the interests of the other.

A.D.

The grand conflict, as yet unrivalled in the history of India both in respect 1759. to the number and power of the combatants, and which was to consign the crown to a Mahommedan or native power, was now rapidly approaching. After his defeat of the Mahrattas, Abdalla returned to Dehli, and had consigned to his original abode the sceptred pageant raised to the throne by Ghazi. He next invited Shah Alum publicly to ascend the throne of his ancestors in the capital; but which that prudent prince, under the present ill-omened auspices, declined.

The Mahratta armies under all their famous chiefs, but subject to the supreme controul of Suddasheo, otherwise called the ***Bhow***, were now rolling in one vast mass on Dehli. On their way thither the Jaut rajah was summoned to join with his forces, who at first hesitated, but on their threatening to ravage his country with fire and sword, Suraje Mull joined them with 50,000 of his best troops, which increased their force to 200,000 men, mostly cavalry. On the approach of these to Dehli, Abdalla moved out, and crossed the Jumna to a more open country for his supplies, and where the Mahommedan troops could more readily form a junction. Among these were the Rohillas, the troops of Sujah ul Dowlah, Ahmed Khan Bunguish, the Patan chief of the Doo-ab, and other Mussulman princes, whose territories bordering on the Ganges had repeatedly suffered from the depredations of these Mahrattas.

The Mahrattas having now exhausted the country of all its supplies and 1760. provisions, had no alternative but the immediate attack of the Mahommedan army; they accordingly moved out of their intrenchments, and advanced towards their adversary's line. The Abdallies were not slow in moving forward to meet them, and on the 14th January, 1761, that desperate battle took place which was 1761. to decide the fate of the empire of India. The onset was made by the troops of Abdalla with an impetuosity so violent, as to deprive them of all the advantage which their very superior artillery would otherwise have given them. The

A.D. 1761. Mahrattas, sensible of their desperate situation, knowing that if death threatened them in front, famine awaited them in the rear, and that their swords alone must cut their way to safety, fought with a fury and obstinate perseverance, which repulsed the allies nearly to their lines. At this important moment a cannon-ball struck off the head of the ***Bhow***, when the Jauts, who had never joined heartily in the cause, immediately deserted in a body; while Sujah ul Dowlah and other of the Mahommedan generals pouring in the mass of their forces upon the enemy's flank, compelled their main body to give way. Still in various parts of that vast army deeds the most heroic were achieved, deeds worthy of the stake for which the adverse parties contended. As one instance of this, of all the Mahratta chiefs and leaders, one only returned home; the rest perished in this tremendous and sanguinary struggle. The carnage in the pursuit was horrible, for no quarter was given to those whose unrelenting rage had spared no one. Fifty thousand are said to have fallen in this battle, and thirty thousand in the pursuit, which continued three days.

The plunder taken in the camp of the Mahrattas exceeded all calculation; all their artillery, camp-equipage, elephants, horses, camels, &c. together with the treasure collected in their march from the Deccan, and the enormous sums extorted from the wretched inhabitants of Dehli, all fell into the hands of the victors.

To the last-named ill-fated city Abdalla, after the pursuit of the enemy, immediately repaired, and received in pompous state the congratulations of all the great Mussulman chiefs, his allies, on the total subversion of the power of the implacable enemies of their government and religion. Abdalla sent for ***Shah Alum*** soon after this from the south, where that prince was engaged in new schemes of conquest, and until his arrival placed his son Jewan Buksh on the musnud to act as regent.

He bsetowed magnificent presents on Sujah ul Dowlah, to whose intrepid courage at the decisive moment the late victory was due, and also confirmed him in the perpetual vizirat. Nujib ul Dowlah was made governor of the city and guardian of the royal family. Abdalla about the close of the year set off on his return to Candahar, nor from that time until his decease in 1773, owing to distractions at home, and the firm barrier opposed to his farther progress by the warlike nation of the Seikhs, was the capital of Hindoostan again cursed with another visit from this worst of scourges. A.D. 1761.

We have already stated, that Shah Alum's first attempt to possess himself of the rich treasures of Bengal and Bahar had been unsuccessful. Sujah ul Dowlah on his return to Oude, loaded with honours and flushed with victory, whatever opinion he might have held of the British troops on former occasions, had now changed it; and he fancied, that under the imperial name and banner he could overwhelm them, as he had done the Mahrattas at Paniput. 1762.

Meer Cossim, the Nuwab of Lucnow, having basely assassinated in cold blood several of the British residents at Patna, and being expelled from that station by the English authorities, had taken refuge at the court of Sujah, who for some time protected, but afterwards plundered and abandoned him. Still he made the deposing of Cossim a pretence for attacking the British force, and preparations were made on a large scale to ensure the conquest of Bengal and Bahar, and for ever expelling the English from the shores of India. 1764.

The British, under Major Carnac, were at this period at Buxar, in a weak and diminished state, from the excessive fatigues of the campaign, in which they had driven Meer Cossim before them all through Bengal and Bahar.

The British fell back at the approach of the immense mass which Sujah ul Dowlah urged rapidly forward from Buxar to Patna, which city they fortified by intrenchments. Here they were attacked several times with great impetuosity

A.D. 1764. by the enemy; but the defence being ably conducted, the latter were repulsed each time with immense slaughter.

Sujah ul Dowlah with his discomfited army retired at night, and no farther attack was made upon the British, and the rainy season speedily put a stop to all operations.

Shah Alum meanwhile was treated at the court of the vizir with great neglect and indifference, until tired of an empty homage, the prince became anxious to throw himself upon the generosity of the English. He being, however, not at freedom at this period, no negociation could be entered into with him.

The rains being ended, Colonel Hector Monro, who had arrived with great reinforcements, assumed the command, and soon after marched towards Buxar, where the enemy had strongly intrenched themselves. Large bodies of cavalry were also dispatched to hover on the English rear; but they steadily moved forward, carrying with them only ten days' provision, being determined in that period to conquer or die.

The vizir's corps, joined to that of Meer Cossim, amounted to 50,000 men, while the British had but 5000, and of these only 1200 were Europeans. Colonel Monro approached close to the enemy and encamped, having a morass in his front. Two days were passed in this manner: on the third day, however, Sujah ul Dowlah moved out with a mass of cavalry to attack the British right; but this was kept in check by the admirable fire of their artillery. The action now became general along the line, and in the midst of it Colonel Monro detached a column to seize a village on the British left, which had much annoyed the line by their fire. This attack not only fully succeeded, but the column penetrating through it, and pushing forward rapidly, turned the enemy's line, and took him in the rear. A scene of confusion ensued difficult to describe, and the Duranny and other mercenaries much increased it by their plundering the baggage: they

A.D.
were, however, soon interrupted in this, and driven completely off the field; 1764.
while Sujah, left alone, abandoned by his army, reluctantly fell back, and did not stop in his retreat until he reached Allahabad. This battle, decisive of the claim of Cossim to Bengal, and also of the ability of the native powers to contend with the British, took place in October 1764. The enemy left 6000 dead on the field and 130 guns.

Shah Alum, once more master of his own actions, now renewed his former offer of throwing himself under the protection of the British. This was granted: he was received in their camp with all the honours due to his rank, and attended by Colonel Monro to Benares, where a handsome stipend was allowed for his maintenance. Sujah ul Dowlah was mean time so unremittingly pursued, that, having in vain invoked aid of the Rohillas and the Mahrattas, he found himself stripped of his territories, and compelled to submit to the mercy of the English. He was received with respect, and all his territories were soon after
restored to him, except the provinces of Korah and Allahabad, which, with a 1765.
revenue of 22 lacs of rupees, about 220,000*l.* were conferred on the Mogul, and the castle of the latter city was assigned to him as a residence. On the arrival of Lord Clive soon after, an addition was made to this, upon the emperor issuing firmans, granting the revenues of Bengal, Bahar, and Orissa in perpetuity to the East India Company. There was paid into the royal treasury an additional sum of 25 lacs, or 250,000*l.* making in all a clear revenue of nearly half a million sterling.

The Company at the same time obtained many important advantages, being appointed a permanent and efficient part of the Mogul empire, with a million and a half as their revenue, after paying all the expenses of the civil and military establishments.

The Jauts, making an attempt upon Dehli, were totally defeated, and the gene- 1767.

ral, Suraje Mull, killed. His son endeavoured to avenge his father, but was equally unsuccessful; and a similar attempt of the Seikhs met with a like result. These successes were owing to the great abilities of Nujib ul Dowlah, who maintained the honour of the royal family until his death, which, to the great regret of the
A.D. 1770. people of Dehli, occurred in 1770.

Shah Alum meanwhile, after a few years' residence at Allahabad in peace and tranquillity, became restless and anxious to be seated on the throne of his ancestors at Dehli. There was at this period near Dehli a force of about 30,000 Mahratta horse, who were ready for any enterprise which favoured their schemes of conquest: to these the emperor applied for assistance. The sum demanded by them was two lacs of rupees, which was to be paid in advance; and for this they pledged themselves to place Shah Alum on the throne of Dehli.

The emperor also collected a force, partly disciplined in the English manner, which, joined to the Mahrattas, made a total of 90,000 men. These entered the capital unopposed, and the promise made to Shah Alum was punctually fulfilled.

On the departure of the emperor for Dehli, the English took military possession of the provinces of Korah and Allahabad.

Sujah ul Dowlah, who had become of great political importance, so as to surpass in influence even the emperor himself, now formed the plan of annexing the province of Rohilcund to his dominions, aided by his allies the English. The pretence employed by him on this occasion was, that forty lacs of rupees promised to him by various Rohilla chiefs for his protection of them during the late war had not been paid. The India Company at Calcutta appears to have entered too readily into this artful chief's designs, while the court of Dehli, bribed by a large sum and the prospect of a share in the plunder, engaged eagerly in the plot. The united forces took the field, and the English soon joined under Colonel Champion. The Rohilla force amounted to about 24,000

A.D.
horse and foot, 4000 rocket-men, and 60 guns; the village of Cutterah being 1774.
in their rear, and a small stream covering their flank. The English moving silently by night, to the surprise of the enemy, appeared formed for the attack. Hazif Rahmut, the Rohilla chief, exerted himself to rally and encourage his troops. A cannonade, in which the superior fire of the British was conspicuous, commenced the action; the contest was long and obstinate, but a ball at length striking their leader, the centre of the Rohillas gave way, and the wings necessarily followed its movement. The enemy left 2000 on the field; but being in general very well mounted, the greater part escaped.

Fizoolah Khan, now the Rohilla general, collected his army, and retired on Loll Dong, a strong fortress, where, being reinforced by some efficient corps, he prepared for a vigorous defence. An accommodation, however, was brought about through the mediation of the British, which was more favourable to the Rohillas than could be expected.

Sujah ul Dowlah died this year, and was succeeded by his son, Asoph ul 1775.
Dowlah.

The Seikhs, now become a great and formidable nation, made an irruption into the province of Dehli, and extended their depredations to the very banks of the Jumna: 20,000 men were sent to oppose them; but this force, ill
managed, failed entirely in its object, receiving a severe check near Patealah, 1780.
a strong fort sixty kos north of Karnal. The Seikhs then moved on Dehli; but Nujif Khan, captain-general, was recalled from a distant service and sent against the enemy, and encountering them under the walls of Meerut, totally overthrew them. This Omrah held for a long time an imperious sway over the weak and imbecile Shah Alum, and continued the same till his death, which occurred in 1782, and freed the emperor from his state of vassalage. Several competitors aspired to the vacant post. Mirza Shuffee attained it; but being

stabbed soon after in the field by Ismael Beg, a very distinguished Mogul chief, Afrasiab succeeded: but the parties at court now ran so high, that to support his authority and that of the emperor, he once more called the Mahrattas. Their famous chief, Madhajee Scindia, who had lately conquered the country round Agra, and had a numerous and highly disciplined army at his command, strengthened much the party of Afrasiab, so that he had hopes of ultimately triumphing over his enemies. But he could not avert the blow of the assassin's knife: he fell by the same hand as his predecessor. Scindia was not discouraged by this event; by dint of large presents, promises of obedience, and a splendid establishment, he persuaded the emperor to place himself under the protection of the Mahratta nation, and to appoint him to the chief command of the army, and to the government of Agra and Dehli, while the emperor was to have an allowance of 60,000 rupees per month.

A.D. 1786. From this period the reign of Shah Alum was a series of sedition, turbulence, and faction, in which he changed masters several times, and was treated by all with marked insult and cruelty. Zabeta Khan, a chief of the Rohillas, was a perpetual annoyance to the emperor, who was unable to chastise his insolence. Zabeta died in the course of this year, and was succeeded by his son, Gholam Caudir, who ascended at once the musnud of his father, without presenting the customary offering to the emperor, or obeying any of the forms so general on such an occasion. Shah Alum, although justly incensed, had no remedy; and Gholam, seeing the weak state of Dehli, conceived the daring idea of collecting a body of troops in haste, expelling the garrison from its walls, plundering the city, and finally gaining possession of the person of the emperor. The great treasures said to be amassed in the palace also tended to excite his thirst for plunder, while he conceived the holding captive the aged monarch would put into his hands all the power yet remaining to the empire. He saw the prize a rich and glorious one, and worth contending for, and he resolved to attempt it at all risks.

The great Mogul nobles, who, from religious and political prejudices, detested the Mahrattas, were most anxious to see the emperor and his court emancipated from their yoke. The Rohillas being of the Mahommedan faith were therefore less obnoxious; and ignorant of the character of the man whom they hailed as their deliverer, when Gholam Caudir appeared with his force before the city, they made no effort in its defence. The Mahratta garrison, aware of their weakness, rapidly retreated. The invader's first act, on gaining Dehli, was to compel the emperor to confer upon him the dignity of emir ul Omrah. He then marched to attack Alligurh, a fortress in which Scindia had left a garrison, took it, and thence directed his course to join Ismael Beg, then besieging Agra. Some differences, however, arose between these chiefs, and Gholam, separating himself from his ally, pursued his own plans of conquest in the Doo-ab. A.D. 1788.

Scindia in the mean time detached a large force under his confidential minister, Rana Khan, for the relief of Agra, which he effected, totally defeating Ismael Beg, and taking from him his cannon, baggage, and stores. Ismael himself narrowly escaped, being compelled to swim his horse across the Jumna. He met on the opposite bank a large body of his routed cavalry, and being soon after solicited by the Rohilla chief to forget their differences, and to rejoin him, he complied with the invitation, and the united armies moved on Dehli. The emperor, fearful of incurring the displeasure of Scindia, ordered the gates to be closed; but they had friends within who encouraged them to enter: the avenues were forced, and they became once again possessed of the city and the person of the emperor.

On being admitted to the presence, they fell at the feet of the monarch,

A.D. 1788. excusing their conduct by their anxiety to free him from the Mahratta yoke. They promised, if he would renounce his alliance with that perfidious race, and appoint them his generals, that they would speedily drive the Mahrattas back to their own territories, restore the lustre of their emperor's faded crown, and add a large increase to his diminished revenue. The dupe of so many projects, and victim of so many adventurers, was at length persuaded to submit; and a treaty being drawn up, was ratified by oaths mutually pledged in one of the mosques of the palace; and in that mosque the doom of the emperor and the empire was sealed.

Gholam Caudir's first demand was for a large sum of money to defray the arrears of pay due to the army. The emperor, as those troops had yet done no service for him or for the state, refused compliance. Incensed at this denial, and being assured that Shah Alum did possess secret hoards of jewels and treasure, he determined to dethrone the unfortunate monarch, and send him into confinement, which would place the whole at his disposal. Having imparted his design to, and gained the assent of, Ismael Beg, early on the morning of the 26th July, 1788, these lawless ruffians, at the head of an armed band, having entered the hall of audience, and seating themselves near the throne, renewed their demand for the sum required. The emperor's reply expressed his inability. They immediately sent for ***Bedar Bukht,*** son of the deceased emperor, Ahmed Shah, who, being placed by them on the imperial musnud, received the presents and salutations usually paid to the emperor on ascending the throne. Shah Alum, with nineteen princes, his sons and grandsons, was then by the barbarous Gholam ordered into confinement in a part of the palace called Noor Mahal, and they were here kept without victuals or drink, until they were near perishing with hunger. The two rebel chiefs next proceeded to search for the treasures, in which they were grievously disappointed, as very little was found in the treasury. The new emperor exerted himself to the utmost to raise the sum required, obtaining by menaces and persuasion the whole of the jewels and wealth from the princesses of the harem. On the 29th Gholam Caudir, having provided five whips, compelled Bedar Shah to take one in his hand, and accompany him to extort a confession of his treasures from Shah Alum. On the following day several of the ladies of the harem were tied up and beaten with whips, to compel a discovery of their effects, and the whole palace resounded with lamentations. A.D. 1788.

At length the fatal 10th of August arrived, when not content with starving, beating, and grossly insulting his sovereign and all the princes, and what was worse, the princesses of the royal family, the monster, attended by five Afghans, ferocious as himself, rushed into the apartment of Shah Alum, and repeated the demand for the treasure, the concealed treasure. The usual answer being returned that he had none, he ordered the ruffians to seize the emperor's children, Solyman, Acber, and others, and raising them on high, to dash them on the ground before their father's agonized sight. He then bade the Afghans to cast the hapless monarch on the ground, and rushing upon him, cut out his eyes with his own dagger. He ordered the princes to be subjected to the same fate, but was restrained by the humane entreaties of an officer in his train. The palace, at the time these dreadful scenes were acting, rang with the screams and cries of women, which the menace of whips and the terror of tortures could not for a long time silence. The bleeding monarch was left in that miserable condition without medical aid: by entreaties, however, two surgeons of the household were permitted to dress his wounds. The city of Dehli, meanwhile, was in the utmost confusion; the bankers' and jewellers' shops were shut, and half the terrified population fled to the country. Parties of Mahratta horse now made their appearance, the van-guard of Scindia's army, with whom it is

A.D. 1788. believed Ismael Beg was in secret correspondence. The Mahrattas approaching nearer, attacked and captured a convoy arriving at Dehli. Still the Rohilla continued his exactions and his cruelties: many ladies died of famine; and Shah Alum, in his dreadful situation, was still denied bread for himself and his family; while this monster indulged in banquets the most luxurious, and caroused all night with his officers in the wildest licentiousness. At length in the beginning of September the rapid approach of the great body of the Mahrattas compelled the Rohilla to think seriously of quitting Dehli. His army on the 7th crossed the river, and having seized all the elephants and horses in the royal stables, and packed up the plunder in boats, mounting his elephant, he joined his troops. Before his departure he set fire to the palace; an act of savage atrocity worthy his previous conduct. The flames, however, were extinguished, and the city and palace immediately taken possession of by the Mahratta chief, who instantly released Shah Alum, and humanely caused refreshments to be furnished to his family, who had tasted nothing for the space of seven days, except some dry grain and water.

The whole of the Mahratta force having at length been concentrated, Rana Khan lost no time in crossing the river Jumna with his whole army to attack Gholam, and rescue the royal victims. That traitor, unable to withstand so great a force, rapidly retired, but was overtaken at Mhirta, where he offered terms of submission, as humiliating as his former conduct had been haughty and arrogant. These were rejected with indignation, and on the 21st December a general assault was made on the place. The Rohillas defended themselves most desperately the whole day, but seeing no hopes of ultimate success, and dreading the vengeance which awaited him, Gholam at midnight, having selected all the most valuable of the jewels, and secreted them about the housings of his horse, made his escape. His horse fell with him, and so injured him, that he lay

A.D. 1788.

helpless on the ground until discovered in the morning by some peasants, who carried him to the Mahratta camp. The Rohillas, deserted by their leader, surrendered the following day. Gholam's horse, after disengaging himself from his prostrate master, galloped off with the treasures of Dehli, and was never more heard of. The princes and princesses of the royal family were liberated by Rana Khan, treated with the greatest respect, and sent back to Dehli, with a proper guard for their protection; while the perfidious Nazir was thrown into chains, and reserved for condign punishment. Gholam Caudir also, when he arrived in the camp, was heavily loaded with irons; and being placed in an iron cage, was kept for some time suspended in front of the army, to be gazed at as a monster of vice and unparalleled barbarity. Soon after, on the arrival of Scindia, that chief ordered the former culprit to be trodden to death by elephants; and the latter, having first had his nose and ears cut off, and then his hands and feet, was sent in this mutilated state to Shah Alum at Dehli; but the miserable wretch died while being conveyed thither.

Scindia, rapidly pursuing his career of victory, reached the country of the deceased rebel, where his army, unable to make any opposition, fled in every direction before him. He speedily took all the forts in the district, and annexed those territories to his own extensive domains in the Doo-ab. Then leaving a strong Mahratta force in the conquered province, he marched to Dehli, where, sending back Bedar Shah to his ancient state-prison of Selimgurh, he with great pomp once more raised the blind debilitated monarch to the musnud, and had coins again struck in his name: but since, by the ancient law both of Persia and India, a prince deprived of sight can never lawfully wield the imperial sceptre, Shah Alum may be considered as having ceased to reign, and the Indian empire itself as being extinguished—the glorious sun of the house of Timour as set for ever!

A.D. 1788. Thus closes the eventful and deeply interesting history of the rise, prosperity, power, and unbounded sway of the Mahommedan lords of Hindoostan; the apparently inexhaustible wealth, the vast resources of whom, with their countless hordes of intrepid and dauntless troops, raised at their nod, and the costly magnificence of their court and state, all have passed away; and where noble palaces and splendid mansions, cities vast in population and in wealth, in their manufactures and commerce, raised their proud and lofty columns under every varied form of pagoda, mosque, and minaret, are now beheld only heaps of shapeless and shattered ruins. Such is ancient Dehli and its gorgeous gardens of Shalimar. Of others, as Oude and Cannouge, scarce a vestige remains to indicate their ever having been the residence of monarchs. These two capitals of ancient Hindoostan each exceeded one hundred miles in circuit, and the present city of Lucnow was but one of the grand gateways to that of ancient Oude. Mausoleums, tombs, and their ruins now alone mark the probable bounds of these once mighty capitals: these can, however, afford but indistinct traces of their ancient extent.

Dehli, the noble, interesting Dehli, still preserves the rank it has, for so many centuries, and through so many dreadful revolutions and awful convulsions, constantly maintained. Dehli is still the imperial city of Hindoostan, still rises proudly and brightly above the ruins of her former splendour, which lie scattered at her feet, like the young phœnix bursting with new life from the ashes of its parent; and the traveller, concerned in her destiny, and that of the once mighty empire which bowed to her decrees, as it were those of Fate, will still encounter within its limits, scenes which must stamp upon the soul impressions, forcible and indelible, of respect and deep interest.

Picturesque Tour

ALONG

THE GANGES AND JUMNA.

CALCUTTA, the capital not only of Bengal but of all India, being the seat of government and residence of the governor-general and council, has been so much talked of, and so often described, that nothing new or interesting concerning it can be offered to the reader. The country in its immediate vicinity is flat and tame, sprinkled for the most part with the different varieties of the cocoa-nut and *palmyra,* or palm-tree. A traveller therefore, who visits Bengal from curiosity and a desire to explore its grander and wilder beauties, will not long tarry in its metropolis, but, deciding on the mode in which he will travel, make his preparations accordingly. These occupy but a short time, the natives being extremely handy and intelligent in all the various conveniences, or rather luxuries, requisite in moving with facility and comfort through this highly interesting country.

There are two modes of travelling used in India from the lower to the upper provinces; the one by land, the other by water. The latter is seldom chosen, except in the rainy season, when the winds are from the south-east, and blow sufficiently strong and steady to enable vessels to stem the very rapid currents encountered in many parts of the Ganges. A description of the establishment of a small fleet for these occasions may amuse such of my readers as have not visited India. The most usual vessels for this purpose are the pinnace and the budjerow. The former is generally preferred by Europeans, as being of a more roomy and stouter build, and as sailing better, when the wind is not quite free, than the other. The pinnace has two masts, the larger or main-mast forward, and a small mizen: some have a top-mast and top-gallant. It is nearly flat-bottomed, and has a shallow keel. Its crew consists of a *mangee,* or master, and from twelve to twenty *dandies,* or boatmen, who tow the vessel by a long line when the wind fails, or trim the sails when it is favourable. These are a hardy race of beings, wear but little clothing, and though exposed in towing the boat for the whole day to a burning sun, and frequently up to the middle in water, their heads are not only without any turban or covering, but literally shaven quite bare. Their skull, probably from constant exposure, becomes hard and thick enough to resist the rays of the sun thus pouring on their naked sconces. The budjerow is a native-built vessel, round-bottomed, and much lighter than the pinnace; it has but one mast and a large lug-sail: it is by far the safest vessel of the two in the hands of the natives, as they better understand its management. Besides these two vessels, there are others appropriated solely for the servants; others as cooking-boats, for stores, &c.; and one for horses, which is fitted up as a complete stable. This fleet, when not favoured by wind, travels usually at the rate of about two miles per hour, so that twenty-five or thirty miles on the average are gained daily. It is customary to come-to close to the river's bank a little before sun-set, to allow the crew and servants to cook their dinners; since there are some sects or casts of the Hindoos who must not eat on the water. At daylight all are again under weigh.

The season of the year, however, at which we were to move, was not favourable for a water excursion, the river being too low. To my great delight therefore a march by land was decided on, and all the requisite preparations for such an undertaking were set on foot with the greatest dispatch. Hands are so plentiful, and servants so numerous, in India, that what appears difficult and likely to occupy much time is performed with inconceivable expedition.

It may not be uninteresting to such of my readers as have not been in this country to give a slight sketch in this place of the retinue of servants, baggage-elephants, camels, horses, which, with a hundred et-ceteras, are indispensable on a journey by land. The best mode in which I can convey some idea of this is, by an enumeration of our party and its train, which, although it may appear large to some of my readers, contained not one individual more than comfort required. None accompanied us for mere state. Our party consisted of seven persons. We had three howdah-elephants, that is, animals trained for riding, hunting, and shooting, well broke, and with able *mahauts*, or leaders. Four others carried the camp-equipage, which consisted of two large marquees, each a sufficient load for an elephant, being about eighteen or twenty hundred weight. There were two smaller tents, besides others for the servants and guard of Sepoys; a light gig and horse, several saddle-horses, four palanquins, a cart, and hackery, or common cart of the country, with two bullocks to each. About two hundred servants and followers, and a guard of Sepoys, or native infantry, of forty men and a native officer, attended us.

The road called the old road was the route we proposed to take, although somewhat longer than the new; but as it was desirable to visit several cantonments of troops on the way, and as the supplies were more abundant upon this line, the former was preferred. The season was the very best for our purpose, having the whole of the cold weather before us. We left Calcutta the evening of the 2d Dec. 1807, and our first day's march was to Barrackpore, where is the country-seat of the governor-general: it is sixteen miles north of Calcutta, and most beautifully situated on the left bank of the river Hoogly, the principal navigable branch of the Ganges, and on which Calcutta is seated. The house is not remarkable either for size or accommodations, but it commands a fine and extensive view of the river, here about a quarter of a mile wide, having the old Danish settlement of Serampore on the opposite bank. The grounds of the domain are extensive, varied in feature, and undulating in graceful swells, interspersed with patches of low wood and scattered trees, among which several neat bungalows, appropriated for the accommodation of the staff of the governor-general, are seen. In one part of the grounds is a menagerie, comprising a tolerable collection of the animals of this country. Among these are two fine young tigers, a large wild boar, a species of bear, native of the upper provinces, and designated by Buffon under the name of ant-eater; and another bear, of a species never before seen in this country, of which it is a native, and equally unknown I believe in Europe. It partakes both of the form and nature of the bear and mastiff-dog, having its body shaped like the former, with the clumsy and awkward action and long claws of that animal; but the round form of the head and short ears, the wiry and sleek black hair on the body, and, above all, the lapping up its drink, would stamp it of the dog kind: it has a deep orange band round its throat. It seemed tolerably tame, and ate roots and fruits with avidity. Here are also several very beautiful neil-gais, antelopes, spotted and hog deer, a moose-deer, and a sloth; and of birds, the flamingo, cyraus, pelicans, and a toucan; also several ostriches and cassowaries.

A short distance below Barrackpore, towards Calcutta, some very beautiful and picturesquely situated pagodas furnish the subject of the ***First Plate.*** They are built with the cutcha, or unburnt brick of the country, and covered with a coating of chunam (a fine stucco), as purely white as marble, and bearing as high a polish. These buildings are backed by a luxuriant growth of every variety of the palm tribe, united with the pliant bamboo, from the dark contrasting masses of which they relieve admirably; and the scene, viewed from the opposite bank of the river, is much enlivened by the quickly gliding boats, of every varied size and model, which are seen passing to and fro in great numbers on the expansive bosom of the Ganges.

Near the governor-general's house at Barrackpore are a large cantonment and permanent huts for four battalions of Sepoys, always stationed here. On the 3d

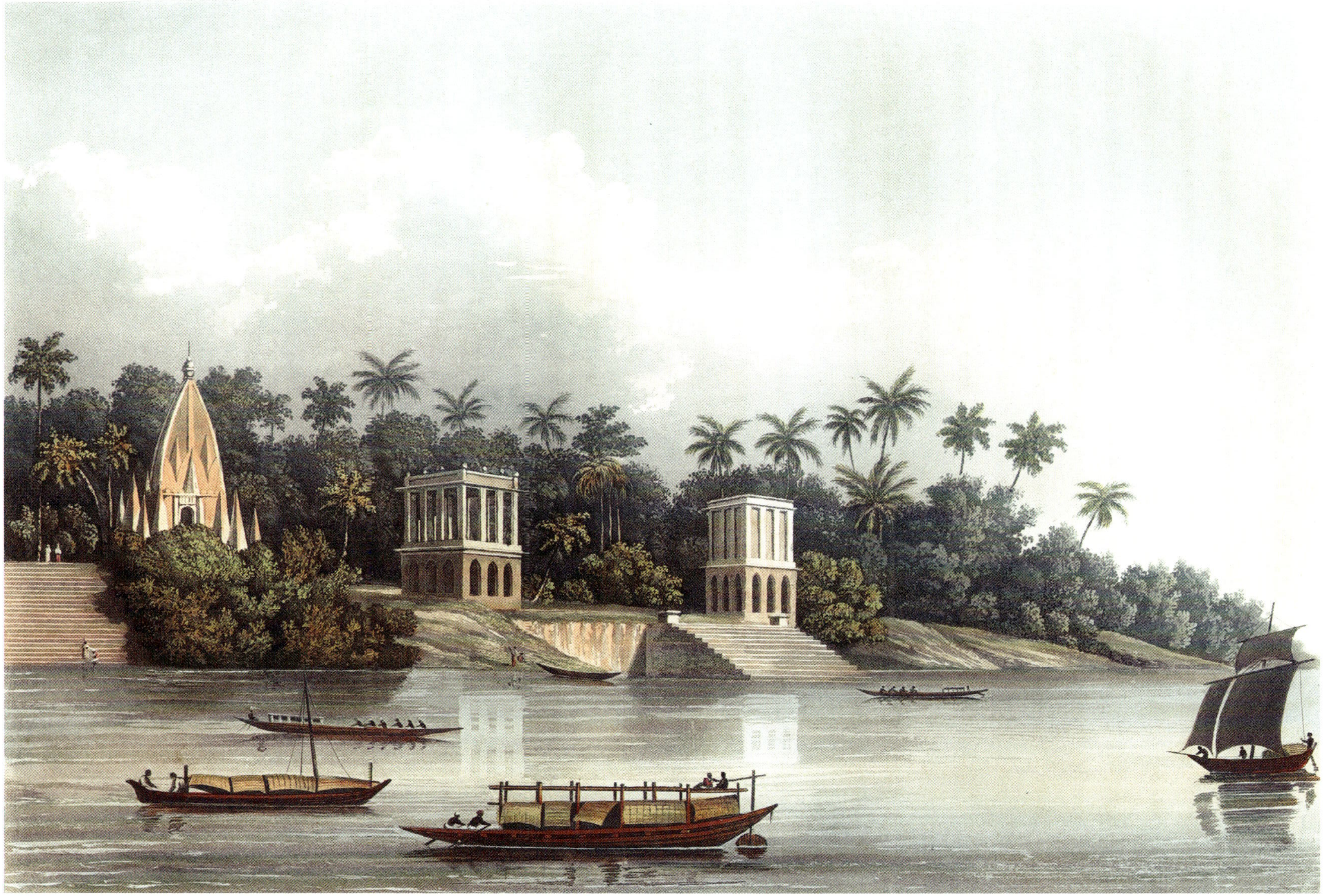

G. Hunt sculp.^t

HINDOO PAGODAS below BARRACKPORE
ON THE GANGES.

London, Published by R. ACKERMANN, 101, Strand, July 1, 1824.

December, having sent off our heavy baggage to await our arrival at Hoogly, we crossed the river at Pulta Ghaut. The current here was so rapid, that to get the baggage, horses, &c. into the boats, crossing them, and swimming the elephants over, occupied three hours. Moved on again, and passing through Ghyretti, the French settlement of Chandenagurh, and also Chinsura, belonging to the Dutch, each containing the remains of a fort, we reached our tents at five o'clock in the evening.

On the following morning at sunrise we again moved on through a finely cultivated line of country, crossing several nullahs or channels, worn by the torrents in the rainy season, now nearly dry. Some of these exceed one hundred yards in breadth, and their beds being very deep, a large body of water must sometimes rush down them. We encamped near the small village of Nia Serai. The early part of this morning was so sharp and cold, that I found a fur pelisse very agreeable. The thermometer stood at noon in the shade at 76°, at night 50° The country over which we passed the following day was mostly cultivated in rice-fields: the crops were off at this time, and the whole of the ground was cracked by the heat of the sun into fissures of a great depth. Near Inchura, where we halted, was a very extensive and beautiful piece of water left by the rains, called a *jeel:* we walked to it in the afternoon; it was covered with vast flights of teal and other birds of the duck kind; but although we had our guns with us, they were so wild, that we could not get one shot. During the greater part of this night we were tormented by the doleful yells and horrid cries of numerous packs of jackalls, who roam in the dark in search of prey, and visit the villages for plunder. Their cry very much resembles what might be supposed to be that of a human being under the most excruciating torture. Sleep was out of the question.

7th December. Road still over rice-grounds, and very bad riding; we were compelled also to ford several wide and extensive jeels, all shallow. Passed Ambooah, a small village on the Hoogly river; and near it, on a projecting point, a small secluded Hindoo village, embosomed in a verdant group of the richest foliage. Its small and pretty pagoda or temple, of a reddish stone, rears its cone-like form above the wooded screen which surrounds it; and, with some of the singularly formed boats, with their matted or bamboo awnings, produced on the whole a scene highly characteristic of this portion of the Ganges. It is represented in *Plate* II.

One mile beyond Ambooah is Culna, a large Hindoo village, close upon the bank. A short distance beyond this, in a bend of the river, the ground was covered, for an extent of full half a mile, with human skulls, washed up and left by the floods in the last rainy season. We here saw a species of the banian tree, called the *peepul:* it was filled with green parrots and monkeys, who seemed to vie with each other which could make the greatest noise. Hence the road was exceeding good to Mirzapore, on high ground; the Hoogly river on our right, and a richly wooded country to our left.

It was our daily practice to send forward a small tent at midnight, with the breakfast apparatus for the following morning, so that on arriving at our new ground we found that meal always ready; and by the time it was completed, unless when the march was an unusually long one, the other tents were up, and in one hour more our little town was perfectly established.

Next morning we were at Commeera, and the following at Aughadeep. We crossed the Hoogly river by a ferry at Chandenagurh, where the stream is about 200 yards wide: it is the westernmost branch of the Delta of the Ganges.

We now succeeded in getting our encampment regularly pitched, and more compact than at our first starting. We had some difficulty to prevail upon the natives to come into our plan, but by persevering they did so; and we found it much easier to guard at night from the expert thieves, who are always on the look-out for plunder, especially when Europeans pass their villages.

On the 10th we encamped, and passed the night on the celebrated field of Plassy,

Plate-11

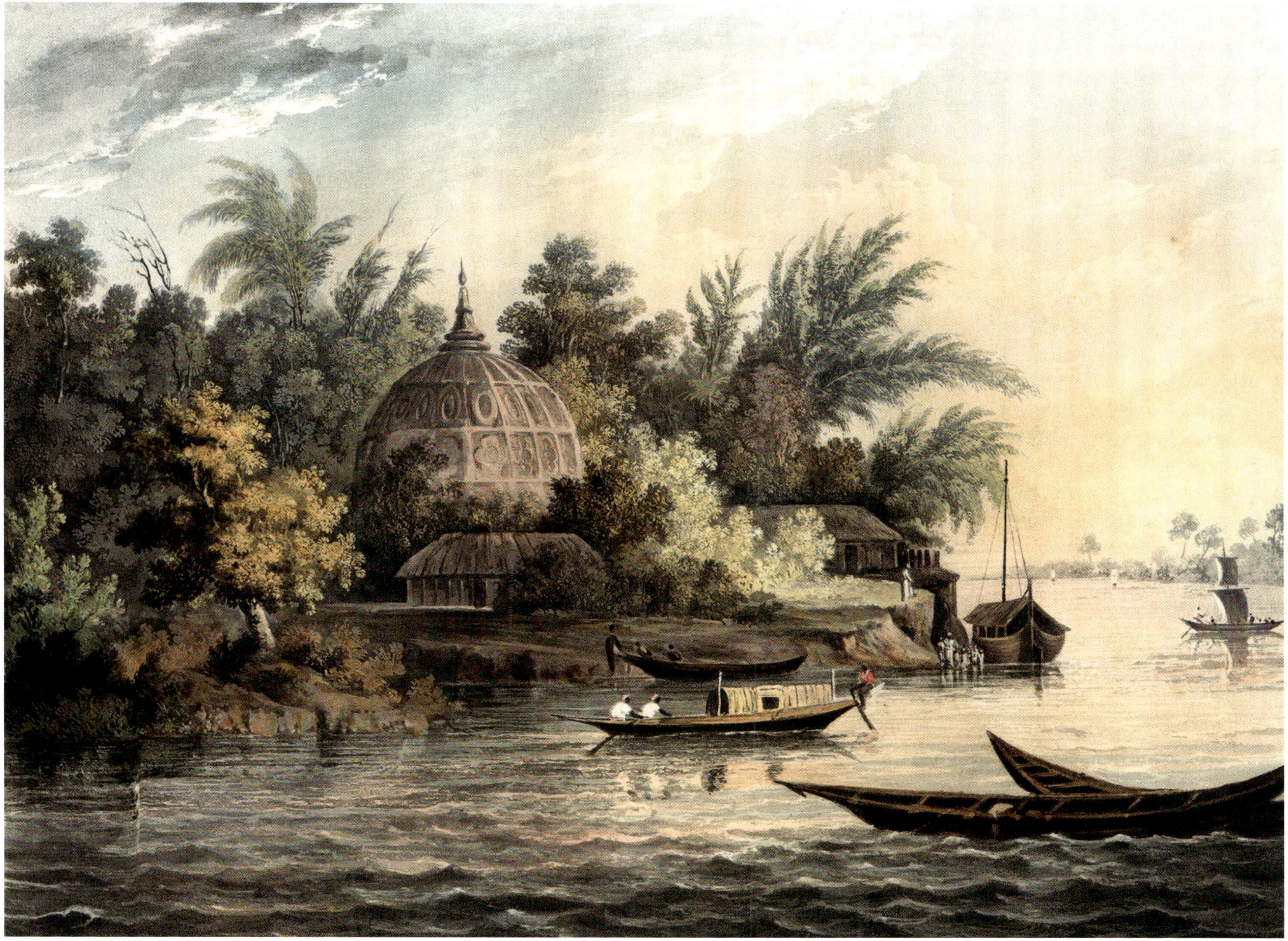

T. Sutherland sculp.

HINDOO VILLAGE on the GANGES.
NEAR AMBOOAH.

London, Published by R. ACKERMANN, 101, Strand, July 1, 1824.

where a decisive and obstinately contested battle took place between the Company's troops under Colonel, afterwards Lord Clive, and the Nuwab of Moorshedabad, in which the latter was totally defeated.

Having passed the village of Burrah on the following day, we turned off the main road, which proceeds to the cantonment of Berhampore, to Jungipore, having engaged ourselves to pass a short time with a civilian of rank resident there, at whose hospitable mansion we remained four days.

On the 17th we again proceeded on our journey, and advancing through the Island of Cossimbazar, passed in the course of our route several of those bunds, or banks, erected for the purpose of preventing the waters of the river from overflowing the island in the rainy season.

I once had occasion to proceed on duty from Calcutta to Berhampore on the Cossimbazar river, a branch of the Ganges, which, uniting with another, the Jellinghy, at Nuddea, forms the Hoogly river, which descends to Calcutta. and is the only free and uninterrupted communication by water between that capital and the Upper Ganges.

I left Calcutta in the month of August, and in the height of the rainy season, it having poured incessantly for six weeks. Our pinnace ascended the Hoogly, and passing Barrackpore, soon after entered a perfect sea, for the expanse of waters had no visible bounds. We continued to run thus over the country through patches of wood, and every now and then passed villages, perched either on the summit of mounds, artificially constructed, or on small natural hills; some of these rearing their spiral pagodas, white as alabaster, with their straw-thatched bamboo cabins, backed by a rich group of wood, in which the palmyra reared its towering height and fan-like leaves, the bamboo waved its graceful and feathery branches, and the plantain threw around its immense leaves of the most vivid green in every fantastic form: these, and the groups of the admiring natives, eagerly gazing on our passing fleet, formed, on the whole, a singularly striking and interesting scene. This apparently destructive flood, an epithet with which it would assuredly be coupled in most regions of the world, is here the greatest blessing heaven can bestow: it spreads fertility and plenty over the tract it seems to devastate, and renders Bengal one of the richest and most flourishing provinces of the earth. We occasionally came upon the river where the channel was deep, and there the current was excessively rapid. We stopped the whole of one day near the village of Cutwah, which is situated on the right bank of the Hoogly, and extends along it a considerable distance: it has numerous ghauts, of one of which a view is given (*Plate* III.), with the Hindoo pagoda attached, and some of the larger boats of the country, used for the transport of merchandise.

The upper part of the Cossimbazar branch of the Ganges is exposed sometimes to more danger: there, when the river has a very sudden rise, it pours so great a mass of its waters into the numerous channels extending from the mouth of the Jellinghy to that of the Cossimbazar, near the village of Sooty, which all unite in the Hoogly below, forming the Cossimbazar Island, that the bed of the latter stream is unable to contain the congregated flood pouring into it from every direction; the waters are arrested, and consequently rise far higher than they can do below this obstacle.

To guard against this pressure of the waters, bunds or banks, of great height and immense solidity, have, by the direction of the East India Company, been constructed, and are kept up at a vast expense: still, the art of man is not equal to cope with the efforts of Nature; massive as these bounds are, they are but too often carried away, when a scene of destruction ensues not easily to be described.

I have passed, in descending from the upper provinces, through some of these branches of the Cossimbazar river: the velocity with which the stream hurried us onwards, and the wonderful effects evident at every turn on the soft yielding matter of which its banks were composed, produced an indescribable sensation of admiration

Plate-III

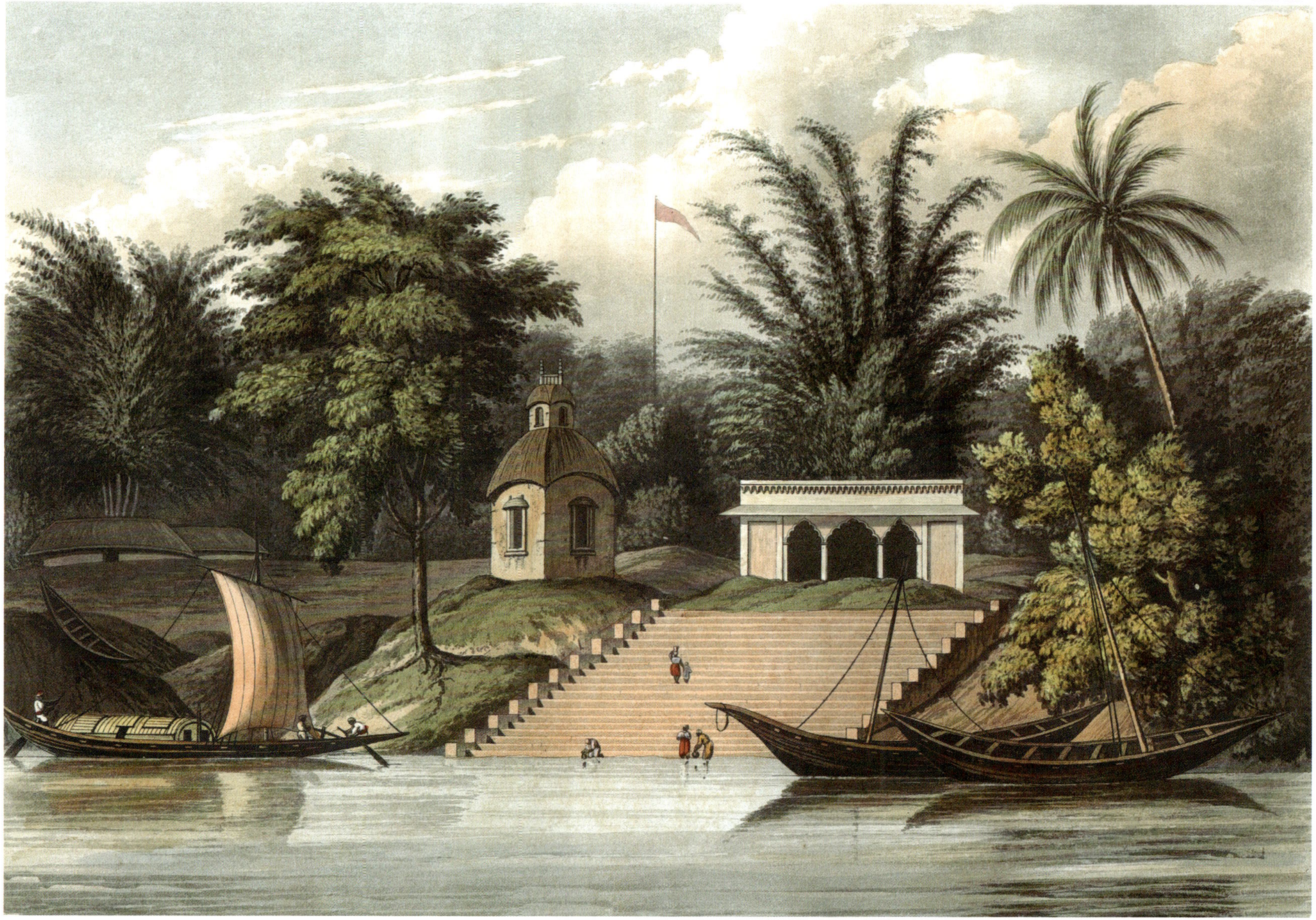

G. Hunt sculp.t

GHAUT OF CUTWA.
ON THE GANGES.

London, Published by R. ACKERMANN, 101, Strand, July 1, 1824.

Plate-IV

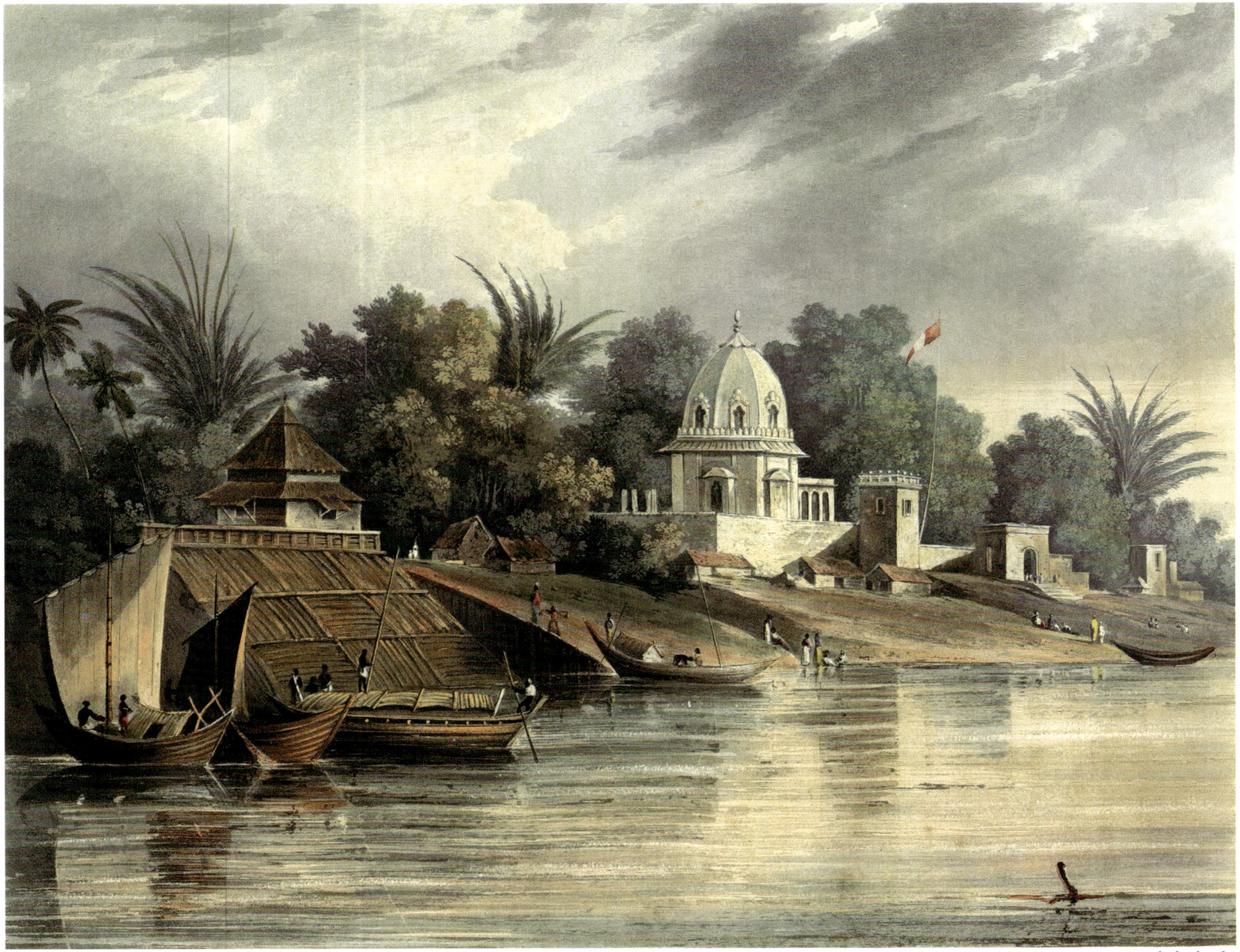

T. Sutherland sculp.t

PART OF THE CITY OF MOORSHEDABAD.
ANCIENT CAPITAL OF BENGAL

London, Published by R. ACKERMANN, 101, Strand, July 1, 1824.

mingled with terror, as we contemplated the foaming and furious torrent, lashing in the most angry manner all obstacles which it encountered in its course, hurrying banks and rocks and large trees before it like straws, while our boat most rapidly glided over its turbulent bosom in perfect safety.

The skill and judgment of the crew of our vessel were wonderful where the river took a sudden turn: the helm was useless, and here the greatest presence of mind was requisite in the one at the head, who, with surprising force and agility, darting his long bamboo pole against the opposing bank, turned the vessel in an instant into the new direction. Never can the impression made by this scene be effaced; never have I seen it equalled, save in the rapids of the mighty rivers of the Canadas. They not only equal but surpass it, in the superior vastness of their torrents, and the more wild, imposing, and gigantic character of their scenery.

Being anxious to see the ancient capital of the soubah of Bengal, always esteemed the finest, most important, and richest province of the empire, I this morning rode in that direction, though our party took a shorter route by the direct road, when I soon reached and entered Moorshedabad by a large and massive gateway of brick, covered with a coating of stucco; the parapet was pierced with embrasures for cannon, but there were none mounted. The city itself is wretched in the extreme, a mass of poor and mean sheds, some having the walls built of mud, others of the bamboo split and interwoven: there were a few brick square-built houses of one story, with flat roofs. The streets were narrow and filthily dirty, and I found the ride through the city sickening and tiresome in the highest degree. Its length is full seven miles. The view from the river is the best, and is given in ***Plate*** IV.

On the following day, the Nuwab of Bengal came in state to pay a visit of ceremony to the general officer commanding the station. He was received with a royal salute from the guns of the garrison of Berhampore. His train of attendants were attired in very gaudy, though at the same time shabby, apparel.

The order of the procession on this occasion was as follows: Several *hircarahs* or out-runners with silver staffs led the way, proclaiming aloud the titles of the Nuwab. Two men mounted on camels, called *shutur sewars,* followed; then a drum and trumpet on horseback, succeeded by the banner of the soubahship, carried by a man on a very large elephant. Then followed a number of smaller flags, which designated the rank his highness bore in the empire; the body guard of cavalry, and a guard of native militia; next his highness's state palanquin, borne on men's shoulders; a band of music; and immediately behind this the Nuwab, in a magnificently gilt and splendidly decorated car, followed by his prime vizir in a smaller one. Several of his officers came next mounted on horseback; and the procession was closed by about twenty elephants, as many camels, all in state trappings, and some state *ruths* (or small waggons used for carrying the women), drawn by the Hindoostannee bullocks of a large size.

On the following day we came upon the main body of the Ganges, which we had not yet seen: it is here an immense and grand expanse of water, rather resembling an inland sea than a river. The opposite shore, being very low and flat, was scarcely to be distinguished; and looking up the stream, it had apparently no bounds.

After marching mostly by the bank of the Ganges for four more days, we began to lose traces of cultivation, and to encounter occasional tracts of jungle. On one occasion we came to a nullah, 40 or 50 yards wide, which for a time puzzled us to cross. There was a wooden bridge over it, and all the horses, carts, and persons on foot passed in safety, although its construction did not appear very strong: but no inducements, no urging, could prevail upon the loaded baggage-elephants to attempt it; when brought up to it they expressed the greatest alarm, striking the flooring of the bridge with their trunks, which seemed to convince them at once of its insufficiency to bear their ponderous bulk. The bed of the nullah was too shallow in water for them to swim, and too deep in mud to ford. No resource remained but to try the experiment of unloading the elephants, pass them over the bridge light, and carry their loads after them. This was accordingly done, and perfectly comprehended by these sagacious animals, who now walked over cheerfully and confidently.

In expectation of some sport, being now in the vicinity of the Rajmahal hills, a group of mountains, which in this part separates the provinces of Bengal and Bahar, we halted one entire day at the village of Futhipore, and having procured from thence a *shekarri,* or in plain English, a poacher, well acquainted with the haunts of the different species of game with which these hills abound, we mounted our elephants, for it is thus that Indian sportsmen take the field, and formed a party of eight or nine persons. Several baggage-elephants with our servants accompanied us to beat the jungles, and a great many persons from the village with long bamboo poles volunteered for the same service, with a tribe of their common pariah or village dogs.

We saw, on entering the jungle, a great quantity of game of various sorts, as the wild buffaloes, hog-deer, wild hog, deer of different kinds, partridges, and chuckores (a large species of the partridge); florikens, a small species of the bustard, and the common domestic barn-door fowl of England in great numbers, called here the jungle fowl; and when we found open spots with partial cultivated fields, quail in great quantities, and very tame. We had a very pleasant day's sport, but our reward was only some of the partridges and quail. We got several shots at the buffaloes, and several we could hear distinctly hit; but the common leaden ounce-ball has no effect on these tough-skinned animals, unless it chances to hit a vital part, behind the ear, or fore-leg. The two-ounce rifle, with pewter balls, to be certain of your shot, the tiger and buffalo both require.

In the course of the day we came upon the tracks of a rhinoceros, several of which are found on these hills; we followed them some time, in hopes of coming up with him: in some parts he appeared to have very recently passed, since the water was still muddy where he had trodden. Our pursuit was, however, in vain.

I had never entered so deeply into the jungles as I did this day, and I felt much delighted with the extremely curious scene they in several parts presented. The height of the grass struck me as particularly wonderful. I was mounted on a very fine elephant, not less than eleven feet high; the howdah, or seat fastened on the animal's back, must have been full two feet higher, it being strapped on a very thick pad: this would give thirteen feet. Now when standing upright, the attitude usually adopted by sportsmen when beating the jungle in order to see better around them, my head must have been near nineteen feet above the ground; but the grass was generally three, and in some places six, feet higher than my head. The stalks were full an inch and a half in diameter, and it would be almost impossible, certainly very fatiguing, to attempt to force a passage on foot through such a thicket, independent of the chance of meeting with a tiger on a sudden—by no means a pleasant *rencontre.*

Having satisfied ourselves with sporting, at the first open spot we found, which I perfectly recollect was a beautiful small natural meadow, surrounded on all sides by high jungles, and having a sweet clear stream trickling through its centre, we alighted from our elephants, sending them to get some forage for themselves, and then sat down very sociably to examine the contents of our provision-basket: we found it very well supplied, and our long ramble through the jungles made us do full justice to its contents. We were in fact enjoying ourselves much; our elephants had gone out of sight, and we were occupied with an ice-cold bottle of most excellent madeira, cooled in our spring, when a sudden and angry snort, not far from us, made us jump up in a hurry on our feet. We saw an immensely large and fierce male buffalo, wild and savage, who was glaring upon our party with his eyes of living fire and his scowling angry front. The male wild buffalo, when met in this solitary state, is supposed to have been driven from the herd of favourite females by more powerful rivals: he is therefore always inclined to mischief, and is said to be more bold and ferocious than the tiger himself. Whether our present visitor was in this state or not, we were uncertain; the number of our party perhaps awed him. We called out lustily, however, for our elephants: they were, fortunately, within call. The first that came up were mounted by some of our party, who made for the buffalo with their guns all ready: he, however, turned tail, and entered the low jungle, declining battle. They got two shots at him, but whether they took effect or not, he disappeared, and we saw no more of him.

On the following day, 24th December, we passed the Ouda-nullah by a handsome Pucka bridge. This nullah is very large and deep, and a vast torrent must rush through it after the rainy season. Six miles further is the village of Rajmahal, and the ruins of a very grand and fine palace, the former residence of the nuwab, soubah, or viceroy of the province of Bahar: it is well situated on a most commanding eminence, its foot washed by the Ganges, here a noble river, of which it commands a fine view on one side, and on the other an equally grand one of the Rajmahal range of mountains.

Next day we passed the large nullah of Sirkunda, near which is the ruin of a noble building, a ***dowlut kana,*** or palace erected by Shah Jehan, emperor of Hindoostan, which must once have been a grand pile, and encamped at Mussaw. The Rajmahal hills were now very close to us, and presented a beautiful sight. Their forms are varied, but all swelling in gentle undulations. They are clothed with wood apparently throughout almost their whole extent: nevertheless there are cleared spots within their retired valleys, and some of the mountains even are deprived of their wood. It is singular that the race of people inhabiting these mountains, by no means inaccessible, should totally differ in stature, feature, language, manners, customs, and religion, from the Hindoos all around them. I walked one evening into the country for some three or four miles, and met a few of these people: one of them talked a little in the common Hindoostannee. They were all nearly naked; the hair tied in a knot at the top of the head. They were well made, but rather low in stature, and carried bows made of bamboo, and arrows. They appeared mild and friendly, and their manner was prepossessing.

A corps was formed from among the natives of the Rajmahal group of mountains, and called the Hill-Rangers: they behaved well, and were far from indifferent soldiers.

I took a small boat this evening, and rowed out to some distance from the shore, to obtain a better view of the hills, and judge more accurately of their height. Several very beautiful breaks offered themselves as the sun sank behind them; and one, which I have included in the views (***Plate*** V.) was the most picturesque.

Having now reached the northern confines of the province of Bengal Proper, and being about to enter that of Bahar, a few observations and remarks on the ancient and modern state, productions and general features of the surface of the province we have just traversed, may not be here inappropriate.

The rich and beautiful valley of the Ganges, extending from the bay of Bengal on the south, along both banks of that river, to the point whence it issues from the mountainous chain which bounds Hindoostan on the north, a distance of nearly fourteen hundred miles, is at present in possession of Great Britain.

This wonderfully fertile tract of country originally formed the empire of the Prasii and Gangaridæ, as described by the earlier Greek historians. These empires, being swept away by the enterprising and sanguinary Mahommedan invaders from the western parts of Asia, became transformed into mere provinces of the new empire of which these warriors were the founders. These comprised the provinces of Oude, Bengal, Bahar, Allahabad, and part of Agra; and as such they exist to this day. At the early period we have alluded to above, from the best authority to be obtained, the city of Cannouge was the capital of this vast empire: it is considered by some

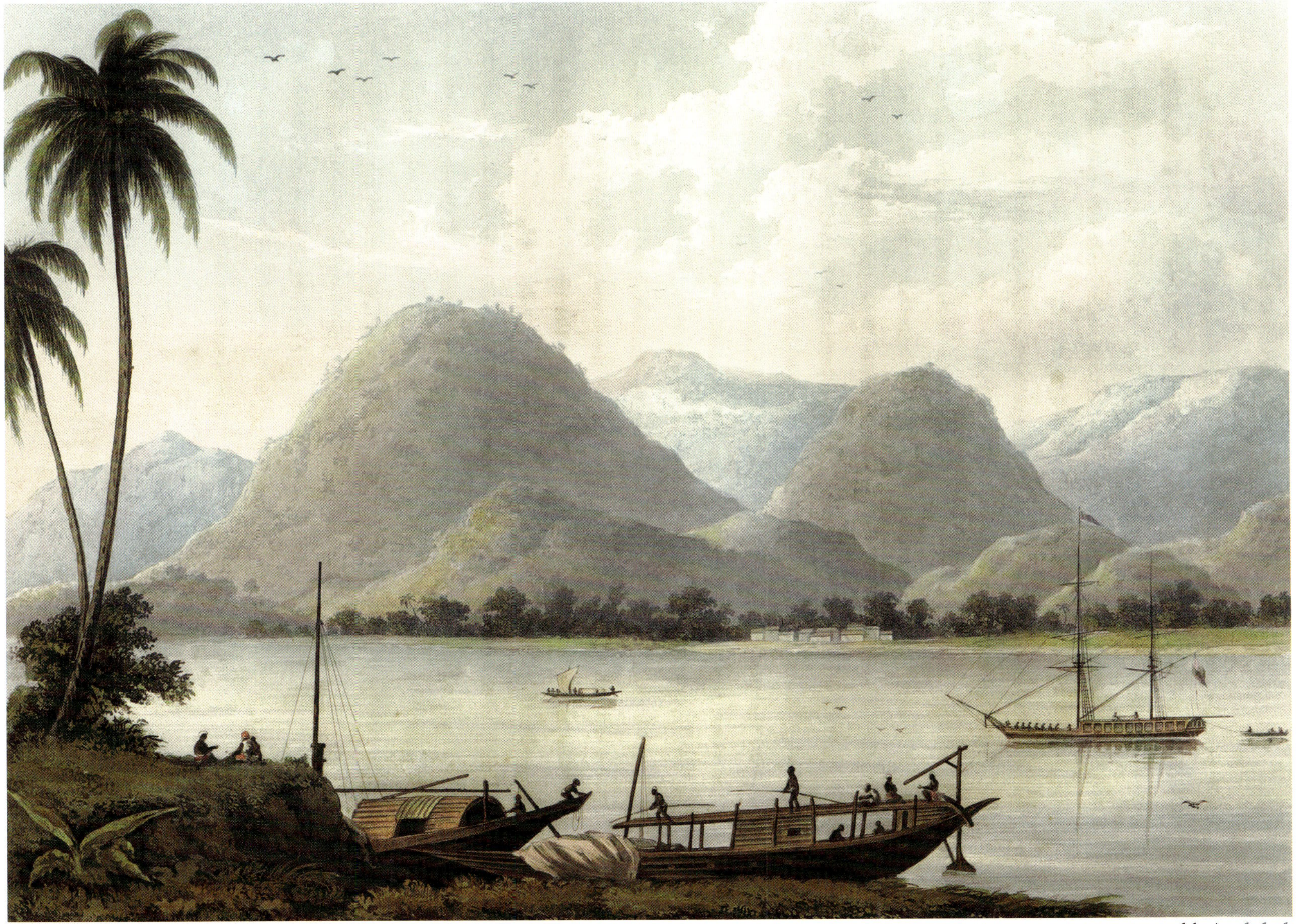

Engraved by T. Sutherland.

MOUNTAINS OF RAJEMAHAL
WHERE THEY DESCEND TO THE GANGES.

London Published by R. ACKERMANN, 101, Strand, Aug.[t] 1, 1824.

writers as the same to which the ancients gave the name of Palibothra. Strabo describes it as situated at the confluence of another river with the Ganges, and its form as that of a vast quadrangle, in length eighty stadia, equal to about ten English miles, and in breadth fifteen stadia, or two miles, surrounded by a fortification constructed with wood, on which were built five hundred and seventy high towers. Its number of gateways amounted to sixty-five; and the whole circumference was protected by a vast fosse or ditch, exceeding 200 yards in breadth, and 45 feet deep. Pliny and Arrian both concur in this account.

The province of Bengal Proper is bounded on the south by the bay of that name, on the north by a range of mountains, on the east is Aracan and part of Assam, and Bahar borders it on the west.

The *Ayeen Acberi,* a book compiled by order of the great Acber, emperor of Hindoostan, at the close of the fifteenth century, when that country was at its highest pinnacle of glory, and which gives a very clear and detailed account of every province of the empire, their produce, population, and every thing connected with them, has estimated the extent of the soubahship of Bengal at four hundred koss in length, and two hundred in breadth, the koss being nearly two English miles.

There is not perhaps in any part of the world a tract of country which can compare with it in fertility, if we except Egypt, which in this respect it very nearly resembles. It is watered by the vast and majestic Ganges, which glides through its centre, and which, on the subsiding of the waters of its periodical floods, spreads a rich deposit to a considerable extent from its banks, and joined by several smaller streams running at right angles nearly with this their great channel, descends to the ocean. Numerous canals also, formed by the industry of man, intersecting in all directions the vast plain of its valley, diffuse a most luxuriant verdure and abundant harvests throughout its whole extent.

The climate of Bengal is comparatively temperate when contrasted with that of the upper provinces: it is not subject to the hot and parching winds of the latter, which prevail for three months in the year, from March to June; and from its situation south of the tropical line, the sun twice passes it within a short space of time, producing a long rainy season, and consequently much cloudy weather. The rains on an average are computed to continue for nearly six months. The violent and frequent storms of thunder also tend, no doubt, to refresh the atmosphere and reduce its temperature. These rains sometimes commence so early as April, but more commonly in the beginning of June.

The Ganges itself has been held in such repute from the earliest times, that the Hindoos entertain a sacred and religious veneration for its waters. One of their most solemn oaths is on its holy stream; and the wealthy Hindoos, who reside many of them at the distance of several days' journey from its banks, have a daily supply of its waters for the purposes of religious ablution.

Some particular parts of this river are considered far more sacred than others; and here immense crowds of the Hindoos, at stated periods, or at their great festivals, are collected for the purposes of devotion, and pass hours and even whole days in its purifying waters.

Independent of these supernatural qualities, however, applied to the water of the Ganges, it has properties really valuable to mankind: it is sweet and wholesome, and may, it is said, be kept for years without being subject to putrefaction.

The rice is the species of grain most cultivated in Bengal, as it delights in a moist soil, and flourishes particularly within reach of the periodical floods. This plant is sometimes so luxuriant and prolific, that the produce of one single grain has been known to yield a measure equal to four pounds weight. The rice possesses another remarkable quality, which deserves notice in this place: in proportion as the inundations of the Ganges rise, the rice extends its stalk even to the length of fifteen or twenty feet, and never permits its head to be immersed in the water.

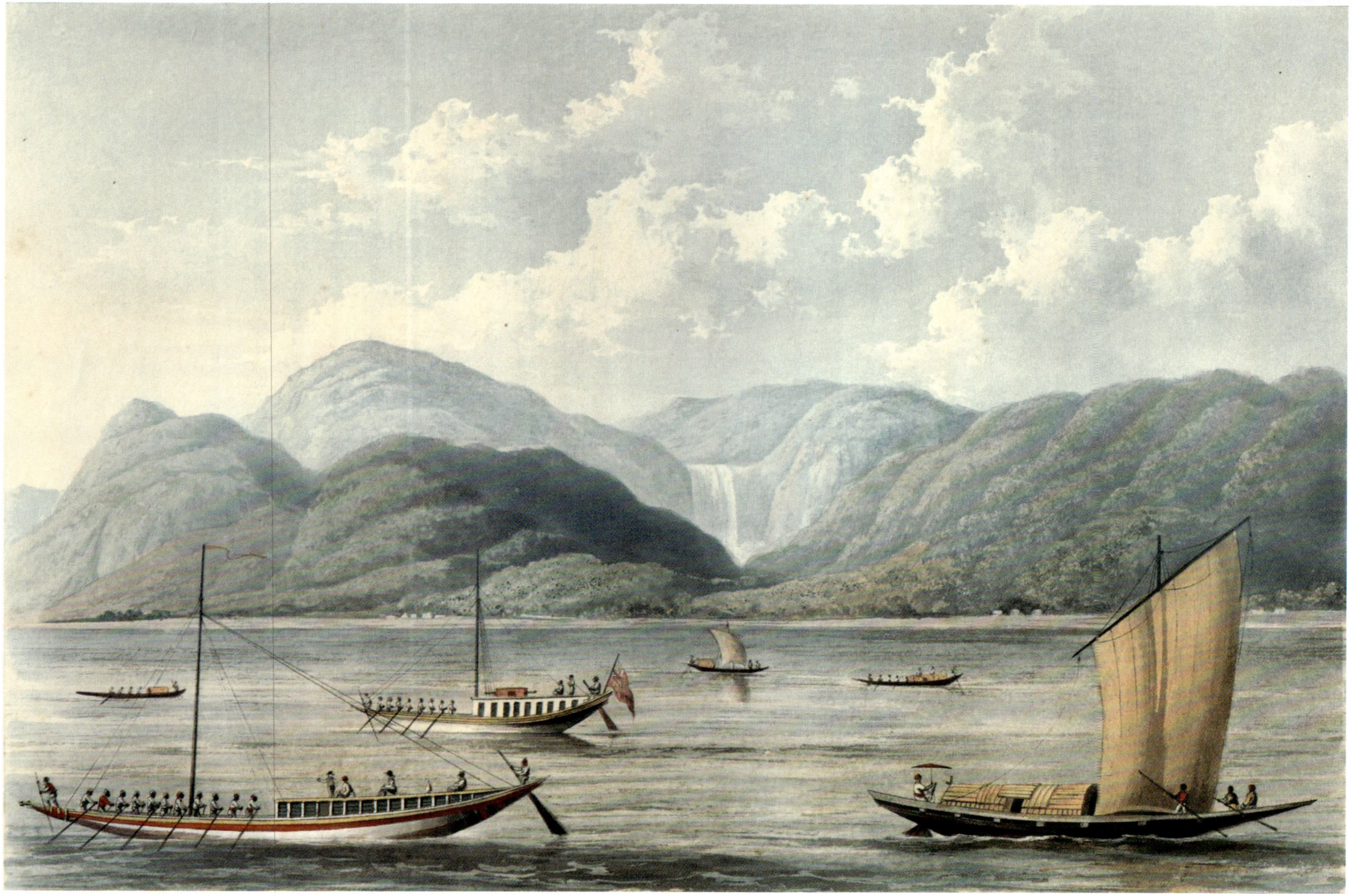

T. Sutherland sculpt.

THE MOTEE GIRNA.
OR FALL OF PEARLS IN THE RAJEMAHAL HILLS.

London, Published by R. ACKERMANN, 101, Strand, Aug.t 1, 1824.

These periodical inundations of the Ganges are usually at their height in August and September; they sometimes continue until October, but this is unusual. I cannot precisely state their perpendicular rise, having had no opportunity of ascertaining it by actual experiment; but I am confident I am much within the mark when I place it at fifteen feet.

The road runs mostly by the right bank of the Ganges to the confines of the province of Bengal Proper, approaching which the country becomes less cultivated and more wooded. The Rajmahal hills shew themselves in the distance on the left of the road, and bending round towards the river, soon run down upon its very banks. Here is a pass, which, winding through a labyrinth of low and thickly wooded rocky hills, is called the Sicre-Gully Pass (represented in the ***Vignette*** at the end of the work); and beyond, at a little distance, is that of Terria-Gully. The road through both is stony, and bad for wheel-carriages. On passing this obstacle, the province of Bahar is entered, which was formerly of equal importance, and now even surpasses Bengal in fertility. There are commonly five distinct crops of grain in the year, and the wheat is of the purest and finest quality. I have seen near Patna sixteen quartern loaves sold for one rupee, 2s. 6d.

Proceeding on from the Terria-Gully Pass, we found the country more open as we entered the province of Bahar. We obtained two beautiful glimpses of the Rajmahal hills: the first soon after rounding the point of land where this ridge of mountain falls abruptly into the river; the other a few miles further on, where, in a profound ravine of the thickly wooded mountains, may be discerned, from near the river's brink, a beautiful cataract of water, which, apparently bursting from a deep chasm, descends in a sheet of silver for some distance, and then breaking into showers of sparkling spray, has received the appropriate and beautiful appellation of the ***Mootee Girna,*** or the Fall of Pearls. A view of it is given in ***Plate*** VI. We had passed in the course of this day's march a very fine ***birkut,*** or banian tree, which, stretching its gigantic limbs across the road, supported on their slender and graceful living columns, and crowned by a thickly interwoven mass of the richest foliage, seemed, as we moved beneath its cool and refreshing porticoes, the temple of some sylvan deity. Seen at a distance, these singular trees have the appearance of a grove of several joined together. The Hindoos regard it with superstitious veneration. To the traveller it is ever a welcome sight, when, fatigued with the burning hours of a midday march, he seeks with eagerness its friendly shelter.

On the following morning we took the field on our elephants at an early hour, in hopes of some sport: we met with vast numbers of peacocks, but they were very wild, and we only brought home a few brace of the chuckore-partridge. We afterwards continued along through the jungle, and parallel with the road, getting an occasional shot, till we reached Colgong, about twelve miles from Pialapore, well situated on the main Ganges. This place is remarkable for three singular masses of rock, which stand in the body of the river, and about two hundred yards from the right bank. The principal of these has a perpendicular height of about eighty feet, and all are composed of irregular rolled masses, as far as I could judge, of different sorts of granite. Their summit is overspread with a luxuriant growth of trees and shrubs. Procuring a *dinghy,* the smallest kind of boat, I passed over to the largest rock, and with a little scrambling attained its summit. The Ganges is here a noble river, and has a breadth, when at the highest, of nearly two miles. But the most singular circumstance connected with these rocks is, the change which has occurred in their situation with respect to the Ganges. Some forty or fifty years ago they were not only on *terra firma,* but considerably inland and remote from the river.

The Ganges, having its sources in a very mountainous region, is subject to periodical, vernal, and autumnal floods, and its bed being a very rich alluvial soil, is constantly changing by the force and rapidity of the current. Some trifling accident generally commences this deviation, as the falling in of a portion of the lofty bank

Plate-7

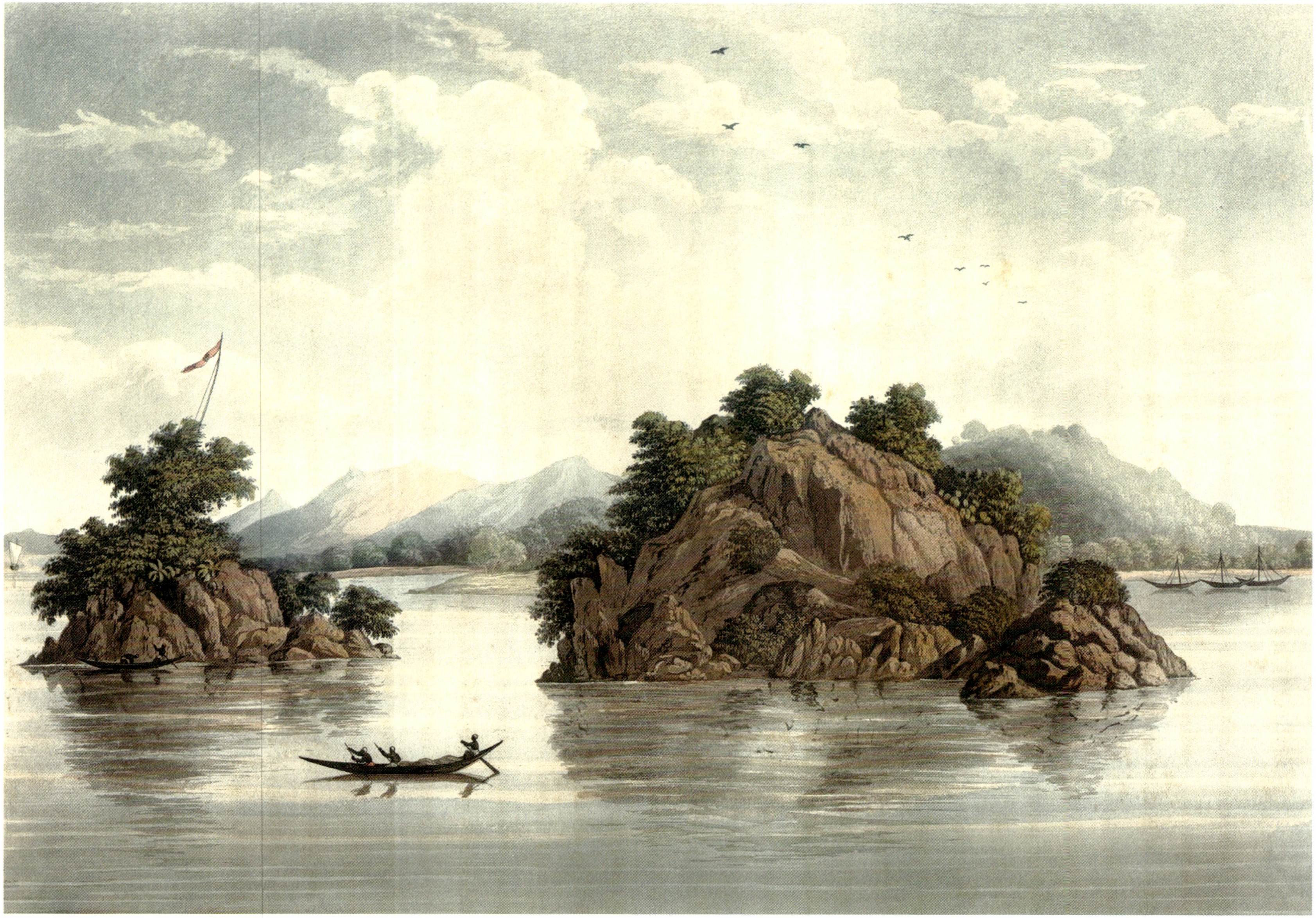

G. Hunt sculpt.

THE ROCKS OF COLGONG.

London, Published by R. ACKERMANN, 101, Strand, Aug.t 1, 1824.

by the undermining of the river; this, forming an obstacle to its usual course, diverts the current, and perhaps directs it against a soft and yielding bank: the work of destruction then is most wonderfully rapid, and an entire village has, in the course of one night, totally disappeared. I have frequently seen this occur in my voyages in the upper provinces, where banks and cliffs of fifty or sixty feet perpendicular height are precipitated in masses of hundreds of tons at a time into the river below. The rocks of Colgong owe their present situation to a gradual change of this nature; formerly they were high inland, now they are in the bosom of the mighty Ganges, and the depth of water close to the largest exceeds sixty feet. A Fakeer, or wandering mendicant friar, occasionally takes up his abode on one of these rocks, for a view of which the reader is referred to *Plate* VII. Our direction from Moorshedabad to Sicre-Gully had been about north-west; but there the river takes a bend nearly due west, forming three large elbows to the northward between this and Surajgurh.

Two more stages brought us to Boglipore, a considerable town, and the residence of the civil servants of the Company, the magistrate, and collector of the district of Monghyr, which is in the province of Bahar.

Having now taken our leave of the province of Bengal Proper, and entered and arrived at the chief station of that of Bahar, we propose to give the same sketch of its general features, produce, and manufactures, as has been already given of the former. It has been long celebrated in India as the most fertile part of Hindoostan, and there is a greater diversity of surface comprised within its limits than in its sister province of Bengal, the western parts being much broken, and rising in some places to hills of a commanding height and form. These give birth to several rivers, which, descending into the plains, tend much to their fertility and verdure. Bahar, throughout the long and grievous disputes and dissensions which convulsed the greater part of the empire, removed to a distance from the focus of these evils, the proud but unfortunate Dehli, was seldom visited by the scourge of war; and it was only in the few expeditions of the more enterprising Acber and ambitious Aurungzebe that it witnessed scenes but too familiar to its neighbouring provinces.

Bahar is stated, in the time of the emperor Acber Shah, to be bounded on the east by the province of Bengal, on the west by Allahabad and Oude, and on the north and south by mountains. Its length is given as one hundred and twenty, and its breadth from the mountains on the north to Tyroot at one hundred and ten koss.

The chief rivers of Bahar are the Ganges and the Soane. The Soane, the Nerbudda, and the Chelun, all take their rise near Kurrah. The first runs in a southern direction as far as Mouneah, where it joins the Ganges. The Gunduck river comes from the foot of the hills to the north, and falls into the Ganges near Hajipore. The summers are very hot, the winters temperate, and the rains continue nearly six months. The whole province is covered with the richest verdure, and the soil being hard and compact, little dust is raised by the storms of wind. Agriculture is in high perfection, and rice flourishes particularly in this province. Many houses throughout Bahar are roofed with tiles, and the inhabitants are famous for building boats and the manufacture of gilded glass. Horses and camels are not numerous, but the elephants are fine, and in great numbers. The hawk, parrot, and fighting-cocks celebrated for giving great sport, abound. The air, water, and climate of Tyroot are much spoken of: it has large and delightful groves of orange-trees extending for thirty koss. The fort of Rhotasgurh is another singular feature of Bahar. It is situated on a lofty mountain, of difficult approach, and twenty-eight miles in circumference; the inclosed land is cultivated, and watered by a variety of springs. The only access to it is by a very narrow road up a steep ascent of two miles from the base of the hill to the gates, which are three in number, one above another, defended by guns and rolling stones. The square contents of the fortified table-land on the summit is ten miles: in this space are included towns and villages, corn-fields, &c.; and water is found a few feet from the surface. On one side, at the foot of a tremendous precipice, runs the

Plate-VIII

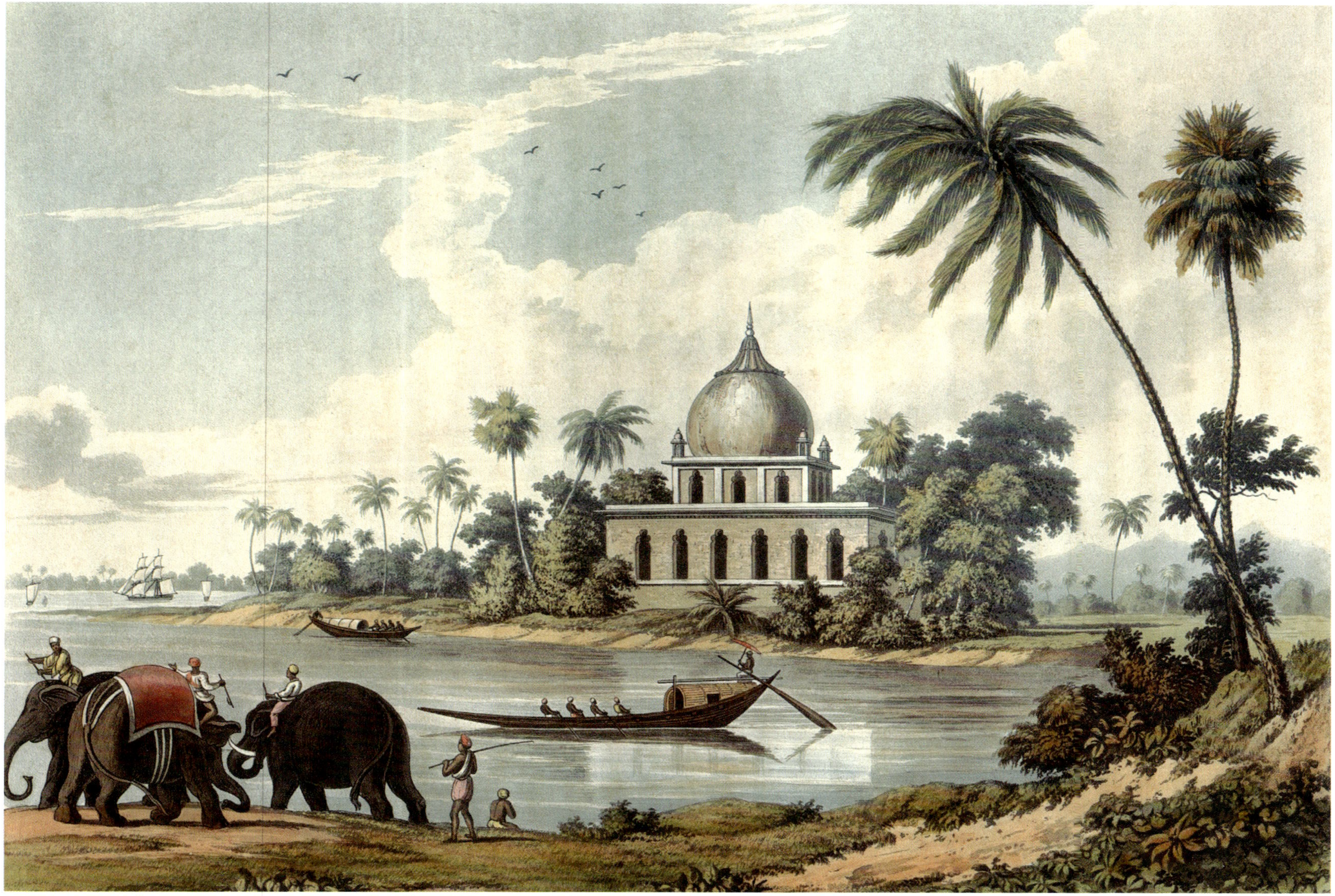

G. Hunt sculpt

ANCIENT TOMB
AT THE CONFLUENCE OF THE BOGLIPORE NULLA AND THE GANGES.

London, Published by R. ACKERMANN, 101, Strand, Aug.t 1, 1824.

river Soane, and on the opposite another river; both meeting after passing the fort, form the hill into a triangular peninsula. A deep valley, full of impervious woods, closes the approach to the third side; and these spreading all over the mountains, render access in that direction next to impossible.

The Ganges at Boglipore forms a considerable elbow, not only by the tracing of its coast, but by shoals and banks of sand, which stretch out a considerable distance, and are constantly shifting at every rise or fall of the river. There is a small branch of the river, which, at some period, has been formed by nature, which cuts off this point, and being still water, offers a far easier and more certain passage in all states of the wind. This branch is called the Boglipore nullah, and admits boats and vessels of the ordinary size used in the transport of various articles of merchandise, grain, &c. This nullah has a course of from twelve to fifteen miles, from its entrance above the projecting point to its reunion with the Ganges. Near the latter spot are situated the remains of a large mausoleum, which, furnishing a specimen of this style of building, is given in the accompanying *Plate* (VIII.) The bank of the nullah winds in a serpentine course, and being in many parts thickly wooded, in others open and cultivated, with huts of the natives interspersed at intervals, forms a pleasing scene, which is constantly changing, and presenting new objects to the traveller's notice. Emerging from this, the tomb alluded to above is seen embosomed in foliage; and a distant peep is caught at the same time of the lowest part of the Monghyr hills, a stony ridge of considerable elevation in another part of the chain, and on the extremity of which, where it abruptly descends to the Ganges, the old native fort of Monghyr is built. From Boglipore, after a few days' halt to rest with the hospitable residents, civil and military, we turned off from the direct route to the upper provinces, to visit a district on the opposite bank of the Ganges, well worth the notice of the traveller who would view the freaks which Nature sometimes in her most capricious mood has here played. This district, named Tyroot, is situated between two clear and rapidly flowing rivers, which descend from the mountainous country towards the north-west, and run in very winding but parallel channels into the Ganges.

This tract of country, for a very considerable extent towards the hills, enjoys an almost equal temperature of climate, which produces the following singular effects: a constant verdure in the hot season, when other parts are scorched and brown; a total absence of the oppressive hot winds; and a temperature of climate favourable to the production and culture of most of the British vegetables and smaller fruits; the currant, raspberry, and strawberry flourishing with very little care, when in most other parts of India they cannot be brought to perfection without great expense and trouble.

In this district of Tyroot, and in the most favourable situation, a stud for the breeding of horses, as remount to the native cavalry of Bengal, had been long established. There were near eight hundred mares and colts of different breeds; Arabs, Tazzies, Turkoman, English, and Persian, and the crosses of these. This establishment was, about a year after my visit to it, broken up, and a selection of the best horses was sent to the coast, to be incorporated with the Hon. Company's stud at that presidency.

We returned thence to the banks of the Ganges, and in our route stopped for the night at a small village called Mojumpore, where we encamped in a most extensive and beautiful *tope* of mango-trees. In the neighbourhood of this place we observed a number of those mounds of earth, daubed over with red paint, which designate the spots where women have sacrificed themselves, according to the barbarous law misconstrued, but not less rigorously enforced to the present day, by the ignorant and bigoted Brahmins, or priests of the Hindoos. This usage has, from the number of these monuments, been too prevalent in the vicinity of this place; for several of the outskirts of the neighbouring villages have their memorials of the same description and import. It is deeply to be lamented that a custom should be tolerated so contrary to

Plate-IX

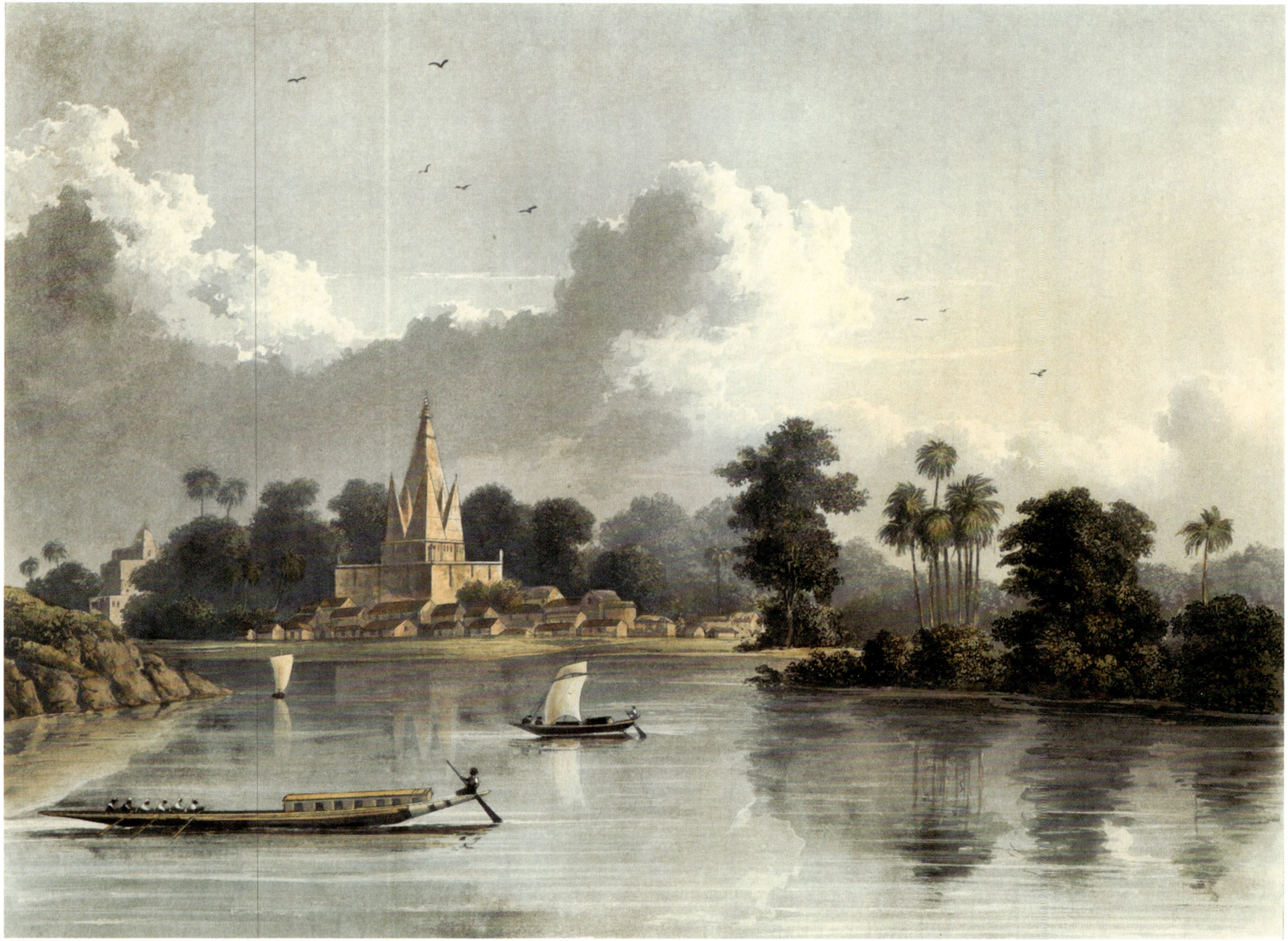

T. Sutherland sculp.t

A Village on the Ganges above Boglipore

London, Published by R. Ackermann, 101, Strand, Sept.r 1, 1824.

reason, so disgusting to humanity, and which no Brahminic law authorizes; it being decidedly condemned by many of the better informed natives, who permit its use only in cases where the self-sacrifice on the part of the woman is perfectly voluntary. It is an omission on the part of the authorities who rule this country to permit its occurrence; the mass of the Hindoos must abhor and dread its enforcement: the Brahmins no doubt are eager for its continuance from motives entirely selfish and sordid, they inheriting the bulk of the property of the wretched family thus cut off. It is sincerely to be hoped that this disgraceful and cruel custom will be speedily and effectually put a stop to wherever the British power and controul extend through this vast empire.

We crossed to the Boglipore side of the Ganges once more, and landed from our ferry-boat near a small village, represented in *Plate* IX. It is very prettily situated in a creek, which runs inland from the river, and is some few miles above the station of Boglipore. We got some good peacock-shooting near this place, the country being for the most part wooded, and abounding with those birds. We experienced this evening one of those violent storms or hurricanes which not unfrequently occur after a hot and sultry day. The rapidity of its approach, the violent impetuosity of its blast, the heavy pour of rain, with the vivid lightning and awfully loud and crashing thunder, conspired to produce an effect sublimely terrific. The boats of different classes which were in the river were blown like straws irresistibly on shore, and two pinnaces fastened near the bank shared the same fate.

Moving on the following morning early, we soon obtained a distant view of the fortress of Monghyr, a place of great strength and importance in former times. It is of vast extent, being nearly two miles square: it was a considerable station, and occupied by a large British force in the earlier part of the progress of our arms up the country. It has a deep ditch quite surrounding it on the land side, while the river Ganges protects it on the north: this ditch is full fifty feet wide. This fortress has of late years become an invalid-station: there is also within the fort an hospital, for the advantage of such men of the native troops as are afflicted with insanity.

Monghyr is also celebrated for a manufactory of wooden work of a variety of form and nature, tables, chairs, sofas, teapoys, and other articles of furniture, made of a wood called the *tchikrassee,* in some measure resembling mahogany in colour, but of a coarser grain and less durability. Toys of all sorts are also here manufactured; some very well executed, and all remarkably cheap. Guns, matchlocks, pistols, and articles of cutlery are also made here, of good form and appearance, but which cannot, in point of finish and durability, vie for a moment with those of England.

At some distance before reaching Monghyr, we saw in the river Ganges on our right a singular mass of rock standing in the water, and somewhat resembling those of Colgong. It is distant about two hundred yards from the right bank, immediately opposite to the village of Sultangunge, and forms the subject of the ***Tenth Plate.*** It rises about seventy feet above the level of the water, towering abruptly from its bosom: there is one place only at which a boat can be put in, and where there is a landing-place, and a very steep and winding path leading to its summit. Here is found a small building, a *madrussa,* or college of Fakeers, or wandering monks, who reside in it. This remarkable rock has doubtless been of more consequence at some remote period than it is at present; for on examining its abrupt and weather-worn sides by passing round it in a boat, a variety of sculpture, comprising the principal Hindoo deities, men, and animals, is seen covering nearly the whole face of the cliff. The same may be observed on the opposite shore of Sultangunge. Some of these figures are tolerably executed, but the greater part are rudely and grotesquely designed, and point out their origin to have been very remote. The whole forms a pretty object as you run past in a boat; and the thick and luxuriant foliage which crowns the summit, adds much to the effect of the picture.

Plate-X

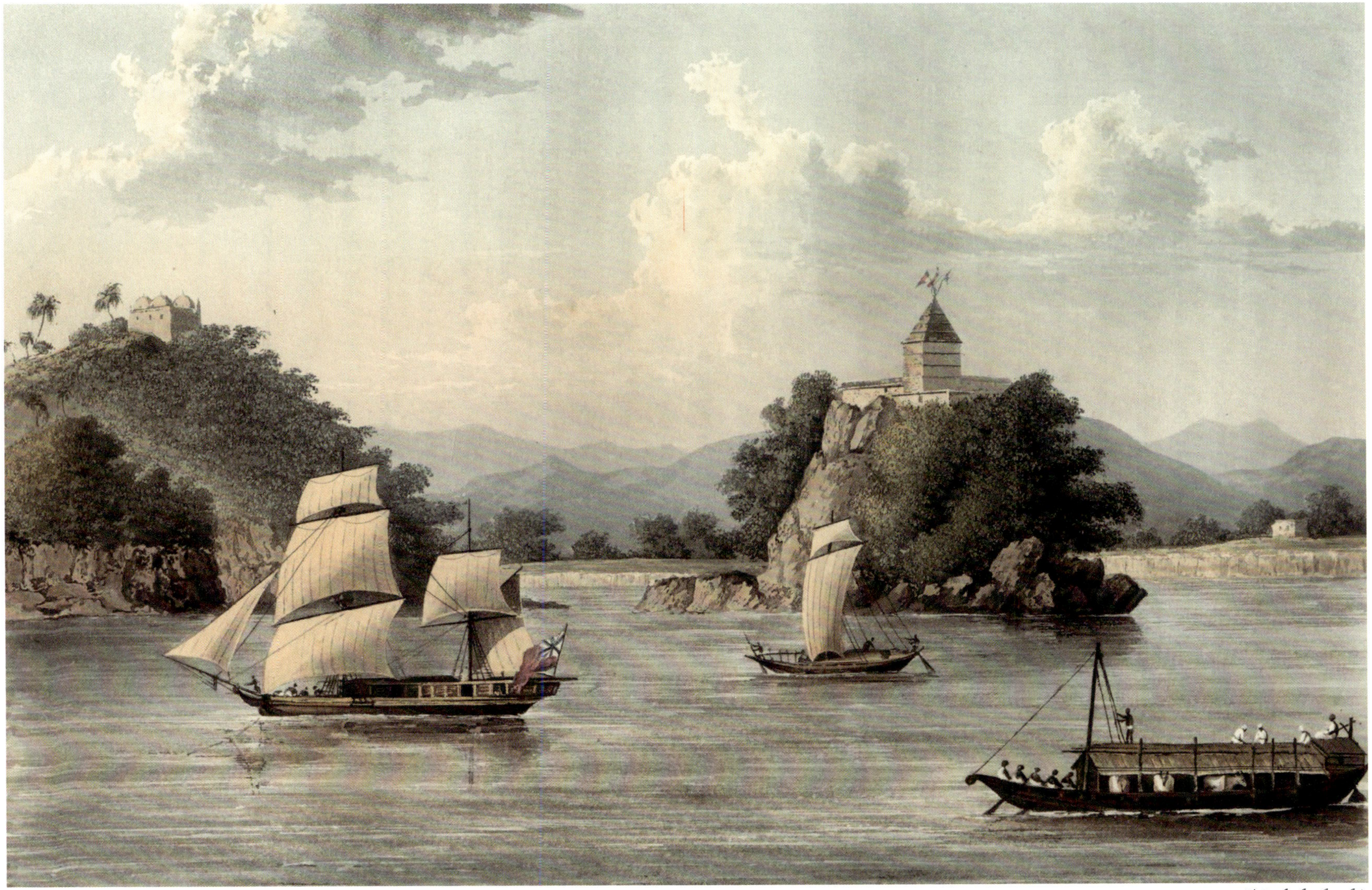

T. Sutherland sculp.

The Fakeer's Rock at Janguira.
NEAR SULTANGUNJ.

London Published by R. ACKERMANN, 101, Strand, Sept.r 1, 1824.

Continuing our journey upwards, we soon left the Ganges, which, a little above Monghyr, makes a great bend to the southward; while the main road to Hajipore on the left, and Patna, Bankipore, and Dinapore on the right bank, takes a direction straight to those places. This is still Bahar, of which Bankipore is the chief civil, and Dinapore the principal military, station: these two and Patna, or Azimabad, are in one long line, and close upon the bank of the Ganges, extending full thirteen miles in length. Azimabad is the most ancient part, and was the capital of Bahar: it is surrounded by a wall and ditch, now quite out of repair; and contains a Roman Catholic chapel, a *madrussa* of Seikhs, and an English and Danish factory. There are also the ruins of a fort. In the churchyard there is a handsome monument, in the form of a pillar, erected to the memory of the English here inhumanly murdered by Meer Jaffier Khan in 1763. At Bankipore is a large building called the Golah; it is in the shape of a beehive, ninety-six feet high, and one hundred and twenty-six paces in circumference: it has two flights of stone steps to ascend to the summit; and here is a large opening, by which it was to have been filled with corn, to serve as a supply in the event of a famine, and which, when wanted, was to have been dug out from four doors at the bottom: it has, however, never yet been filled. The road from Bankipore to Dinapore, a distance of seven miles, is beautiful, the greater part being through a very richly wooded country. At the latter place a king's regiment of infantry is usually quartered.

Leaving Bankipore in the evening, we encamped that same night in a most extensive and beautiful *tope*, or grove. These *topes* are mostly of the mango-tree, and have a very beautiful appearance. They are all regularly planted, like our orchards. The mangoes rise to the height of between forty and fifty feet, and generally branch out into three or four stems. They resemble in some measure the mulberry-tree of England, but their leaves are smooth, and of a very dark green; their foliage is very rich and thick, and at about the age of twenty years, these trees form a very picturesque group. In travelling through the country, more especially in the upper provinces of Bengal, these *topes*, some of them covering an extent of several acres, are met with every three or four miles on the principal routes. They are chiefly planted by men of rank and wealth among the Hindoos, who, at their death, usually bequeath a certain sum for the planting a *tope*, digging a well, or forming a tank or large reservoir of water; and these are mostly situated on the road-side, as a convenience for travellers, and a general benefit and advantage to mankind. These works perhaps have, in their foundation, a portion of self-pride, since they serve to commemorate and hand down to posterity the name and rank of their author: but whatever be the motive of their creation, they prove most welcome to the traveller, whether native or European, in the burning summer heats; affording to the former a cool and refreshing shade for his noontide nap, and to the latter a delightful spot in which to form his camp, as he travels either for duty or pleasure along the otherwise exposed and burning tracts of arid country, which the hot season here for three or four months invariably produces.

A few miles below Patna we passed a very prettily situated village, with its pagoda of a most picturesque form, its ghaut of the red stone, and its native Hindoos performing their ablutions in the sacred stream of the Ganges. The varied forms and tints of the foliage surrounding this romantic spot give a good relief and effect to the white buildings, as may be seen in the annexed view (***Plate*** XI.)

We reached Mangee-Ghaut, a village situated very near the confluence of the two mighty streams of the Ganges and Gogra rivers, where we have an instance of the very wonderful change that has been wrought, by the united efforts of both, in the bed of the former, which, since the season of the rains last year, has been shifted near half a mile more to the eastward. The road continues from Mangee-Ghaut along the left bank of the Gogra river as far as Mindeegunj, about seven miles, where is a ferry and good establishment of boats for crossing it.

Plate-XI

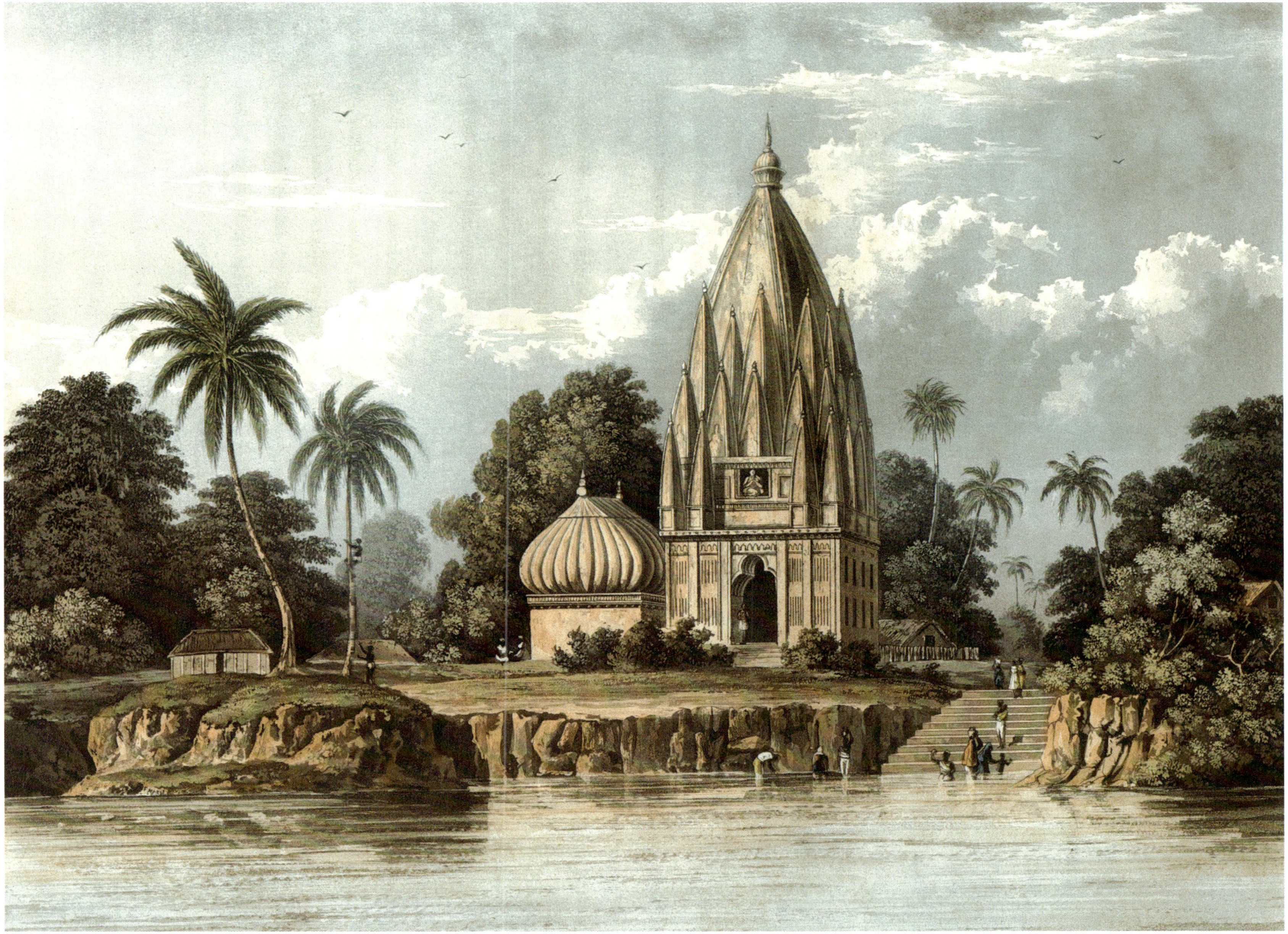

T. Sutherland sculp.t

VILLAGE and PAGODA below PATNA AZIMABAD.
ON THE GANGES.

London Published by R. ACKERMANN, 101, Strand, Sept.r 1, 1824.

Before we take leave of Mangee, however, it would be unpardonable to omit noticing the magnificent ***birkut,*** or banian-tree, for which this ghaut is so celebrated, and which, in point of extent, variety of form, and grand and highly picturesque groups of mighty stems and pendent rope-like columns, far exceeds any tree of the kind in this part of India. It is situated close upon the banks of the Gogra, and at a short distance from its point of junction with the Ganges, and viewed from a distance, has the appearance of a vast ***tope,*** or grove. It rises to a most gigantic height, and its large limbs stretch out to a great length in every direction, supported by their columnar shafts in graceful clusters, which they send downwards to the earth for this purpose.

At the time I visited and examined this wonderful production of nature, some natives, who had been cutting wood in the neighbourhood, happened to pass under it, and seeing me attentively examining its various parts, accosted me, and expressed some surprise at my admiration of its wonderful structure. We entered into conversation, and in the course of it I learned the history of this great natural wonder, which is religiously and implicitly credited by the inhabitants of the surrounding districts.

About one thousand years ago, they very gravely told me, there lived on this spot a very religious and holy Brahminee woman, famed for the austerity and sanctity of her life: her name was Gunga Purrain: she lived to a very great age, and did not die, but the earth opening swallowed her up, and on the spot where she disappeared this tree in one night sprang up. In the centre of this grove, formed of one tree, is now a large open space; and where the original trunk stood there is a small building, consisting of four low mud walls only, eight or ten feet square, without a roof; inclosed in which is a small rude kind of mound, or altar of earth, over which some flowers were strewed when I saw it. The original trunk has perished, no doubt by gradual decay; but its children, its descendants, encircle the spot on which their parent stood, and clasped in each other's embraces, joined and united as one family, form a perfect circle, a magnificent screen, consisting of lofty white and shining columns, crowned with masses of the richest and most luxuriant foliage. Rich festoons of the same hang in every varied and graceful form, interspersed amidst these natural pillars; while beneath long galleries and noble arcades extend in all directions, and form deep and shady recesses, grand porticoes, and large and lofty halls, like the pictured palaces of Fairy-Land. The circumference of this mighty tree round the outer stems is four hundred yards, and it is calculated that ten thousand men can repose beneath its shelter.

There is another of these trees in the province of Sirhind, equal in bulk to the one above-mentioned; but it is less ancient, and being quite perfect, and without any decayed parts, does not produce by any means so grand and varied a picture as this at Mangee.

In five marches from this we reached Ghazipore, on the left bank of the Ganges, here about four hundred yards wide. This place is celebrated for its excellent and high-flavoured rose-water. All the neighbouring fields are planted with this lovely shrub; and it may be conceived how fragrant to the sense, how delightful to the eye, must be these extensive plains of many thousand acres when the rose is in full blossom. There are here cantonments for a regiment of native cavalry; and at no great distance the remains of a very beautiful palace, built by the emperor Aurungzebe. The only part at all perfect is the *chalees setoon,* or hall of forty pillars, an edifice of much elegance, and which, placed on the edge of the Ganges, on a bank rising fifty or sixty feet perpendicular, and backed by some fine large trees, has a very grand and imposing effect.

We rapidly approached Benares, and before we got sight of its venerable pile, we came unexpectedly, on a sudden turn of the road, in view of one of the ghauts so often met with on the Ganges, and the small pagoda of the village, which latter was

Plate XII

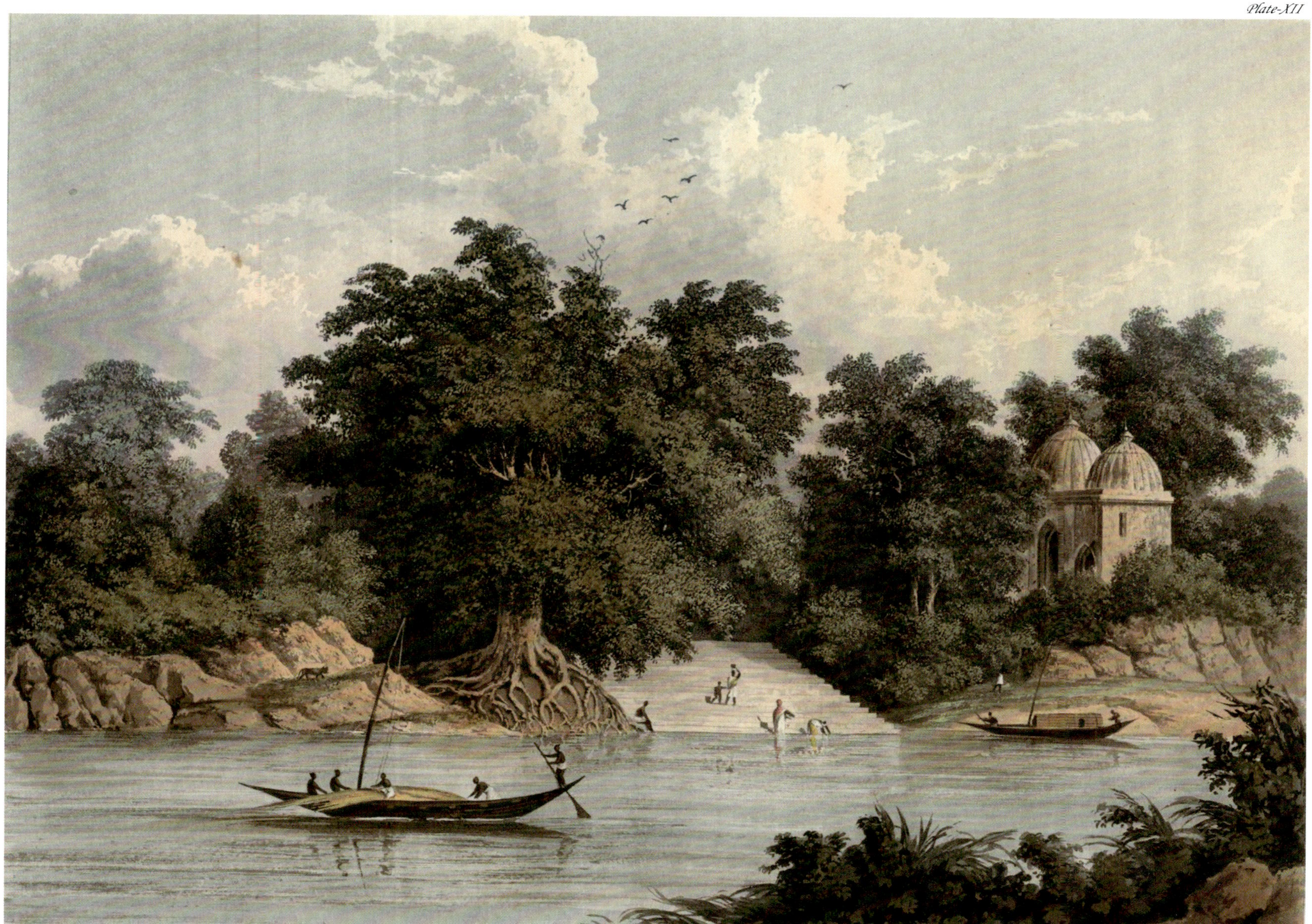

T. Sutherland sculp.t

HINDOO GHAUT on the GANGES.
BELOW BENARES.

London Published by R. ACKERMANN, 101, Strand, Sept.r 1, 1824.

concealed from our sight by the thick and luxuriant foliage. This sweet and quiet scene forms the subject of the view, ***Plate*** XII. The large tree is a ***peepul,*** of the birkut or banian tribe, but which does not throw out those pendent shoots on which the other supports the weight of its overgrown branches.

At length a turn in the river and the road we were travelling, which followed the windings of the former, shewed us Benares. Of all the cities of Hindoostan Benares is held the most sacred by the Hindoos: here their principal pagodas or temples are situated, their most revered and celebrated Brahmins reside; here is the centre and seat of Hindoo learning ; and here is the celebrated observatory, which is said to have been erected by command of the emperor Acber, and is well known from the description of Sir Robert Barker in the ***Philosophical Transactions.***

Benares is likewise one of the most ancient cities of India. It is there that Brahminic influence exerts unbounded sway; while its opulence and trade entitle it to rank among the principal cities of the world. It is situated on the left bank of the Ganges, here a noble stream, and its extent along the bank of that river is full five miles; its breadth inland being in proportion. Built upon a rising ground, sloping gradually upwards from the water's brink, its buildings appear very lofty when seen from the boats in passing it. Some of the ghauts are very fine edifices; one especially has six stories. Indeed the whole face of the city towards the river is one continued line of these ghauts, which, exclusive of the ornament they are to Benares, are highly commodious and useful in the facility for bathing which they present to its vast population; and the immense crowds of all sexes, in their varied and graceful costumes, who constantly frequent these public resorts, is truly wonderful.

Towards the east end of this, and near to the Ganges, the Jumeh Musjid, or chief Mahommedan temple, rises in great grandeur. It was built by the emperor Aurungzebe on the ruins of an ancient and highly venerated Hindoo pagoda, which the fanaticism of this bigoted Mussulman destroyed. This building is seen on the right of the view here given (*Plate* XIV.), with its two lofty minarets and three noble domes of pure white marble. One of the smaller Hindoo pagodas may be observed very much out of perpendicular: this is occasioned by the foundation being undermined by the river, whose freaks and depredations have been before described.

As we are now in the city of Hindoostan which is considered by every sect of Hindoos their most holy station, some of the peculiarities of character of that very ancient and singular race of people will not be inappropriately noticed in this place.

There are four principal casts or sects of the Hindoos, which are commonly denominated the ***Brahmin,*** the ***Chehteree,*** the ***Bice,*** and the ***Soodra.*** These great casts are divided into many others by the intermixture of one with the other; and these are so numerous and complicated, that it would be as troublesome as needless here to notice them. Suffice it to say, that thirty-six is considered about the number. These four principal casts are in a great measure restricted to certain occupations and modes of living. The ***Brahmins*** are confined to the teaching of the ***Vedas,*** or religious and moral tracts of very ancient standing. The ***Cshatriga*** (vulgarly ***Chehteree***) are the military cast; their profession is arms. The ***Vaisya,*** or ***Bice,*** attend to commerce, agriculture, and the care of cattle. The ***Soodra*** is the lowest, and the duty attached to it is servile attendance on the higher casts.

A Brahmin unable to subsist by his duties may become a soldier: if he cannot find employment in either of these, he may apply to tillage, the care of cattle, or traffic; but in the latter certain commodities are to be avoided. A Chehteree in distress may resort to all these means; but he must not aspire to the higher functions. Medicine and other learned professions are allowed to be practised by the two superior casts, as are likewise painting and other arts, work for wages, menial service, alms, and usury. A Bice may descend to the servile acts of a Sooder; and a Sooder may gain a subsistence by handicraft, as joinery and masonry, or by the arts of painting or writing. He is also expressly permitted to become a trader or a husbandman.

Plate-XIV

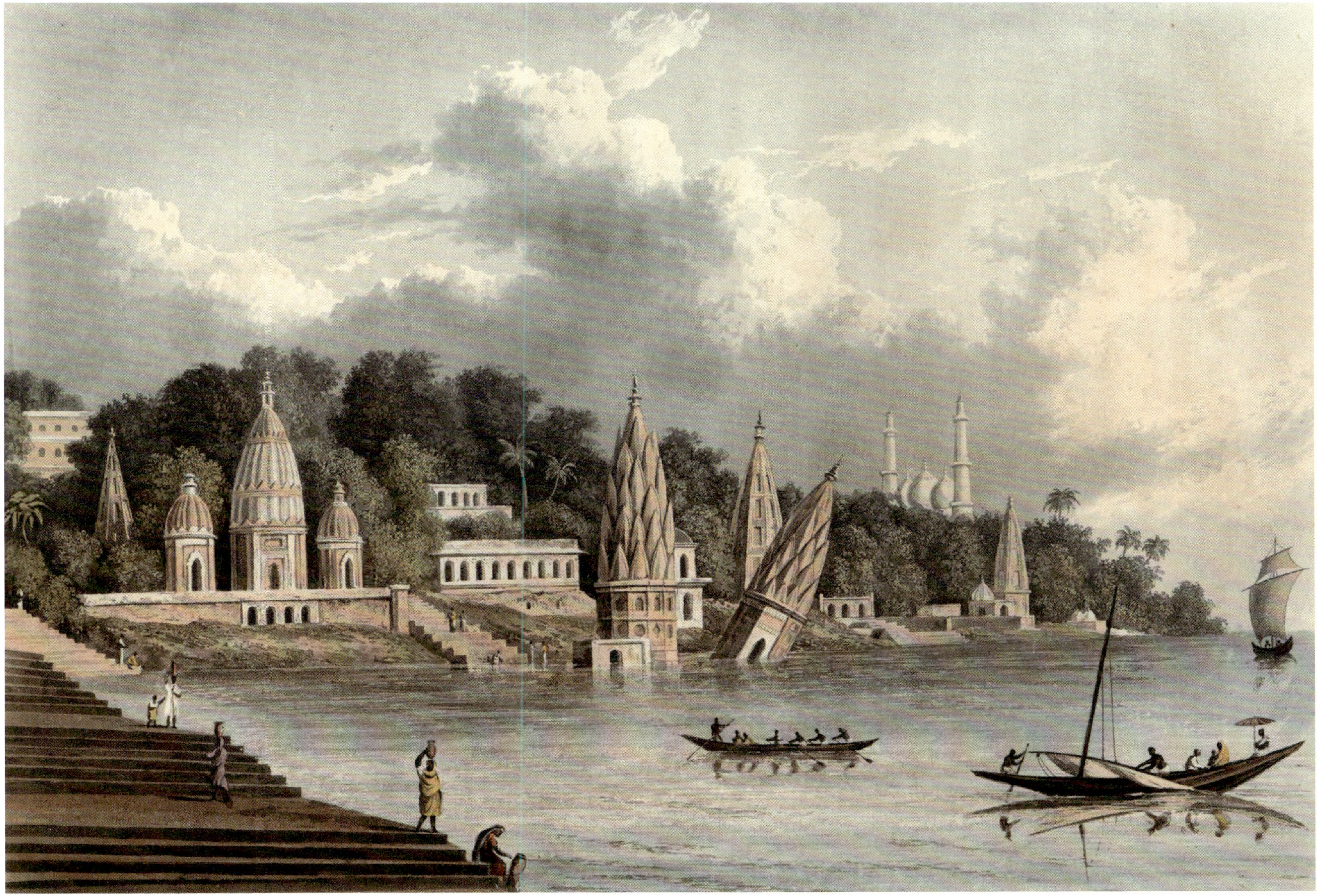

Engraved by T. Sutherland.

CITY OF BENARES.
FROM THE GAMGES.

London Published by R. ACKERMANN, 101, Strand, Oct.r 1, 1824.

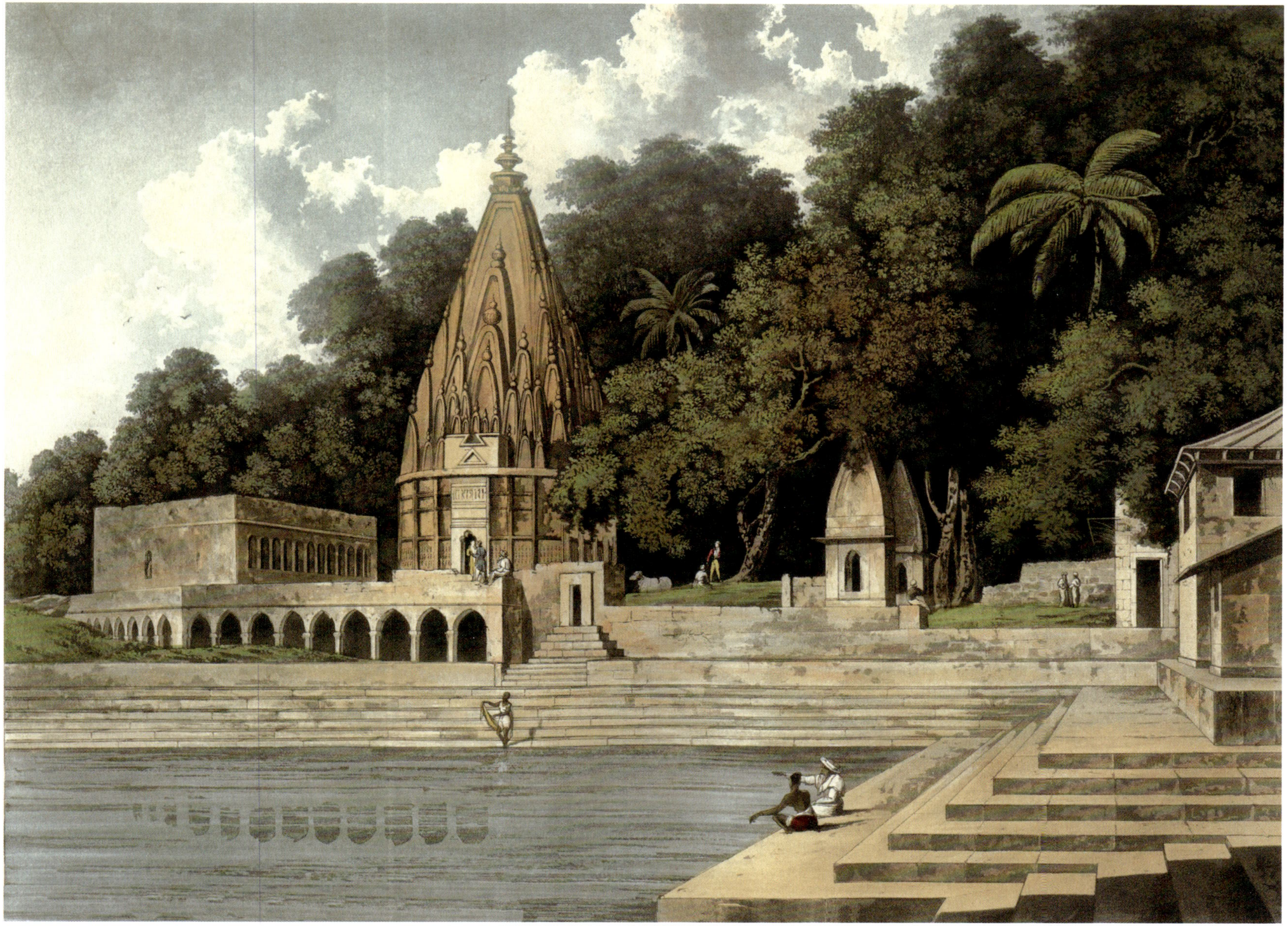

T. Sutherland sculp.

SACRED TANK and PAGODAS near BENARES.

London Published by R. ACKERMANN, 101, Strand, Nov.r 1, 1824.

The distinctions of families are important in regulating their intermarriages. Genealogy is made a particular study; and great attention is given to regulate this ceremony according to the established rules, particularly in the first marriage of the eldest son. The chief points to be observed are, not to marry within the prohibited degrees; nor in a family known by its name to be of the same primitive stock; nor in a family of inferior rank.

Exclusively of the grandeur of the appearance which the city of Benares exhibits as seen from the river, by walking round its environs a number of other objects, of great architectural beauty, are scattered in the path of the stranger: tanks on a noble scale; ***topes*** of the sacred ***birkut,*** or banian-tree; pagodas of all sizes and descriptions, interspersed with a variety of the richest foliage, offer views highly interesting and beautifully picturesque. There is one in particular which is highly valuable as a perfect specimen of the pure Hindoo style of temple; and we here see grouped together the main edifice of a very rich style of sculpture, the inferior and detached pagodas or chapels, the sacred ***tope,*** and the extensive and noble tank, with its expansive sheet of water and its grand flight of steps, which, for the purpose of ablution, lead down from the four sides into the water. The accompanying ***Plate*** (XIII.) will give a better idea of the grandeur and solemn beauty of this scene than any further description can do: to it therefore we refer the reader.

Returning one forenoon from a tour round a considerable part of the environs towards the north of the city of Benares, I turned down to the river's side, to examine some ghauts and pagodas which I had not yet seen. I here perceived, that not only has the Ganges undermined and thrown out of perpendicular the pagoda so singularly removed from its base in the view already given of Benares from the water, but a very considerable part of these ghauts are also fast following the same course; and many appear as if blown up, their masses in huge fragments lying scattered about by the violence of the currents during the season the Ganges is at its height. The general quality of the soil throughout the whole course of this mighty river, a rich loam, renders it extremely liable to injury from a body of water to which it is always exposed: at times the river is full sixteen feet higher than at others; and at that period it is most rapid. While contemplating this scene, I was much amused by a mode of travelling quite novel to me; though it is, as I afterwards found, an every-day occurrence. I heard, although I could see nothing, the voices of several persons apparently near us; and as no canoe or vessel of any kind was in sight, I was at a loss to divine whence they proceeded. I was soon, however, made acquainted with the apparent mystery, and speedily perceived half a dozen natives floating in the water about breast-high, each having a long bamboo, with something attached to its upper extremity. I found on inquiry that their contrivance was an ingenious one, being as follows:

An earthen pot, called a ***kedgeree*** pot, commonly used for their cooking, is inverted in the water, its mouth downwards; to this is firmly tied a stout bamboo of five or six feet long, so that the thicker end of the pole shall be even with the mouth of the vessel. On the latter the man mounts, and it buoys him up considerably: he has little clothes of course on him; but to the upper end of his pole is attached his ***lootee,*** or brass vessel, and a change of dress to put on when he goes ashore, and which is kept perfectly dry. The party on the present occasion evinced great good-humour, and chatted and laughed right merrily, seeming to trust their course entirely to the river's current.

After a stay of five days at Benares, where we were kindly received and hospitably entertained, which is ever the traveller's reception through Bengal, be he friend or stranger, our party left this celebrated and interesting city, and resumed the route towards the upper provinces, proposing to visit in our way the fortress of Allahabad,

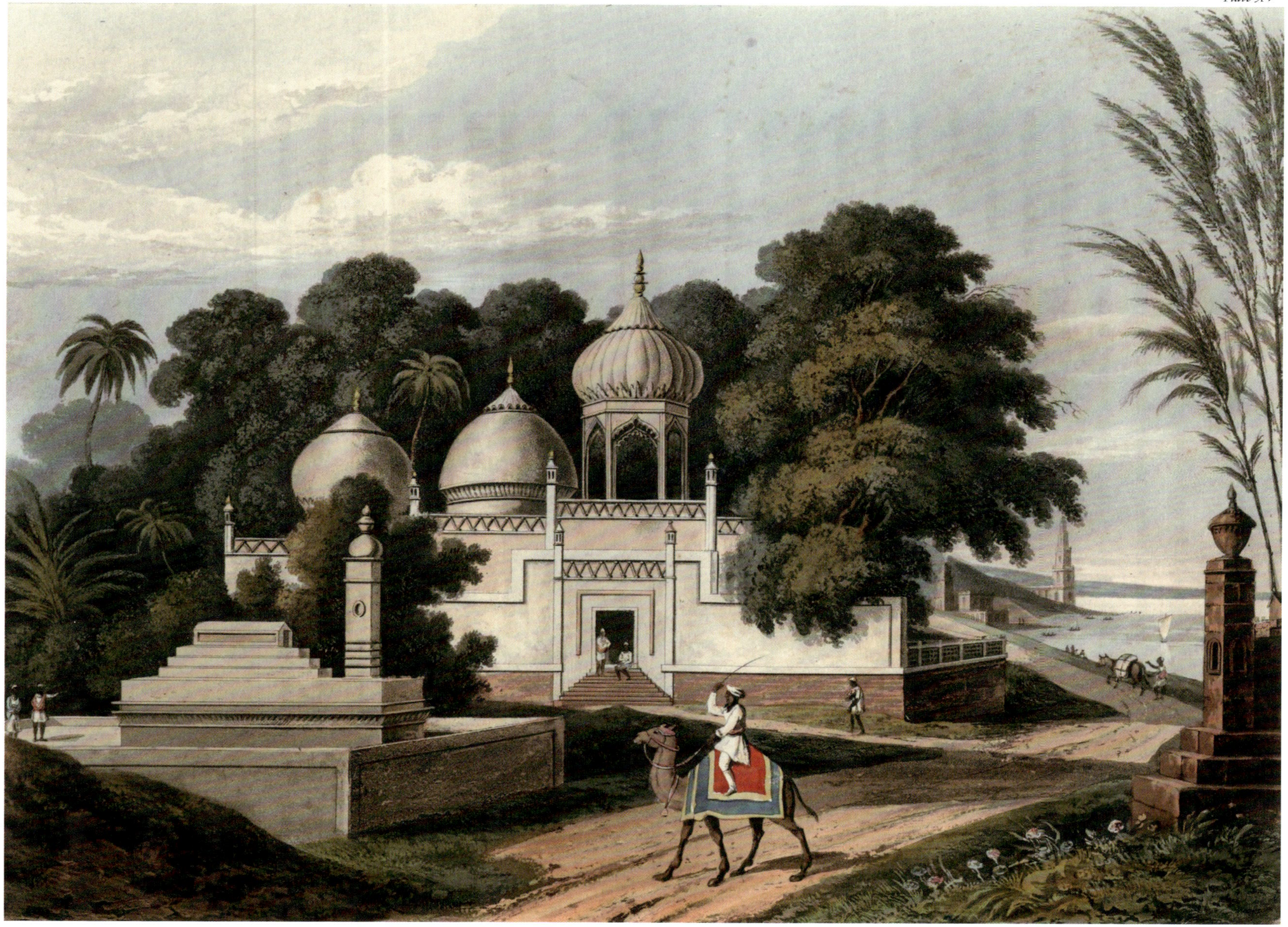

T. Sutherland sculp.

MAHOMEDAN MOSQUE AND TOMB.
NEAR BENARES.

London Published by R. ACKERMANN, 101, Strand, July 1, 1824.

celebrated both in ancient and modern times as a city of the first rank and consequence in Hindoostan. Our route for the first day was through the outskirts of Benares chiefly: still in many places we paused, either to admire some group of pagodas, tank, or fine grove of trees; now a distant peep at the city we had left arrested us for a moment; while the face of the country gradually became more rural, now diversified with village, farm, and *topes* of great extent and beauty.

We had also many grand and widely extensive views of the Ganges, that noble stream, never to be seen without interest, as it rolls in solemn grandeur its deep and golden volume towards the ocean through one of the richest valleys of the globe, and during a course navigable for an extent of nearly two thousand miles, without one single obstacle or impediment, enriches and fertilizes the vast provinces of the Bengal presidency through which it takes its way.

After proceeding about four miles, at a gentle rise in the road, looking round towards Benares, we caught a most beautiful distant view of its principal ghauts, the larger pagodas, and, beyond all, the Jumah Musjid, towering over all in proud superiority. The fine sweep of the Ganges on which the city stands was also visible to the extreme wooded point some distance below. Our fore-ground was at the same moment singularly magnificent: it consisted of a fine group of tombs of Mahommedans, of an elegance and lightness I have not seen equalled in this country, and which can scarcely be surpassed in any other for their form and style of building. The figure represented in the accompanying ***Plate*** (XV.), which gives a correct view of the scene I have above described, is a ***shutur sewar,*** or person appointed to carry dispatches, &c.: the camel on which he is mounted will go at the rate of six or seven miles an hour. His action is at the same time very violent, and it has been said, that those who ride these extremely rough-going animals are seldom long-lived. They are trained expressly for this purpose; for the baggage-camel, if loaded, moves at the rate of not more than three miles an hour. He is an animal, however, most peculiarly adapted for burthens in a hot and parched-up climate, as he can undergo great fatigue, and carries about seven hundred weight. This quantity, if a camel is lamed or otherwise injured, can be easily divided amongst the others; but a baggage-elephant failing, and they often bruise their feet if the country is stony and rough, throws a weight of incumbrance on the ground, which cannot readily be otherwise disposed of. On this account chiefly I would always prefer the camel, which is, besides, more easily fed and supported, and can go a long period without water.

As we continued our route upwards by the main road on the left bank, we passed the fortress of Chunar Gurh on the opposite side of the river, which is not here very wide. It is situated on the extremity of a long range of hills, of moderate elevation, composed throughout of a stone of a red colour, and called Chunar stone, which is hard and very durable, and is much employed in building. Their summits are bare, but there is some wood about their base, which creeps in parts up their rugged sides. The fort of Chunar has a very singular appearance when viewed from a boat immediately opposite; for you can see into the whole interior of the works, although they are elevated full one hundred and twenty feet above the level of the Ganges. The fact is, the fort occupies the slope of a hill, which rises with a regular ascent from the river. The appearance both above and below, however, is far more respectable, and especially from the latter point, whence the view given in the accompanying ***Plate*** (XVI.) is taken.

This fortress is wholly of native construction; it is a place often named in the military history of the country in ancient and modern times. It had dwindled at the period when I saw it to an invalid-station. The view here given will convey an idea of its position on a projecting mass of rocky hill. The vessels seen nearer to the eye are a small fleet, which would accompany a civilian or military officer of rank on an excursion of business or pleasure.

We arrived at length at Allahabad, a celebrated city of very ancient date, and

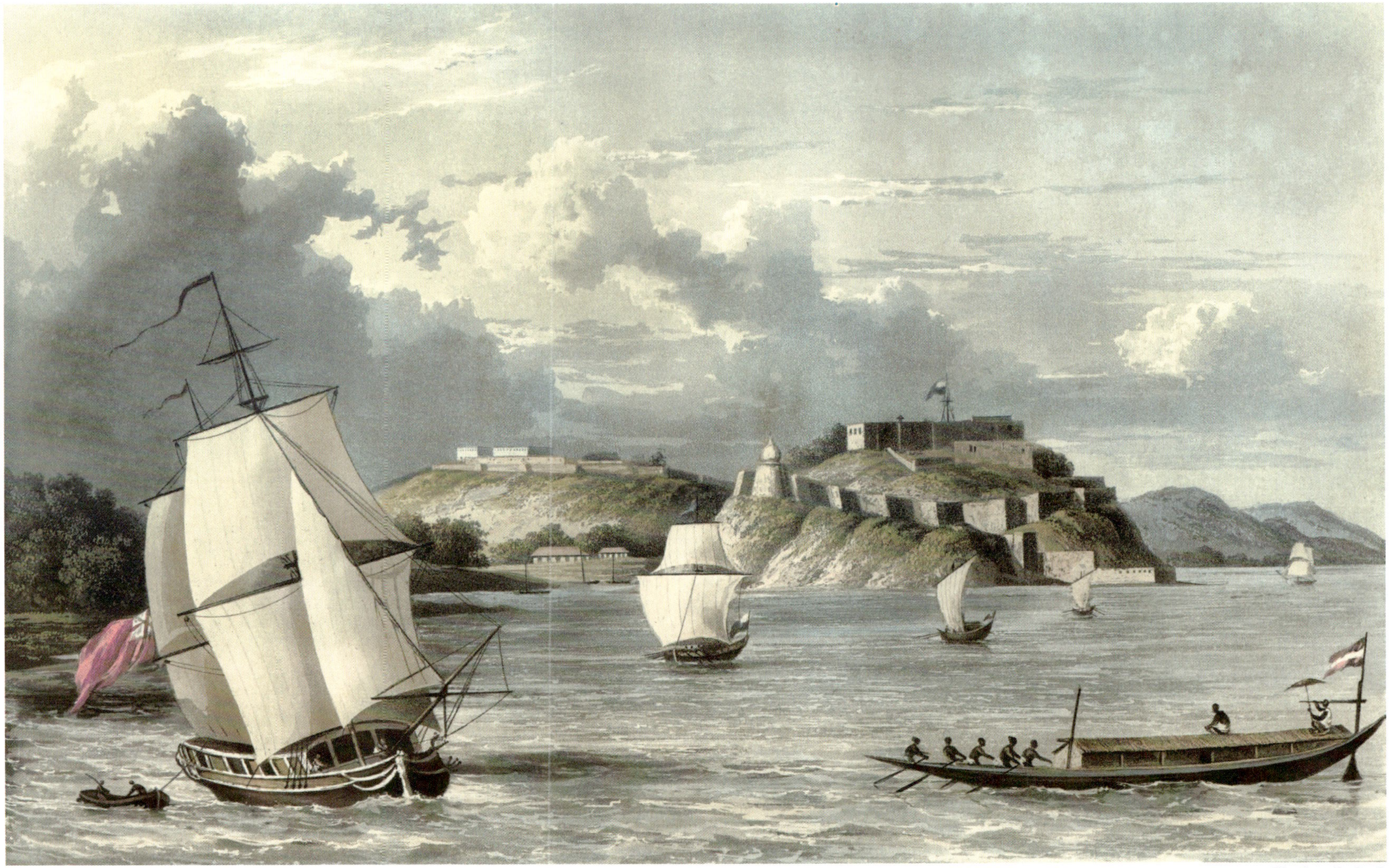

Engraved by T. Sutherland.

THE INDIAN FORT OF CHUNARGURH.
ON THE GANGES.

London Published by R. ACKERMANN, 101, Strand, Oct.r 1, 1824.

Plate-XVII

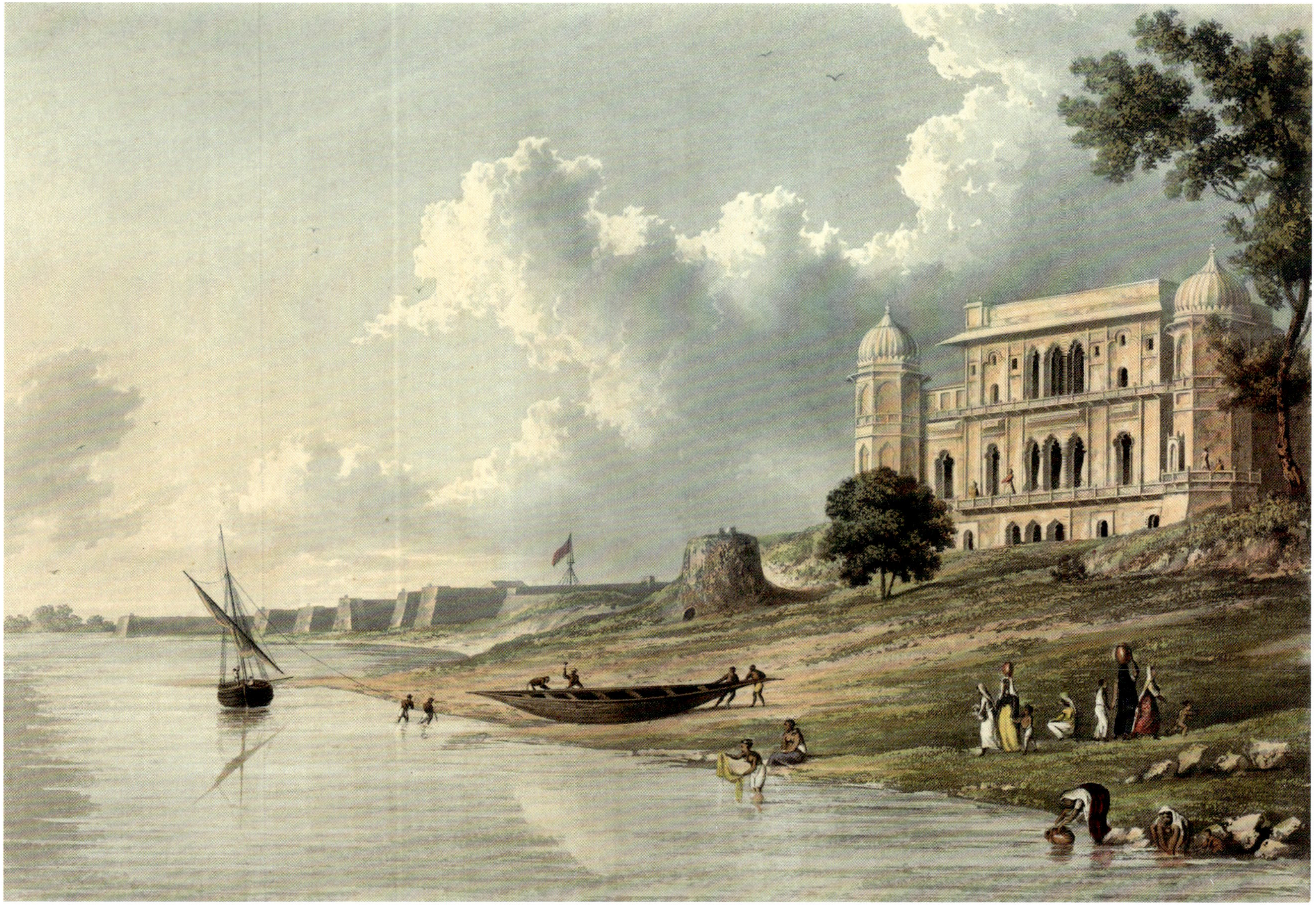

T. Sutherland sculp.

RAJ GHAUT and FORT of ALLAHABAD.
AT THE CONFLUENCE OF THE GANGES AND JUMNA RIVERS.

London Published by R. ACKERMANN, 101, Strand, Nov.r 1, 1824.

renowned in history. It forms one of the soubahships, or provinces of the empire of Hindoostan, and, according to the *Ayeen Acberi,* is one hundred and sixty koss in length, and one hundred and twenty-two in breadth. It is bounded by Bahar on the east, Bundhoo on the south, and Agra on the west. This province is very productive in fruits, flowers, and rare plants. The vine flourishes, and its grapes are delicious. Melons also come to great perfection. Various and beautiful cloths are made in this province, and also woollen carpets.

Allahabad ranks almost equally high with Benares in the estimation and religious prejudices of the Hindoos; for, according to their belief, it is the spot where Vishnu, the adored and darling deity of the Indian women, first descended from heaven, and took upon him the mortal form. This fortress and city is situated at the immediate confluence of the two great rivers, Ganges and Jumna, which here mingle their mighty bulk of waters. The fortress is nearly triangular in shape: each of the two lower faces is covered and washed by a river; and the walls of both are of native work, of great solidity and strength, and further fortified by round towers from distance to distance. It was built by the great Acber, and was long the residence of that renowned warrior and statesman. On the land side, the fortifications have been altogether new-modelled on the improved modern system, and it may now be considered as entitled to a high rank in the scale of fortified places. A view of it is given in *Plate* XVII.

The point of junction of the two rivers, Ganges and Jumna, also shewn in the view, is a great resort of pilgrims, who come in vast crowds from the most remote parts of India to bathe in the sacred waters, and purify themselves from worldly sins. Many of these weak and superstitious wretches, urged on by their Brahmins, and deluded by the hope of eternal happiness, plunge into the holy stream, and sink never to rise again, with the firm conviction on their minds that they will go immediately to heaven.

Within the fort is the Peetulpooree, a very sacred and highly revered subterraneous temple of the Hindoos. It is approached by a descent of eight or ten stone steps; and turning to the left along a vaulted passage, five feet wide and seven feet high, for about forty-five paces, the temple is entered, in whose centre stands the Lingham of Mahadeo on an altar of stone. This apartment is about twenty feet square, and is supported by numerous pillars, its walls being covered with roughly executed half-finished images of Vishnu, Ganesa, and other Hindoo deities. From this temple is a passage, which the Brahmins pretend leads to Dehli: it seems, however, rather to have been designed for a drain to carry off the surplus water in the rainy season, which would otherwise lodge in the temple.

There is in front of this an edifice constructed of the ***sungh soorkh***, a red stone resembling jasper, which is inhabited by a society of Fakeers, who subsist on the credulity of the people in perfect idleness.

This city was anciently called Piyaug. In the view of Allahabad from Raj-Ghaut on the Ganges, given in the last ***Plate***, beyond the fort may be perceived the Jumna river, where a small vessel is at anchor. The part of the fort here seen is Indian.

From Allahabad we proceeded up through the Doo-ab, or country of the two rivers, it being situated between the Ganges and Jumna. I here left my party, who proceeded direct onwards for Khanpore, while I followed the course of the Jumna upwards, anxious to see its character and scenery, and in what respect it differed from the Ganges. I passed through the provinces of Allahabad, Currah, and Manickpore, a line of country beautifully diversified in surface, and interspersed with woody tracts and rich patches of cultivation. The Jumna pursues a much more devious and winding course than the Ganges; but its waters are not so turbid, its bed being for a great length through a sandy soil, bordering the desert. The Cane, the Betwah, and the Sinde rivers join their tributary streams from Bundelcund on the south-west and

Plate XIX

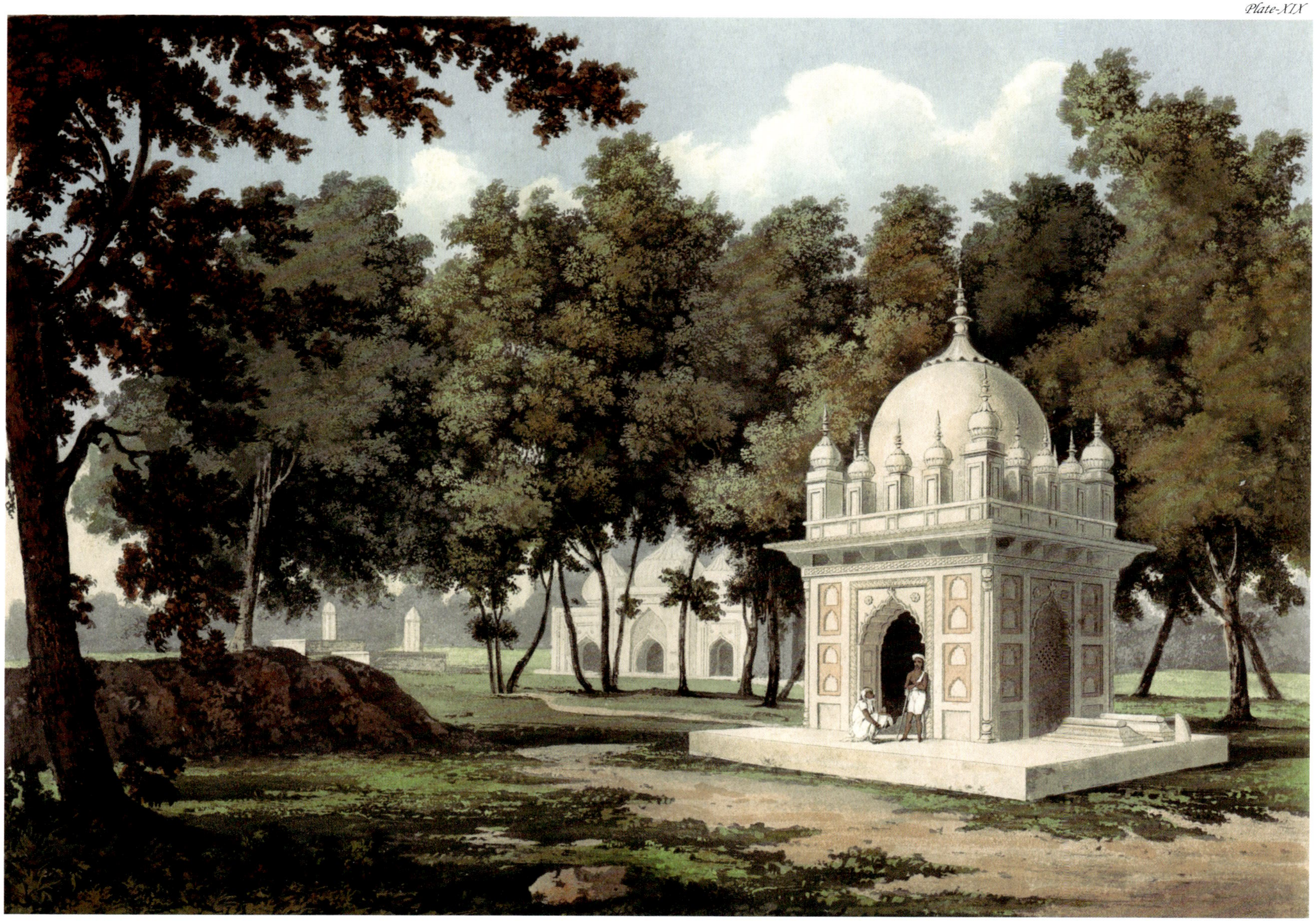

T. Sutherland sculp.

TOMBS near ETAYA.

IN THE DOO-AB, ON THE JUMNA RIVER.

London Published by R. ACKERMANN, 101, Strand, Nov.r 1, 1824.

opposite bank of the Jumna, during its course past the province of Korah; while the Rinde river, which has run a nearly central course through the Doo-ab, pours its waters from the north into it near the village of Abidpore. Proceeding on thence as far as Etawah, passing on the left Kalpee, which is the main road and principal military communication with Bundelcund, and taking a new direction by the village of Jeswuntnagurh, where are some very beautiful Mahommedan tombs in a thick *tope* or grove, views of which are given in ***Plate*** XIX. and in the ***Vignette*** in the ***Frontispiece;*** and crossing the Doo-ab, I reached Cannouge on the Ganges, situated on the great road to the provinces of Agra and Dehli, as also on that into Rohilcund and Oude. The passage of the river to the latter is from Mendy Ghaut, where a regular ferry is established.

The city of Cannouge was once (in those remote ages of the Indian history handed down by tradition alone, and involved in the gloomy mists of superstition,) the capital of this vast empire, having a circumference of upwards of one hundred miles, and celebrated for its opulence and splendour. All has passed away like the faint traces of a dream: a few miserable huts huddled into a kind of village are now all that exists. But its ruins, its remains of magnificent mausolcums and tombs, the fragments of grandeur, and traces of foundations of buildings of vast size, powerfully corroborate the traditionary belief, and make it a spot for the traveller to pause upon, and give, as he pursues his way, the parting tribute of a sigh.

From Cannouge I proceeded direct to Khanpore, where I found my party, who had arrived two days previous. Khanpore was at that period the head-quarters of the field-command in Bengal; a command very extensive in its nature, reaching from Allahabad to the north-west frontier, and bounded on the east by the Ganges, and on the south-west by the Jumna, which, however, it oversteps in many parts. The total force in this command, including the King's and Company's troops, artillery, cavalry, and infantry, amounted at this period to 40,000 effective. Considerable changes have occurred since my residence there; and since the late acquisition of the countries of Scindia and the Mahrattas, Agimere has succeeded to the honours formerly possessed by Khanpore. The cantonments at Khanpore are of great extent, being nearly seven miles in length, mostly along the bank of the Ganges; there are barracks for two cavalry and three infantry regiments, besides artillery. The situation is high, airy, and at this time was considered remarkably healthy. The Ganges is here a fine expanse of water, and glides majestically along with a current of about four miles per hour, when the river is not swollen by the rains; but in the months of September and October, which immediately follow the rainy season, its rapidity, breadth, and volume are all proportionably augmented: it then runs five, and in some parts six, miles per hour; and its width at Khanpore, upwards of seven hundred and fifty miles from its mouth, is nearly two English miles.

The style of house generally adopted here is that termed the ***bungalow,*** one now too well known in England to need a description. The heat soon after our arrival at Khanpore increased rapidly; early in March the wind, termed the hot wind, sets in, and blows steadily and unremittingly for near three months: this wind bears a pretty equal temperature of 106° of Fahrenheit's thermometer; it is always accompanied by a thickness like a mist, of a deep brown hue, caused by the infinitely fine particles of sand which, raised by its impetuosity, are borne along with it. This obscures or dims the sun's light, and divests his rays of much of their direct influence. It rises to a hard gale at noon, and then gradually declines with the sun: still the temperature changes very little at night, being frequently 100°; the heat continues intense and parching, every thing retaining a portion of that which it has imbibed during the day, until the rising sun again ushers in the burning blast.

Still this season is considered the most healthy, since there is no possibility of experiencing any check of perspiration. Within the houses are cool, being rendered so by a very simple contrivance of a frame of bamboo, interwoven with a species of

Plate XVIII

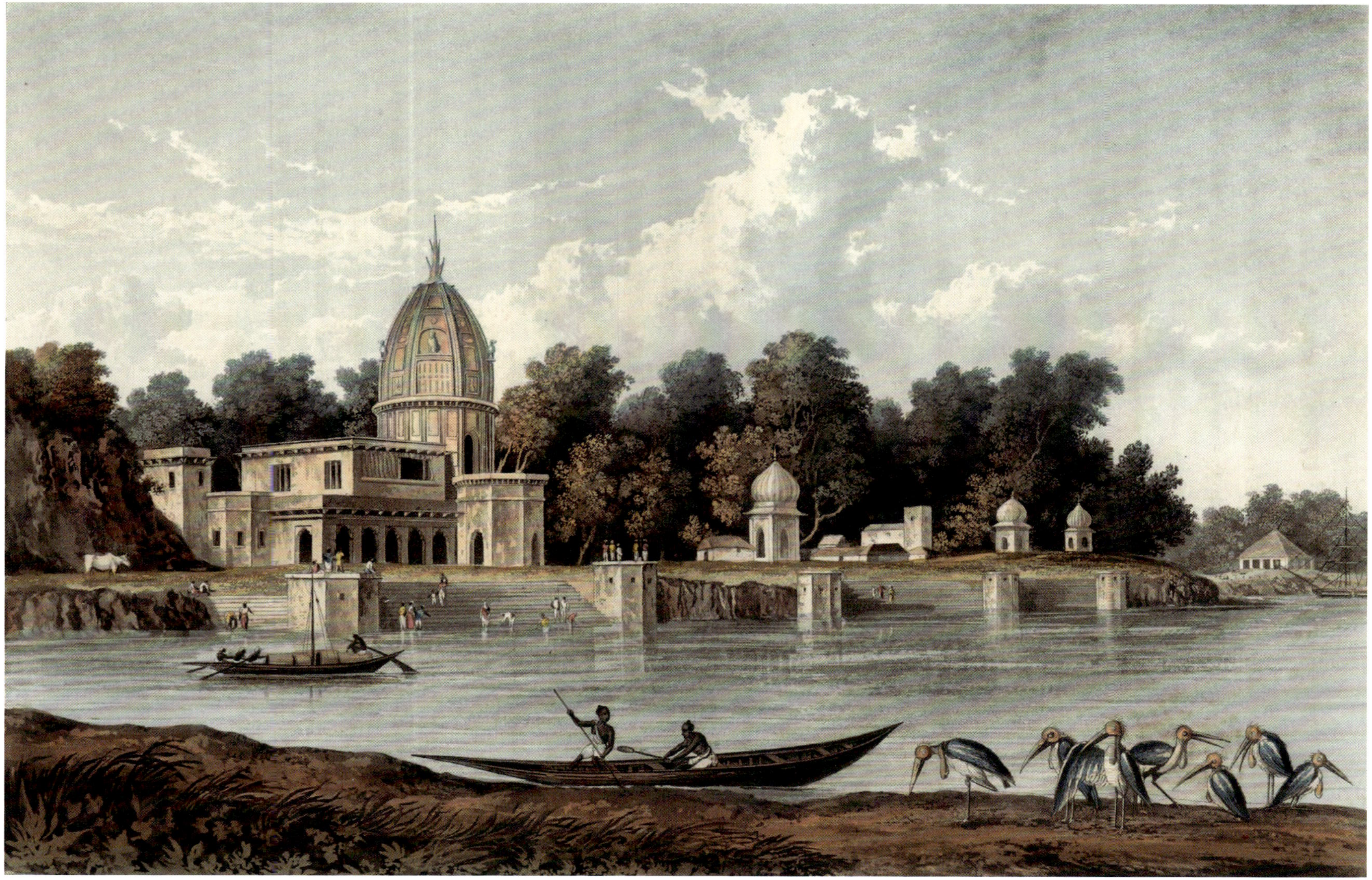

T. Sutherland sculp.

SURSEYA GHAUT, KHANPORE.

London Published by R. ACKERMANN, 101, Strand, Nov.r 1, 1824.

grass, called ***kuss kuss,*** having a very sweet scent, and affixed to all the windows to the north-west, the point from whence the hot winds usually blow. One or two men are employed to throw water on these frames (*tatties* is their name), the hot wind passing through, which is rendered so cool as to lower the thermometer in the interior to 70°. The houses are at the same time kept dark, and one door opened to leeward, to cause a regular and gentle draught; so that one really enjoys, amid this burning atmosphere, an English summer's climate.

The annexed view (*Plate* XVIII.) of Surseya-Ghaut, at Khanpore, is taken from a small sandy island in the Ganges, a short distance from the shore, and which exists only in the dry season when the river is at its lowest. The several ranges of stone steps, or stairs, are for the purpose of bathing; a religious ceremony indispensable with some casts of the Hindoos, and a custom highly conducive to health. The natives of both sexes enter the water in their clothes, and after performing their ablutions and prayers, reascend to the shore, trusting to the warm beams of an ever brilliant and glowing sun to dry their dripping garments. India's daughters, rising thus like Naiads of the flood from the bosom of their adored river, their finely wove simple garb, consisting of one long piece only, and of every varied hue, clinging closely to their figure, exhibit a symmetry of form which might fairly vie with the Medicean. Indeed the mass of the Hindoos of both sexes of the upper provinces of Bengal are perfect models for the sculptor.

Throughout the British possessions in India the customs, manners, society, mode of living, &c. are quite English, although transplanted into so different a soil and to so (in many parts) intensely hot a climate. Though the natives of the country differ essentially, nay, I may say totally, from us in all these points, still there is, as there ought assuredly to be, a friendly intercourse between us and men of rank, education, and learning, who are still found among the natives, more especially the Mahommedans, that is highly gratifying.

There are still remaining, though few in number, some descendants of the great Omrahs and nobles of the court of the emperors of Hindoostan; and these, many of whom sided with the English, retained of course their property and *jaghires*, swearing fealty to the British government in India. There are also some who, independent in a great measure, collect their own revenue, and govern their people with an arbitrary and despotic sway; but instead of being subject to the British empire, are counted its true and faithful allies. Of these, the principal under the presidency of Bengal is the Nuwab of Oude, a man placed on the musnud by the English in opposition to his brother, a turbulent and unprincipled character. At the period I was in India, Saidat Ali was Nuwab of Lucnow and prime vizir of the empire, which, as we have seen, was conferred in perpetuity on his ancestor, Sujah ul Dowlah, and his descendants, for the great services he had rendered, and the shelter and assistance he had afforded to Shah Alum, which was a very principal cause of that prince's accession to the throne of Hindoostan. Stationed almost constantly at Khanpore, the Ganges alone separated me from Oude: I therefore had several opportunities of visiting Lucnow, its capital, and seeing, on a small scale indeed, the usages, customs, and ceremonies of the empire of India in the days of its splendour.

To avoid repetition and prolixity, I shall give the substance of what I saw in these different visits in one narrative.

My first was to accompany a British officer of rank, who had recently arrived in that part of India, and who, as is customary, paid an early visit of ceremony to his highness. Leaving Khanpore, and crossing the river at sunrise, having sent our camp-equipage across the night before, with orders to have the tents pitched and breakfast ready at the proper hour, we got into our palanquins, and after a pleasant run of about nine miles, we reached our encampment at the village of Onow. We remained quiet during the heat of the day, when the thermometer stood at 90° of Fahrenheit; but towards evening we mounted our elephants, and made the tour of the town, which we found larger than its first appearance indicated. There are some mausoleums of Mahommedans to the westward; there are also the remains of a brick fort in the centre of the place, and the ruins of a large *serai* near it. A temple dedicated to Siva was just finished.

Our second day's march was fourteen miles, to Jellootra; and the third to Futteh-gunj. This morning, after having proceeded about half way, near the village of Vizir-gunj, we received notice that two of the Nuwab's sons were approaching to receive us, and conduct us to their father's presence. Soon after, we perceived their tents under some trees, and themselves coming towards us on their elephants. On meeting, the elephants of both parties fell prostrate, and we descended, and were severally introduced to the two Sahebzadehs, who were the younger sons, and were accompanied by a brother-in-law of the Nuwab, named Ramjan Khan. The ceremony of embracing took place; we were then conducted to a complete set of very elegant tents erected for our accommodation, where we found a handsome English breakfast laid out ready on the table; after which we were summoned to the tent of the princes, who made a present, as is usual on these occasions, of some shawls. We then retired, embracing as before, and, resuming our journey, reached our own tents at Futteh-gunj.

Mirza Hosain Ali Khan and Mirza Meendeh Khan, the fifth and youngest sons of the Nuwab who appear in public, have much of the gentleman in their manner, especially the youngest, who conducted himself with that ease and dignity so eminently possessed by his father. We saw the lofty minarets of Lucnow this evening. The Sahebzadehs dined with us, and confirmed the good opinion with which their first appearance had impressed us. Indeed, no European gentleman could conduct himself with greater propriety and good-breeding. Ramjan Ali Khan also proved a most pleasant companion, a complete man of the world, possessing great urbanity and politeness.

On the following morning, we all mounted our howdahs at five a. m.; the Nuwab having intimated his intention of meeting our party at the Chahar Baug, one of his highness's gardens. We now made a very respectable appearance, having twenty elephants gaily caparisoned in our train, the greater part of which had been sent for our accommodation by the Nuwab.

As we approached the grand gateway of the Chahar Baug, the massive folding doors flew open, and the Nuwab advanced, surrounded and followed by his principal courtiers, all on elephants richly caparisoned, and they in their most splendid and costly costume. This spectacle was uncommonly grand and impressive; the richness of the housings of the elephants, fifty in number, the immense and gaudy banners, the spirited and beautiful Arab horses; all this splendid pageant, bursting at once from a noble gateway embosomed in a wood, had an effect at once magnificent and highly picturesque.

On a signal from his highness, every elephant knelt down, and he, dismounting from his splendid howdah of solid silver richly embossed, advanced towards us. All present dropped like lightning from their elephants and horses, the greater part falling prostrate on their faces, those higher in rank bowing the head, while our chief and his highness embraced. At a second signal all rose and mounted, and we set off in a confused crowd, which, by the awkward motion of the elephants, so many in number, raised a dust that was almost suffocating. We soon, however, reached the palace on the Goomty river, where we sat down to an elegant breakfast, at which seven of the Nuwab's sons, and most of his principal *ameers* or nobles, were present. Breakfast over, we were conducted to a separate room, where we were severally introduced to the Nuwab, and had the honour of embracing him. The usual present of shawls for a dress, and an ornament called *goshwara* for the turban, was presented to each of us. His highness's reception was most handsome, and marked by every kind attention.

On the following day we were left to ourselves, and this I passed in visiting the public edifices and various parts of this fine city. In making use of this epithet, I apply it only to the palaces, mosques, gateways, &c.; for the town itself is as filthy a hole as I ever put foot in: the streets narrow, the huts miserable; while a nauseous odour, arising from the piles of dirt and rubbish which frequently obstructed the passage, was in the extreme disgusting: add to this, the frequent meetings with elephants in these narrow roads, a *rencontre* which more alarms a horse than any thing else could do. The elephant, however, has on his part as great apparent dread of a horse, especially if the latter comes up quick behind him.

The next day we went with a large party to visit two large pleasure-gardens belonging to the Nuwab, one of which is called the ***Hazar i Baug***, or the Thousand Gardens; the other, the ***Nashar Baug***, or Garden of Delight. These are both very considerable, running round a great part of the suburbs of the city. They are planted with orange and rose-trees, marigolds, and other common flowers. There are two very fine Pucka tanks, one of which is said to contain alligators.

We also saw this day the Imaum Baureh, the mausoleum where the late Nuwab was buried. We entered it by a lofty gateway, highly ornamented with sculpture, and passing into a sort of garden, very much neglected, ascended a long flight of steps to the main body of the building. On entering, in lieu of a place costly and splendid, as might have been expected in the tomb of the late prince of this country, we found a large room, filled completely with rubbish, which appears not to have been cleaned out since it was built; and it is besides crowded with pigeons, who build their nests all round the cornice, and cover the floor with their dirt.

In the centre of this room is the grave of the late Nuwab, Azof ul Dowlah: it is a small bed of mould, in which grass has been sown, and was springing, surrounded by four slabs of white marble at right angles, forming a long parallelogram. The direction of the grave does not correspond with that of the building, varying nearly twenty degrees. At the head of the grave are placed the *Koran* open, and the state turban of the deceased; his sword and shield are on his left side, and several vessels of rose-water on his right. *Chowries*, or fans of peacocks' feathers, are strewed about the grave, and over the whole is a canopy of scarlet cloth, supported at the four corners by poles.

The mosque attached to this tomb is a pretty building of pure white, with its three domes and its minarets all of the same material, which I believe to be marble. We were not allowed to ascend these minarets, no person being permitted to do so without public notice being given. The cause is, that, from their great height, these minarets overlook the whole city, and among other parts, the *balakhanehs*, or apartments of the women, which are on the flat tops of most of the native houses, and which have four low walls only, and no roofs.

We passed from the Imaum Baureh to the gate called the *Room i Durwazeh*, or Gate of Rome, built after the model of one at Constantinople, which city is denominated Rome by the natives. It is a showy and splendid ornament to this approach to the city, a view of which is given in *Plate* XX.; but its style does not display any architectural chasteness. The old Dowlut Khaneh, or palace, now no longer inhabited, next drew our attention: it contains one kitchen, however, of a circular form, having a balcony round its interior circumference, and is fitted up much in the English style: it is said the Nuwab sometimes dines here.

In the evening the Nuwab dined with the British resident: he came in state, and the procession on this occasion was one of the most striking and magnificent I had yet seen in India. Notice being given of his highness's approach, the resident, with a large suite, placed himself at the top of the steps to receive him. About one hundred *hircarrahs*, armed with spears with silver handles and silver maces, preceded,

Plate XX

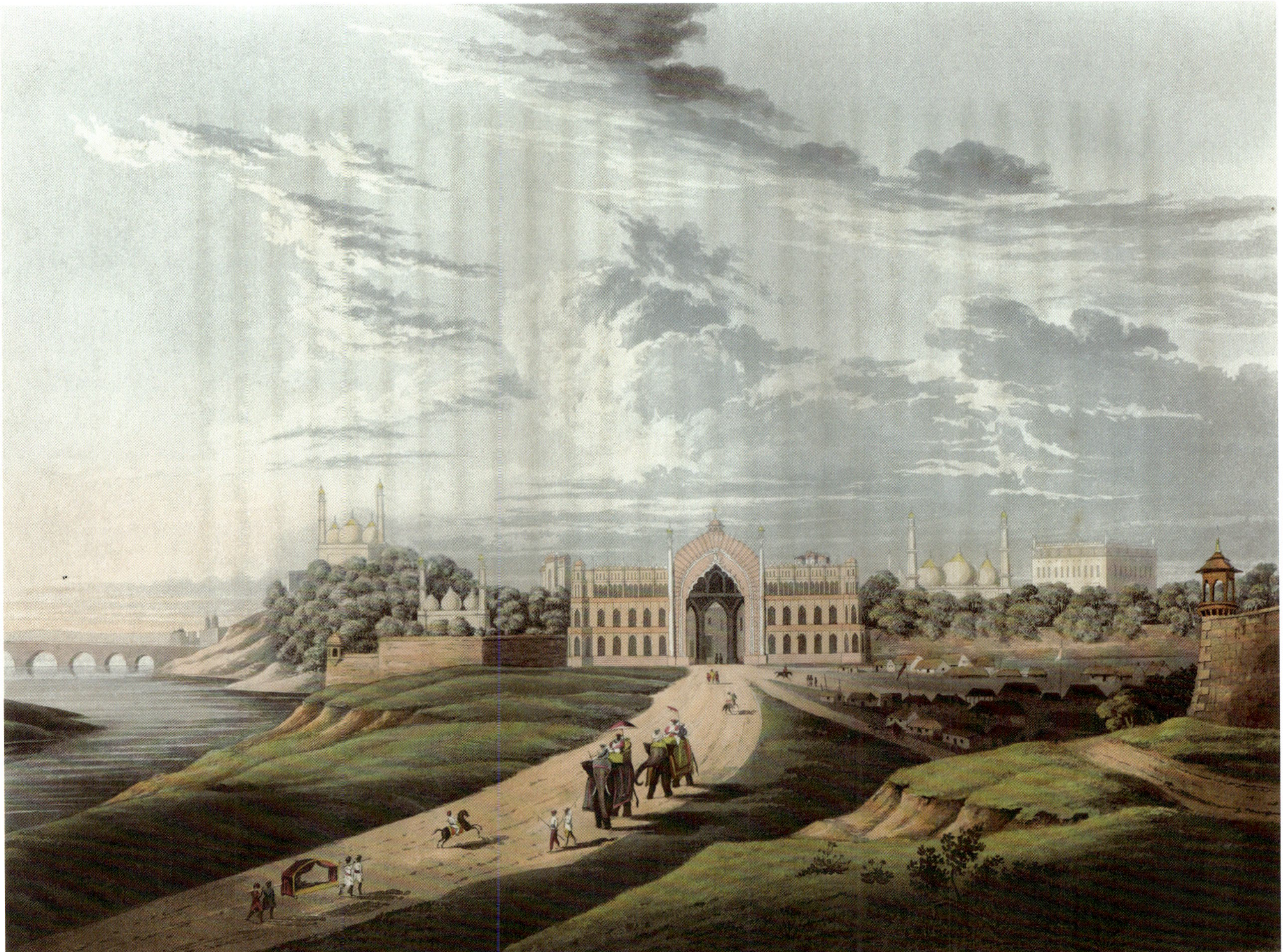

G. Hunt sculp.^t

CITY OF LUCKNOW.
CAPITAL OF PROVINCE OF OUDE ON THE GOOMTY RIVER.

London Published by R. ACKERMANN, 101, Strand, Nov.r 1, 1824.

crying aloud his titles: these were followed by several attendants on horseback, and others on foot carrying flambeaux; then came the body-guard, armed with spears and swords. His highness followed these on a superbly caparisoned elephant, and in a splendid *howdah* or seat. He was accompanied by five of his sons, each on his own elephant, with their respective attendants, and about ten of his principal nobles; the lights placing themselves on each side the steps leading up to the door, where he was received by the resident, and conducted to the drawing-room. During dinner his highness did not appear to have lost his appetite, though he was far outdone by one of his nobles, named Cossim Ali Khan, who sat opposite to me at table, and ate as much certainly as would have satisfied any five English farmers. He was a good-looking man, of about five feet ten inches in height, but immensely large, so as to weigh upwards of twenty stone. His own servants brought his dinner, which consisted of a large dish of boiled rice, with butter, spices, and a variety of vegetables, which being all placed in a semicircle around him, he took of the several ingredients, and mixing up a portion of them with his hand, he began to chuck this into his mouth; part he swallowed, but a large portion was denied entrance by his mustachios, and descended on his plate. What amused me most was, this *bon-vivant* in the midst of his repast threw handfuls of this mess on the plates of his fellow-nobles, who seemed to receive this substantial mark of his favour with profound respect. He described a favourite dish which he often indulged in, enumerating the several items like a professed epicure. He gave also the exact measure of the different ingredients, which amounted in all to seven pounds weight. After stuffing himself thoroughly, his servant brought a ponderous ewer and bason, when his lordship washed his beard and hands, and rising with a *salaam* to his master, retired to take his nap. The Nuwab retired about nine o'clock: the procession was the same as on his arrival, except that there was a much greater display of flambeaux, almost every attendant, servants, guards, &c. bearing one. The night being very dark added to this scene, and produced a brilliant effect, which time never can efface from my memory.

The following day was the Mahommedan festival of the ***Ede,*** corresponding with our Easter, as it is celebrated on the appearance of the new moon after the month ***Ramazan,*** which resembles the Lent of the Christians. During its continuance the Mussulmans eat nothing from sunrise to sunset; and some are said to be so punctilious, as not even to swallow their saliva during that period. The festivities at the conclusion of this fast are sumptuous; some very curious in their nature: but in consequence of the death of the Nuwab's mother, his highness did not attend, and much of the splendour of the festival was lost in consequence.

Another day was dedicated to a new species of amusement, quite novel to Europeans, and well worthy of notice—an elephant fight. We mounted our horses at an early hour, and proceeded to the palace to meet the Nuwab, who was on horseback also; and followed by a large retinue, we set off for a palace of his highness's, called the Barouoon Baug, where there is an area appropriated for the combats of elephants and other wild beasts. This palace is delightfully situated on a gently rising eminence, commanding a most extensive view over the surrounding country; and, in point of splendour combined with elegance, far surpasses any thing of the sort in this part of India. There was a well-judged union of the comfort of the English with the splendour and magnificence of the Asiatic style, throughout its numerous and extensive apartments.

An elegant breakfast awaited our arrival; after which we passed to a spacious verandah on the east side of the palace, which looked down into the area prepared for the combat: the latter was nearly surrounded by a paling of bamboo, eighteen or twenty feet high. Soon after we were all seated the crowd were admitted, and presently filled the circumference of the theatre below us. Two very large war-elephants were now brought forward from opposite sides, each preceded by its favourite female, whose presence it appears is necessary to arouse the anger of these noble animals. The conflict of this pair, however, gave little sport, one of them appearing very shy, and inferior to his opponent in strength; they were therefore withdrawn. Another pair now advanced, led as the first. These approached with a slow and majestic step, until they caught a glimpse of each other; both then raising their trunks, and uttering a shrill and angry cry, rushed with the most tremendous impetuosity together, presenting their heads to receive the first shock. It was awfully grand. The animals, thus stopped in their first career, still continued to strive by every possible exertion of strength and art to force their adversary back, or to attack him in flank. Their heads, however, still were firmly pressed together, and they alternately receded and rallied. One was of rather a smaller size than his antagonist, but he appeared to make up for this deficiency by his greater spirit. He retreated a little for a moment, but it was only to renew the charge with increased rage: again they met; the same tremendous concussion took place, and these attacks were several times repeated, until in a last and most desperate one a tooth of the smaller elephant was broken in two with a loud crash. Still he was not dispirited, and would have persevered longer in the contest; but being now so decidedly inferior to his adversary, the fire-works were cast between them, which ended the combat.

The noble animals kept for this sport are unfit of course for any other purpose, and are almost ungovernable by their *mahauts*. They are fed, to bring them to this furious state, on high-seasoned food and spices, which in a manner intoxicate them, and render them furious beyond description.

The *mahauts*, or conductors, sit upon the elephant's back during the contest, and too often fall victims to the mad rage of their own animal or the opposing foe. There is a large pad like a mattress strongly fixed on the animal's back, and covered over with a coarse netting of thick white cotton rope; to this the *mahaut* clings, and as the elephants approach to the attack, the rider gradually recedes towards the tail, where he usually is at the moment of the shock, stimulating the already furious animal with his voice and the sharp goad with which the elephant is always driven and guided.

We had one more entertainment from the Nuwab previous to our departure from his capital: it consisted of a late dinner, which was as splendid and well conducted as any thing of the kind I had yet witnessed in the country. Six sons of his highness, and several nobles of the highest rank at his court, with some British officers, swelled the company to about forty persons. After dinner, the health of our party and that of the resident was given by the Nuwab; but although the bottle circulated pretty freely, neither himself nor any of his courtiers tasted a drop, it being contrary to their religion to indulge in wine.

Towards dusk we all rose from table, and followed his highness to an open space on the banks of the Goomty river, where sofas and seats were placed on a ***chebootra***, a low terrace of stone or ***chunam***, over which a spacious awning of crimson and white, supported by four lofty gilt poles, and having a curtain or screen of the same behind, was spread. Scarcely were we all seated when a very splendid display of fire-works, in the making of which the natives of India excel, burst forth with great brilliancy, and continued about a quarter of an hour, with as many various and beautiful changes as I have any where witnessed. A ***nautch*** meanwhile was performing by a corps of the Nuwab's dancing-girls: they were, however, very inferior to many other sets I had seen in the lower country.

The next morning we received the farewell presents of his highness, consisting of utter of roses, and an ornament or badge for the neck, suspended on a string of large but very ill-shaped and discoloured pearls. We were detained two days longer by excessively heavy rains, and in our return to Lucnow, found the whole country inundated. It was with some difficulty we made good our way to Khanpore. The Ganges opposite to that cantonment had so much overflowed its usual limits, that it was full four miles broad: it had not been known so high for many years, being five feet above its ordinary level at this season.

A negociation, which had long been pending between the Indian government and the Seikh chief, Rungeet Singh, and which it appeared there was little prospect of adjusting amicably, induced the sending of a British force in that direction, to give our arguments more weight, and present at once the olive-branch and the sword. This corps of troops assembled far to the northward, near four hundred miles above Khanpore, and close upon the north-western frontier of the Company's territory at that period. Being attached to this force, I left Khanpore as soon as possible; and as expedition was highly requisite, I took the resolution of travelling by *dawk*, or what would be denominated in Europe by post. The main difference is, that here you travel much at ease in your own palanquin, and at the very fair rate of four miles per hour. This vehicle admits of your sitting up or lying down; or you can get out and take an occasional walk, without in any way impeding the bearers who carry you. The only preparatory measure to take on starting is, to give due notice of the day and hour you propose commencing your journey to all the postmasters through whose districts you will pass. They will have the regular sets of bearers at every stage, and you are shifted from the shoulders of one to those of another set, frequently without being conscious of it. On most of the routes European settlers are met with, and at the several stations travellers are always welcome visitors to the magistrates or collectors, who abundantly supply your wants. Such is British society in India. I completed without accident the four hundred miles in four days; nor did I feel fatigued so much as I had anticipated. An officer who accompanied me was not so fortunate, as he lost two travelling-baskets with linen and clothes, cut off by some thieves, who follow persons thus moving, and often catch a loiterer. The baggage is carried in two large round baskets covered with leather, slung one at each end of an elastic bamboo, which is carried on a bearer's shoulder. Each set, which consists of eight for each palanquin, carry you about eight or ten miles, sometimes more.

The greater part of the troops had assembled by the time we reached the point of rendezvous, and in a few days the remainder joined. We advanced and crossed the Jumna at Boorea-Ghaut, which is here divided into numerous channels, running rapidly over a pebbly bed, fordable every where, and its stream clear as crystal. The day previous to moving, our heavy baggage and camp-equipage had arrived, having marched from Khanpore the four hundred miles in eighteen days. It was principally carried by elephants and camels. We pursued the route through Mustaphabad, Amballa, and Mogul ka Serai; near which we had a bad and dangerous nullah to ford, where several accidents occurred. The country is level, mostly open, with some jungle, and also fine cultivation. Every village was fortified; a precaution very necessary on a frontier line, which is alternately ravaged by both parties, and by marauders who belong to neither. The fortification seldom surpasses a thick, high, and solid mud wall, with a high tower as a look-out post.

The army thence marched by Patarsi and Rajpoora, a considerable town, surrounded with a wall of brick, and having turrets at the angles. There is also a very fine *serai* close to it. We had been marching for some time past upon the great royal road formed in the days of the greatest wealth and splendour of India, for the annual visits of the emperors to Lahore, Candahar, and Cabul. It is still in fine order, and the distances marked throughout by high pillars of red stone at every two koss, or three and a half miles English. Numerous splendid *serais* are also met with from distance to distance on the road-side, for the accommodation of the traveller at the same period, where for about three-pence a man and horse were fed and lodged well for the night. These *serais* are usually in the form of a square of great extent, some of three or four hundred yards; their walls, surmounted by a parapet, are from thirty to fifty feet high; and their entrance is always by a grand gateway of massive structure, and beautifully ornamented by Mosaic work or sculpture. Our camp this day was in front of the ancient city of Sirhind, once so famous for its commerce and manufacture of silks, and whence silk was first brought to Europe, as also the mode of working it, in the sixth century. I rode through its ruins, which are very extensive, and exhibit traits, although melancholy ones, of its former consequence and wealth. At present not one building is perfect.

Not far from these ruins are those of a very fine palace, used it is believed by the emperors of Hindoostan in their annual excursions to Cashmere. This ruin stands on a rising ground, and occupies with its gardens a square of a full quarter of a mile. Its principal entrance is to the north. On entering you find a court, now under cultivation; at the end opposite is a building of two stories; passing under this through an arched gateway, a second extensive square is entered. A large tank of water occupies nearly the whole of this space, and a causeway on arches leads up its centre to the principal building, containing two fine halls below, and other apartments above. The roof and all the ceilings have fallen in. A third square is behind this, and has been originally a garden, laid out in a very ancient style: down the centre is a broad and fine walk, with a row of fountains on each side, twenty yards asunder. At the end of this walk are the *hummaum,* or hot baths. The whole is terminated by a terrace, running the breadth of the area, and having a turret at each end. One is a heap of ruins; that on the west is tolerably perfect. I ascended its summit, which commands a fine view of the surrounding country and the city of Sirhind. This edifice was erected by the Derveish Sultan Hafiz in the reign of Alumgire.

The army moved from Sirhind, and, preceded by a strong advanced corps, arrived after two marches within about eighteen miles of the Sutlooj river, the first and most easterly of the five which form the Punjab. Our advance was in position on its left bank. The country through which we had for some days been marching belonged, by the right of conquest, to the Seikh nation; but the latter had all retired behind the river, of which they occupied the bank opposite to our advance, and several large bodies could be distinguished dispersed further inland. All are cavalry, and it is said Runjeet Singh can bring into the field 30,000 of this arm. The Seikhs are a fine, manly, and athletic race of men, skilled in all the martial exercises, and far superior in feature and bodily strength to the more southern natives of Hindoostan. Their country is celebrated for its fine climate and its productive soil. It has increased much in power and influence of late years, and at the present day is the only state left in perfect independence and full liberty from British influence; and it is in consequence the only one whose hostility might prove formidable to us.

During our march up from the Jumna, we had once or twice obtained partial glimpses of the hills to the north and eastward, which form the great barrier between India and China: behind the lower hills rises another and more elevated range; and a third considerably overtops these. Lastly towers the mighty chain of Himalaya, which was always considered by men of science to have a great elevation, from their snow-white summits being sometimes seen like a distant cloud amid the vapours of the horizon; but no attempts were made to determine their exact position and distance until within these few years, when the East India Company sent an expedition, composed of engineers and men of science, to solve the mystery. These, after a laborious and most arduous service, perfectly succeeded in the main object of their attempt; and the result is, that this chain of Himalaya is decided by actual observation to exceed very far in perpendicular height the Andes, hitherto considered the most elevated points of the globe. The White Mountain of the Himalaya range is five English miles in perpendicular elevation above the level of the sea.

This chain had been beheld by but few of the British in India. We were more fortunate; for in the position we now occupied, we were considerably nearer to them than a person could be in any part of the lower provinces, having gradually approached them in our movement upwards. Still we had not as yet seen them, until Nature herself drew up the veil which concealed them from our view, and displayed them at once in all their majesty. We had been encamped for five or six days near the town of Pahil; the weather had been fine and warm for the season, the month of February: a considerable haze is the natural consequence of such a state of the atmosphere. On the 6th there fell some showers of rain about noon; and towards four o'clock p. m. this was followed by one of those dreadful and tremendous tornados which frequently occur, and lay desolate the finest and most fruitful tracts of tropical countries. The lightning was most vivid and incessant; the thunder burst in the most awful peals; while the hail, or rather fragments of ice, many of which measured an inch and a quarter in diameter, exceeded any thing that had been before witnessed by the oldest inhabitants of India. This was followed by a deluge of rain, such as I never saw before or since, accompanied by a deep gloom, which rendered the scene more imposing and terrific; while violent gusts of wind speedily laid prostrate a large portion of our encampment, the wet soil being incapable of retaining the tent-pins. The horses, camels, and other cattle, buffeted by the hail-stones, and alarmed at the lightning, broke from their fastenings, and rushing wildly about in every direction through the camp, got entangled in the tent-cords, and tore up many a tent that would otherwise have withstood the storm. The tent I was in was a large and stout one, but it required the whole of my servants to keep it standing by holding on with all their might to the two poles. We thus weathered the storm, which had come from the south-west. Towards sunset it cleared away, and the evening brightened up. As the mists dissipated, the faintly traced outline of the lower range of hills became apparent; and soon beyond these another and loftier tier raised its blue crest, till at length the evening having settled into clear and serene, the light vapours were drawn up, and collected in the form of fleecy clouds; and as they rose, the grand

and lofty summits of Himalaya were seen towering to that height that the mind could with difficulty believe them to form part of our earth; they more resembled the clouds of heaven. Their mass was covered with a clothing of everlasting snows, which, tinged with the last beams of the declining sun, that had long disappeared to us, and assuming that pure and aërial rosy blush, never seen but on the more elevated summits of the earth, sweetly contrasted with the deep and calm blue of the Indian summer sky. It was a scene, contrasted with the horrors of the forenoon, that inspired sensations of delight, which those only who witnessed it can fully appreciate. All were fascinated; it was the topic for many days. The whole camp were out, with eyes riveted in admiration on the magnificent effect before them; nor did they cease to gaze until the sober veil of evening wrapped all nature in its soft and silent folds, and left them to dwell in imagination on the magnificent and enchanting fairy scene.

Our division of troops never advanced further than this position near Pahil. The Seikh commander, convinced that we were in earnest, and alarmed by the near approach of our main body, consented to the terms offered by the Company's envoy. The army consequently returned by the route they had advanced, leaving a strong post at the village of Ludhiana; and assuming the line of the Sutlooj river as the boundary of the Seikh country and our provinces, a strong field-work was thrown up there, sufficiently respectable to withstand a *coup-de-main.*

The army received orders to break up at Dehli, and the corps to resume their former quarters and cantonments. My shortest route would have been through the Doo-ab, by the road I had already travelled by *dawk:* I, however, obtained permission to accompany a regiment of cavalry, which was to follow the route by Dehli and Agra, renowned in the pages of history as the capitals of the Indian empire in its days of power and splendour.

We passed in this route many places of interest as the scenes of events highly famed in ancient times; many remains also of magnificent works of art, now scarcely to be traced even by their ruins. Among others the field of Panniput, the theatre of that dreadful and destructive battle already recorded in this work, where the great struggle took place between the Mahratta hordes and all the Mussulman powers. We thus approached Dehli by rapid marches, and entered the ruins of that city in fifteen marches from the frontier. On this route their extent is not great, and we soon entered the new city, which was built and named by Shah Jehan, Shah Jehanabad. This is the modern Dehli, and the capital of Hindoostan: we passed through a great part of this city, and out at the Water-gate, and encamped near the beautiful tomb of the emperor Humaioon, built by his son Acber. Dehli has now a circumference of about six English miles, including the palace of the emperor. It has seven gates, the Lahore, Dehli or Water-gate, Agimere, Moor, Turkoman, Cabul, and Cashmere.

On the morning after our arrival I waited on the British resident, who received me with the kindest attentions: after breakfast, he told me he had obtained the emperor's permission for my seeing the palace, and introduced to me a native gentleman of rank, who was to be my guide. The first visit was to the Jumah Musjid, the cathedral of Dehli, that is, the principal mosque, situated on a high mound of rock, and nearly in the centre of the city. It has three grand gates, the principal one to the eastward; by this, ascending a flight of forty steps, we entered: its doors are of solid brass. The area in which this magnificent mosque stands is about fourteen hundred yards square. The building itself is an oblong, two hundred and sixty-one feet in length, and surmounted with three white marble domes, banded with black; and at each of the two front extremities is a lofty and graceful minaret of three stories, of red and white stone striped, and one hundred and thirty feet high. I ascended the minaret on the right hand, and from thence had an extensive and grand view of the city of Dehli, the palace, and the country beyond to a great distance. The erection of this building, by Shah Jehan, cost 125,000*l.* Near it is seen the mosque of Roshun ul Dowlah, of red stone, with three golden domes, in which Nadir Shah sat during the massacre of the inhabitants, when in one morning 100,000 persons of all descriptions were slaughtered.

We next proceeded to the palace, a view of which is given in ***Plate*** XXI. and entered by the West-gate. The walls are about forty feet high, composed of blocks of the red stone. We then entered the gate called the Nia Khana: here we were requested to leave our swords and ***chattah***, or umbrellas.

The first principal building we came to was the ***Dewan Aum***, or Hall of Audience, at the upper end of a large paved square. Here is a throne of pure marble, on which the emperor sits; and below a large slab of marble, nine feet by five, and once inlaid with precious stones, on which sat the vizir, the Bukshee, the Jyepore, and Joudpore rajahs: this hall is supported on marble pillars.

Thence we went through a handsome gateway to the Dewan Khass. It is at the further end of a beautiful square, and elevated on a terrace of marble: its dimensions are one hundred and fifty feet in front, and forty feet deep. The roof is flat; the ceiling, exquisitely painted and gilt, is supported by rows of columns of white marble, finely sculptured, and which have once been richly inlaid in mosaic. In the centre of this splendid edifice is the musnud, or low throne on which the emperor sat; and near it is a large block of pure crystal, four feet long by three wide, and two feet thick. It is I think the most beautiful stone I ever saw. Near this are the royal baths, consisting of three spacious rooms, with domes of white marble, and lighted from the top through windows of stained glass. The walls are of marble, as is also the floor; and the latter very beautifully inlaid with patterns of flowers in mosaic, all composed of cornelians, jasper, and other semiprecious stones.

Not far from these baths is the private mosque of the emperor, a small highly

Plate-XXI

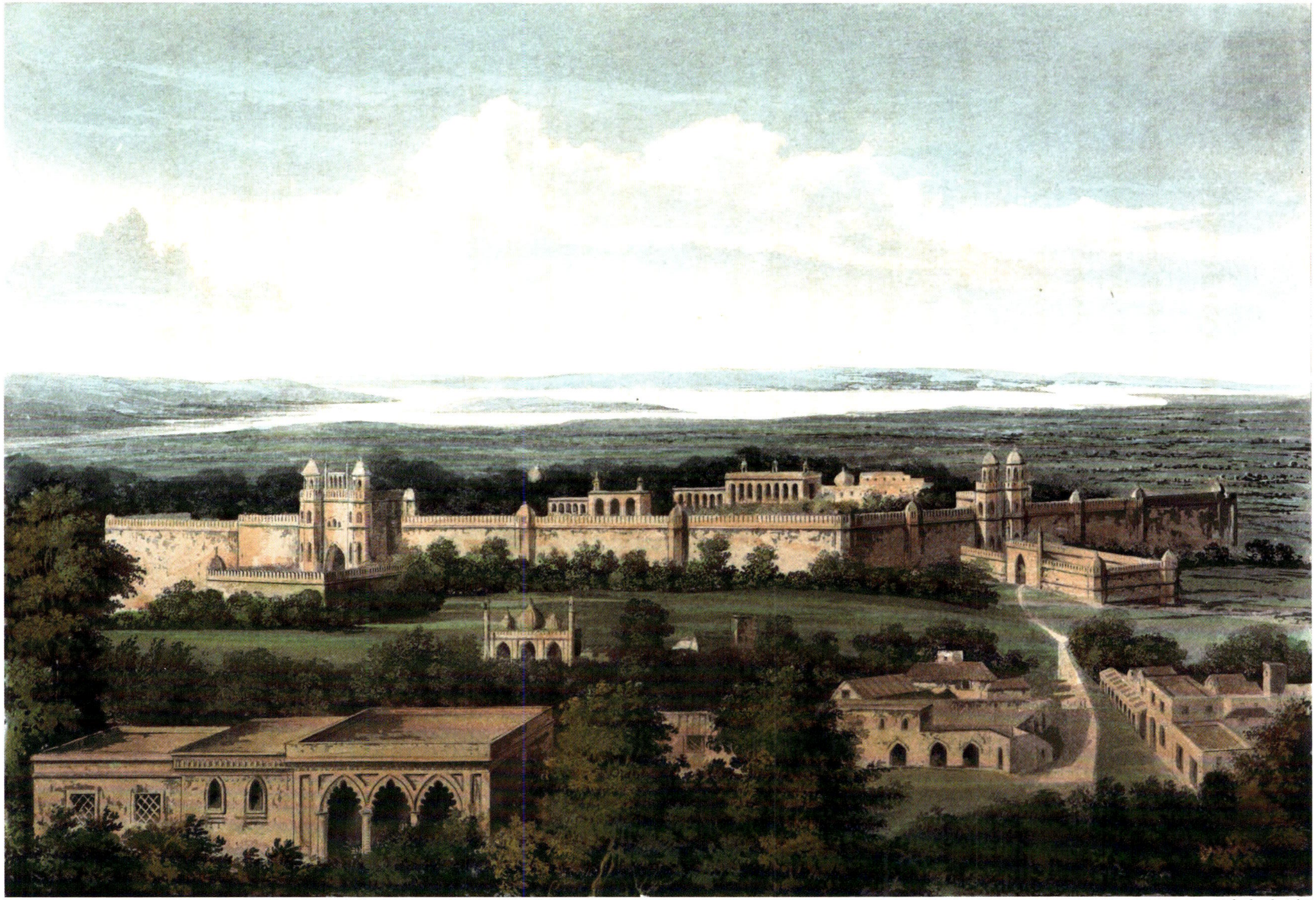

T. Sutherland sculp.t

PALACE of the KING of DELHI

Taken from the Principal Mosque

London: Published by R. ACKERMANN, 101, Strand, Dec., 1824.

Plate-XXII

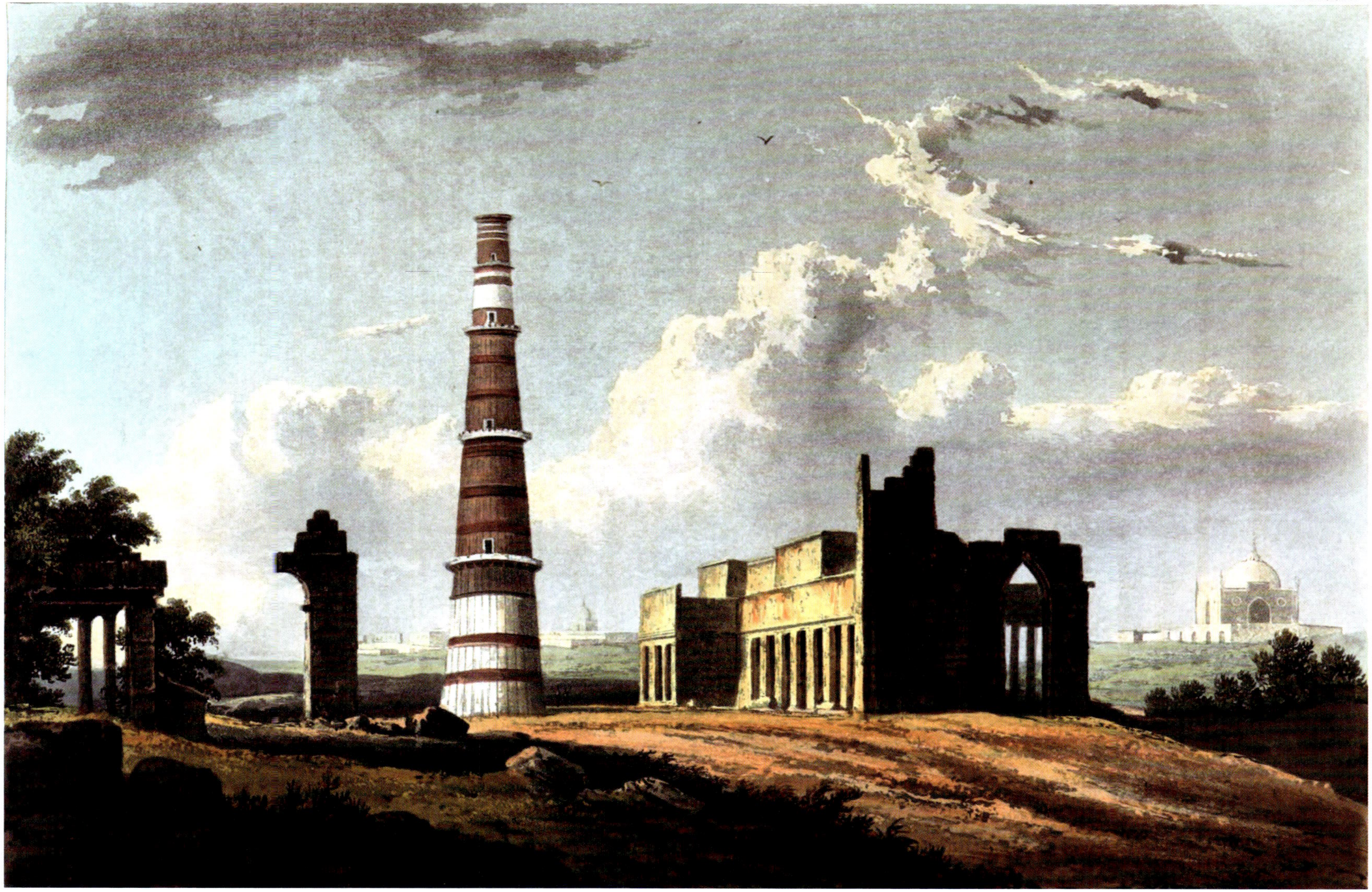

T. Sutherland sculp.t

THE CUTTUB MINAR IN THE RUINS OF ANCIENT DELHI

London Published by R. ACKERMANN, 101, Strand, Dec., 1824.

finished edifice of white marble, surmounted by three golden domes. This palace is about one mile in circumference.

The gardens were next visited: they contain, however, nothing remarkable. There were some wild beasts, of the leopard and lynx species, kept for hunting the deer. There is also one block of marble, formed into a reservoir, nine feet square, and four deep.

The following day I accompanied an officer to see the remains of part of ancient Dehli; and among other works of art erected in the olden time of India's glory, one object is particularly worthy of remark: this is the Cuttub Minar, a pillar of stone, which equals, if not exceeds, any other known both in form and height, and is situated in the midst of the ruins of the ancient capital of India. It is represented in *Plate* XXII. Little remains at the present day of its palaces; nothing of its private buildings but rubbish: but its tombs, those grand piles of masonry of various, of noble, and some of elegant form and proportion, being always erected without the walls, mark very correctly by their vast circuit the amazing extent which old Dehli embraced in the days of its splendour.

The height of this pillar is two hundred and forty-five English feet, and its circumference at the base is one hundred and fifty-six feet. It had formerly five stories, with a spiral staircase of three hundred and four stone steps leading up to the very summit. The earthquake, however, of 30th September, 1803, seriously injured the upper story, having thrown down a part, and strewed the remains on the stairs below, so as much to impede the passage up. This pillar appears to be cased on the exterior with stone, of the red granite kind; and this casing, after a close inspection, will be found of a different quality, and of more modern workmanship, than the mass of the interior. The view from the summit is very grand and extensive over a vast plain, in which remains of buildings and tombs are seen as far as the eye can discern.

It is to this day a subject of doubt and discussion at what period this column was reared, for what purpose, and by what prince, and whether it owes its existence to Hindoo or Mussulman. It is claimed by both sects. The form of the building, which quite resembles the minaret, would assign it to the latter; but the Hindoos contend that it was erected by them previously to the arrival of the Mahommedans, and the latter, jealous of the beauty of the pile, gave it the casing of stone which covers it. There are certainly the remains of a very large and grand Hindoo temple surrounding this pillar, and some colonnades with stone pillars are evidently the sculpture of that people. It is equally certain that the period of its erection must be long anterior to the era fixed by the Mahommedans, the reign of Behadur Shah.

To the north of the Cuttub Minar is a lofty pillar of solid iron, twenty-six feet above ground, and the size of a man's body. To the east is a building surmounted by a dome, in which the sculpture is exquisite; the whole of the red stone. On the bands of darker stone which encircle this pillar are characters beautifully cut in alto relievo; and each story has a door to the west. On the whole it is an interesting object, well deserving the attention of the curious, and the researches of those learned in the language and history of this extraordinary country to trace it to its origin.

Having satisfied myself with the view of the antiquities and splendid remains of ancient Dehli, I proceeded down the Doo-ab to visit the fort and palace of Agra, for a long period the rival city of Dehli. When the emperor Acber Shah in 1570 returned from his expedition towards Lucnow to punish the rebellious chiefs, Zeman Khan and Behadur Khan, who had erected the standard of revolt, he returned to Agra, which place he determined for the future to make his principal residence; and accordingly commanded his whole court to be moved thither from Dehli. The old part of Agra being much gone to decay, and the palace, the former residence of the Patan kings, very incommodious, he resolved to rebuild them both, and in a style becoming the founder and the monarch of so mighty an empire.

As the building of Agra, and of the stupendous and noble fortress, decidedly ranks among the most magnificent works of Acber's reign, the following account, taken from *the Indian Antiquities,* will perhaps be acceptable in this place to the reader:

Agra, called Agara by Ptolemy, who, however, by no means placed it in his map of India in a latitude corresponding with the modern maps, which is marked in 27° 15′ north, owed its importance, and indeed its existence as a capital, to the munificence of Acber. That emperor, pleased with its situation on the bank of the Jumna river, and incited perhaps by its proximity to the kingdoms of the Deccan, raised Agra from an inconsiderable fortified town to an eminence in splendour, beauty, and renown, which no city in India, not even Dehli itself, had ever before enjoyed. This monarch had far advanced in the completion of the proud structures of the palace at Futtehpore Sicre, of which the remains still shew the original grandeur, when on a sudden he relinquished them, to execute his more noble and extensive projects at Agra. Indeed the projects of Acber were all vast and comprehensive, like the mind that formed them. In the important plans for which peace gave leisure, as well as in the more dazzling scenes of martial glory, his genius and his abilities seemed to soar alike superior to the rest of mankind.

Acber, after having determined to make Agra an imperial residence, ordered the old wall of earth, with which the city had been inclosed by the Patan monarchs, to be destroyed, and rebuilt with hewn stone, brought from the quarries at Futtehpore. This undertaking, however considerable, was finished with no great difficulty, and within no very protracted period. But to rebuild Agra and its castle in a manner worthy of the designer, and calculated to render it the metropolis of the greatest empire in Asia, required the unwearied exertions of one of the greatest monarchs whom Asia had ever beheld.

For the full completion of his magnificent plan, Acber, by the promise of ample rewards, collected from every quarter of his dominions the most skilful architects, and the most celebrated artists in every branch both of external ornament and domestic decoration; and some idea may be formed of the great labour and expense required to perfect the whole undertaking, when the reader learns, that the palace alone took up twelve years in finishing, kept above a thousand labourers constantly employed during that period, and cost nearly three millions of rupees. The castle itself, the largest ever built in India, was in the form of a crescent, along the banks of the Jumna, which becomes at this place in its progress to the Ganges a very considerable river. Its lofty walls were composed of stones of an enormous size, hard as marble, and of a reddish colour, resembling jasper, which at a distance, in the rays of the sun, gave it a shining and beautiful appearance.

This palace was four miles in extent, and consisted of three courts, adorned with many stately porticoes, galleries, and turrets, all richly painted and gilded, and some even overlaid with plates of gold. The first court, built round with arches, that afforded a pleasant shade, so desirable amid the heats of a burning climate, was intended for the imperial guard; the second, for the great Omrahs and ministers of state, who had their several apartments for the transaction of the public business; and, lastly, the third court, within which was contained the seraglio, consisting entirely of the stately apartments of the emperor himself, hung round with the richest silks of Persia, and glittering with a profusion of Indian wealth. Behind these were the royal gardens, laid out in the most exquisite taste, and decorated with all that could gratify the eye, regale the ear, or satiate the most luxurious palate; the loveliest shade, the deepest verdure, grottoes of the most refreshing coolness, fruits of the most delicious flavour, cascades that never ceased to murmur, and music that never failed to delight. In the front of the castle, towards the river, a large area was left for the exercising of the royal elephants and the battles of the wild beasts, in which the emperors of India used to take great pleasure; and in a square of vast extent, that separated the palace from the city, a numerous army was constantly encamped, whose shining armour and gorgeous ensigns diffused a glory round them, and added greatly to the splendour of the scene.

But if this palace was thus grand and magnificent externally, what a splendid scene must its interior have displayed! Mandeslo, who visited Agra in 1638, and saw that city in the meridian of its glory, after stating that the palace altogether was the grandest object he had ever beheld, that it was surrounded by a wall of freestone and a broad ditch, with a drawbridge at each of its gates, adds, that at the further end of the third court was seen a row of silver pillars under a piazza, and beyond this court was the presence-chamber; that this more spacious apartment was adorned with a row of golden pillars of a smaller size, and within the balustrade was the royal throne of massy gold, almost incrusted over with diamonds, pearls, and other precious stones. Above this throne was a gallery, where the Mogul appeared every day at a certain time to hear and to redress the complaints of his subjects; and no person whatever, except the sons of the emperor, were admitted behind these pillars of gold. The same traveller also mentions an apartment in the castle very remarkable for its high tower, which was covered with massy gold, and for the treasure which it contained, having eight large vaults filled with gold, silver, and precious stones, the value of which was inestimable.

In a line with the palace, along the banks of the same river, were ranged the magnificent palaces of the princes and great rajahs, who vied with each other in adorning the new metropolis; the majestic edifices of which met the delighted eye, intersected with lofty trees, wide canals, and beautiful gardens. Determined to make it the wonder and envy of the East, and to bury both its former name and obscurity in equal oblivion, the emperor gave his own name to the rising capital, calling it Acberabad; while he enriched it with the noblest monuments of royal munificence that human ingenuity could plan, or human industry could execute.

Our first object, after viewing the noble works we have described, was the tomb of the emperor Acber, shewn in ***Plate*** XXIII. This celebrated mausoleum of the greatest monarch recorded by history as having ever sat on the throne of Hindoostan, when that empire was at its highest pitch of splendour and power, still bears the character of that grandeur which its inmate once enjoyed: it is, however, fast falling to decay, and a few years more will probably see it a mere ruin. It is situated in an inclosure, which was once a garden, and still contains some fine trees. A wall, thirty feet high, and of a quadrangular form, each side being about six hundred yards, surrounds the tomb: in the centre of each face is a handsome gateway, covered with mosaic work in vivid-coloured stones and marbles. The gate to the south is the largest, and is denominated the Grand Gateway: it has white marble turrets at each angle, of a circular form, the building itself being an oblong square, and it is surmounted by a pavilion. Entering this gateway, a fine broad causeway of stone leads up to the tomb.

The tomb consists of five tiers or stories, the four lower of the red granite, the upper of pure white marble in elegant fret-work. The jollies, or screen, which surround the cenotaph placed in the centre, are richly and beautifully sculptured: this upper apartment is open at top.

Below the lower story you descend by a very gradually sloping passage to the tomb of the emperor, a plain white marble slab, of very large size.

Acber was buried here in the year 1604, and on the tomb of this illustrious monarch is inscribed simply—" ACBER."

The site of this noble monument is close to the small village of Secundra, and about five miles from the fort of Agra, the most celebrated fortress in this part of Hindoostan.

At some distance from Agra to the westward, and about fifteen miles from the

Plate XXII

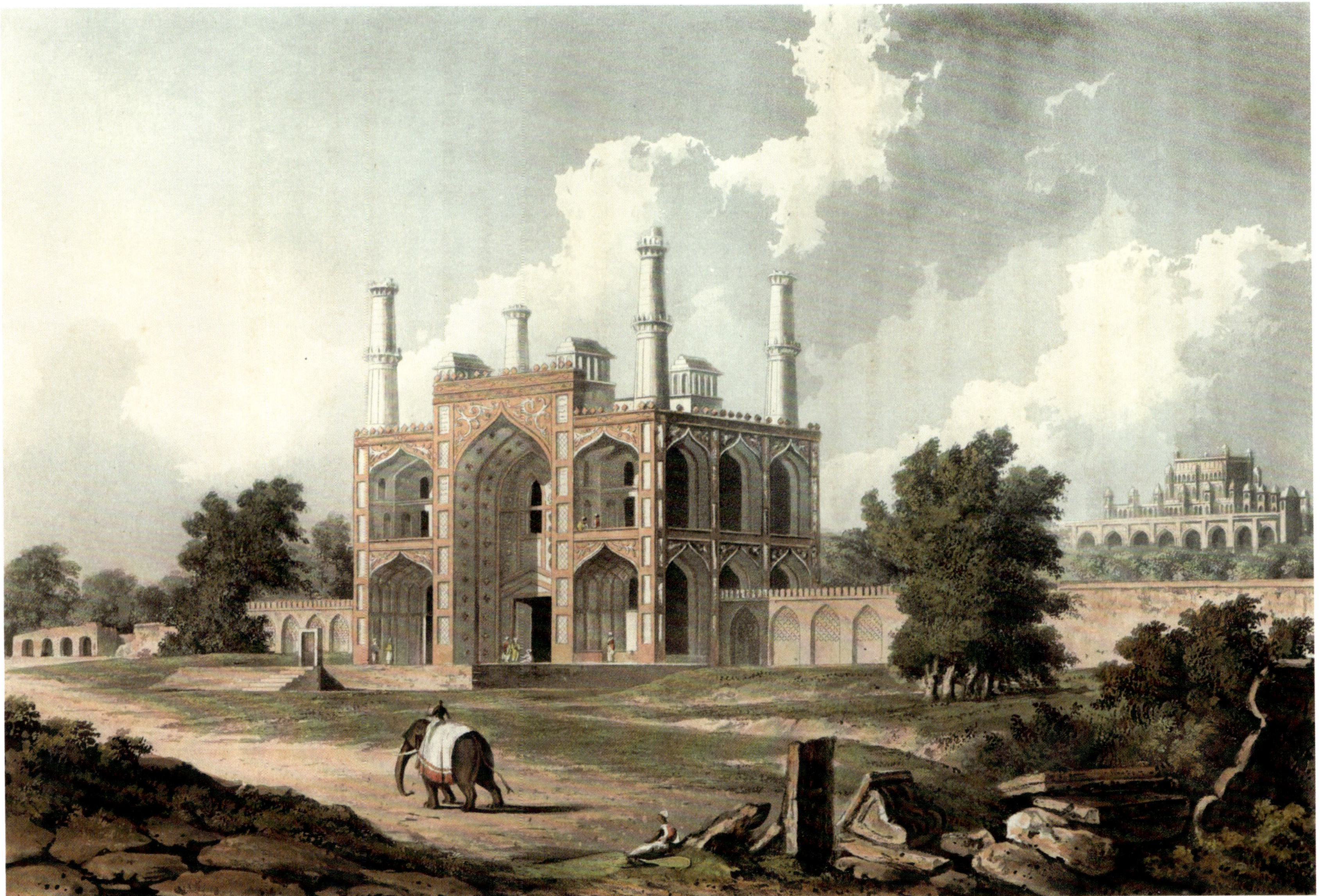

T. Sutherland sculpt.

GRAND GATEWAY and TOMB of the EMPEROR ACBAR at SECUNDRA.

Published Dec.r 1, 1824, by R. ACKERMANN, 101, Strand London.

main road from Dehli to that fortress, are the remains of a palace, called Futtehpore Sicre, built by the emperor Acber. I rode to visit these singular remains of a most splendid and wonderful work, quite worthy of the illustrious founder of Agra.

We have omitted one beautiful and chaste building in the fort of Agra, which deserves to be recorded: it is denominated the Mootee Musjid, formerly the principal mosque of the place. It consists of four parallel rows of nine arches each, and is surmounted with three domes, but has no minarets. Although very inferior in size to the Jumah Musjid of Dehli, it rivals that monument in beauty, and surpasses it in chasteness of design and execution.

I made an excursion from Agra to visit another of the palaces of the magnificent Acber, situated to the westward of Agra, and one of high interest, as containing remains, only in part injured by time, of the grand and noble schemes and plans of this illustrious warrior and legislator. This singular and impressive structure is built of a red granite, and has wonderfully withstood the assaults of time: it forms part of a palace on a very grand and extensive scale, erected by Acber, the greater part of which is now a heap of ruins. These, however, still retain visible traces of its former magnificence and splendour, and in its perfect state it must have exceeded any thing of the kind in Hindoostan.

The approach to this palace is through a very extensive park, once stocked with every species of game; the wall surrounding which is said to have been six koss, or nine English miles, in extent. The gate to enter this park is a fine pile of building of the red granite, surmounted by two pavilions: hence, through the park for half a mile, you see the remains of various buildings scattered around, and making your way through heaps of rubbish, you enter the great square or court, on the south side of which the grand hall of forty pillars is situated. All the buildings are of the same material, and the square is paved with large slabs of the same. The scene presented to the eye is singularly impressive and interesting; there is a grandeur, an awful vastness in the massive buildings which surround it, recalling to the mind by their unique form times far gone by. Add to this the now solemn silence which reigns around these halls, where once every thing was bustle, splendour, and carousing. All is passed away as a dream, but the hall still stands in proud yet gloomy majesty.

The hall of forty pillars consists of five tiers or stories, diminishing as they successively rise; the upper one being a square pavilion supported on four pillars; the lower row consists of seven.

There is a college founded by a Mahommedan saint, Shaik Selim Shaisteh, in the reign of Jehanguire: it is a very fine edifice, and is built in a square form, surrounded by a high wall, having three gateways, of which the grand gateway is magnificent beyond description. This is said to have been erected by a merchant, in consequence of a vow he made to the saint in question.

The village of Futtehpore is close under this gateway, but below it considerably. As we descended to this place we saw a very large ***bhowlee***, or well, used as a habitation during the excessive heats of summer. This was unusually large, having a circumference of ninety feet, with apartments all round, as far down as the level of the water, which might be thirty feet from the surface. There was a fine and broad stone staircase to descend to these apartments.

The tomb of the saint, Selim Shaisteh, is also near the village, formed of the purest white marble, and having round it a screen of the same material in a beautiful and rich fret-work. Entering the tomb, the floor is paved with yellow and white marble slabs. In the centre stands the cenotaph, with a canopy over it, supported by four pillars, overlaid with mother of pearl. Thousands of scraps of rags of all colours are tied to the windows of this tomb, which commemorate the vows and wishes of those who have here offered up their prayers.

Plate-XXIV

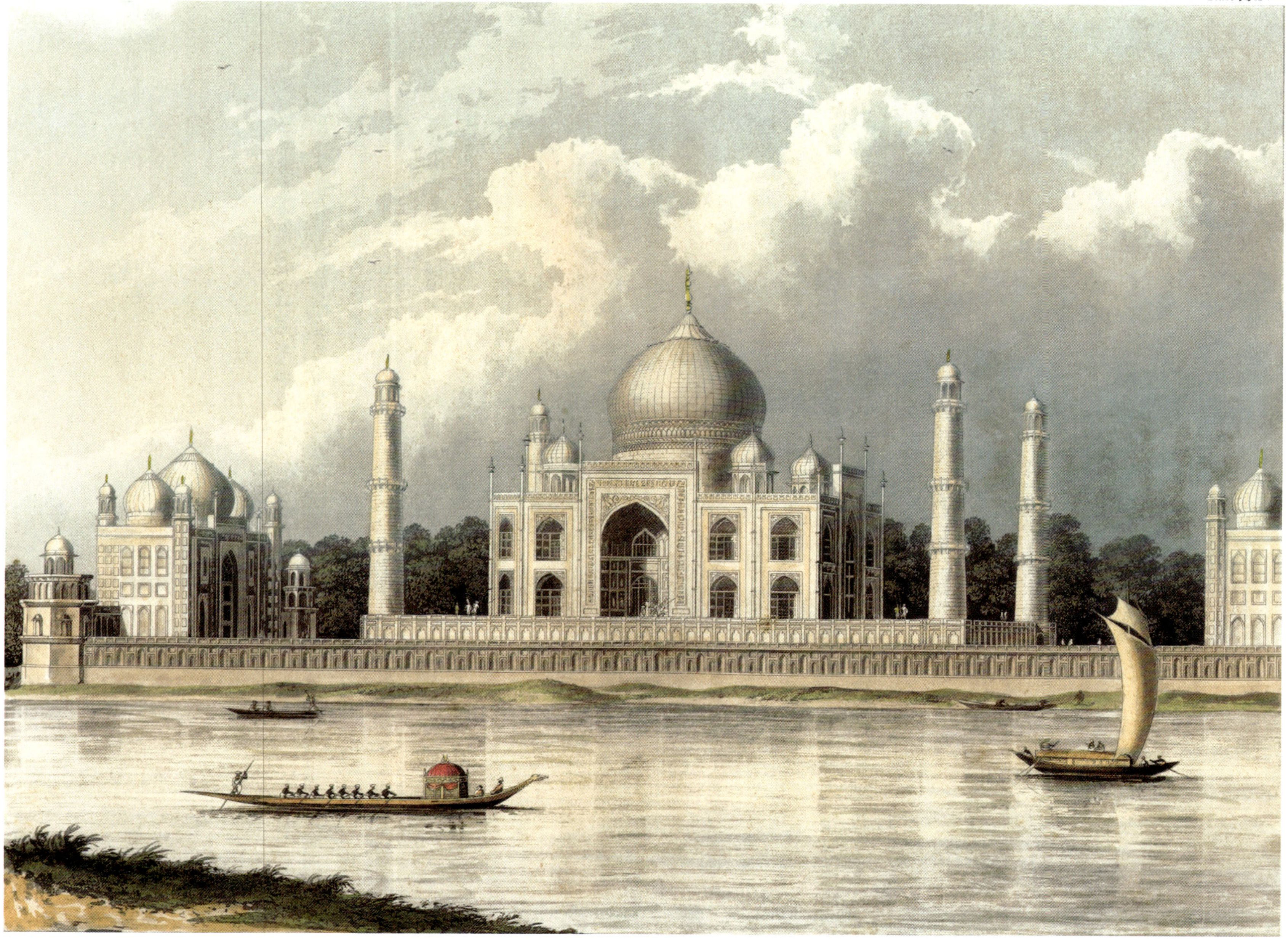

T. Sutherland sculp.t

THE TAJ MAHAL, TOMB of the EMPEROR SHAH JEHAN and his QUEEN.

Published Dec.r 1, 1824, by R. ACKERMANN, 101, Strand London.

The object which now calls our attention is the last in order, but of the highest beauty and interest of any structure yet raised and perfected by man in any region of the earth. It is only a tomb it is true, and contains the mouldering remains of what was noble, powerful, and beautiful: all these have passed away; but their names, their fame, their deeds remain; and these their works promise to hand down to distant ages their well-earned renown.

This tomb, the mausoleum of the emperor Shah Jehan and his favourite queen, Moomtaz ul Zemani (or Wonder of the Age), still exists, and in all its pristine beauty and perfection, as may be seen on reference to ***Plate*** XXIV. Time, with his efforts for a period of two hundred years, has as yet scarcely cast one sullying stain on its pure and lovely mass.

The first approach to this wonderful work by no means gives an idea of the splendid scene which is to be encountered: the road is impeded and the eye bewildered by the ruins of old brick and stone buildings, said to have once been a ***serai***, or place for the accommodation of travellers, or more probably pilgrims who came to visit this monument.

The main gateway is seen after passing these ruins; it faces nearly south, and is constructed with the red stone, but ornamented in panels of rich mosaic in various parts. It is a massive and lofty pile, and has apartments in its upper part, which can be ascended by a staircase, and from whence is a fine view of the tomb. This building is an octagon, and after passing under its grand portal, a scene bursts at once upon the eye, which dazzles the senses, and wraps every other feeling in that of astonishment. The Taje appears embosomed in a mass of foliage of a deep green at the further extremity of a large and handsome garden, with its lofty and elegant minarets, and its dome of extreme beauty and airy lightness; the whole of the purest white marble, richly inlaid in patterns of the semiprecious stones, as cornelian, jasper, onyx, and a variety of others of all hues.

A noble causeway of stone, raised considerably above the level of the garden, leads up to the main building, in the centre of which is a range of fountains, fifty in number; and midway a large basin, in which five other *jets-d'eau* of much greater height are thrown up.

The garden is filled with trees of almost every kind common to India; some bearing fruits, others perfuming the air with the odoriferous scents of their blossoms.

The Taje stands on two terraces; the lower and largest, of an oblong shape, is composed wholly of red stone: this is ascended by a flight of steps, and on reaching the summit, a large mosque is perceived at each end of it, which, in any other situation than so close to their lovely companion, would be considered as noble and splendid edifices. These may be ascended, and from their upper apartments command good views of the main building.

To the second or upper terrace, which has a height of about fifteen feet, you ascend by a flight of white marble steps: of these the upper slab or landing-place is one piece of pure white marble, nine feet square. This upper terrace is floored with a chequered pavement of red and white. Upon this stands the tomb, surrounded by a marble balustrade; at each angle of which rises a graceful minaret of three stories, in sweet proportions. At each story is a door, which opens on a balustraded balcony surrounding it. The summit is finished by a light pavilion, with a small golden ornament on its top.

All that now presents itself to the eye of the spectator is pure, unsullied, white marble, variously ornamented. The entrance to the building is on the side opposite to the grand gateway. It is a lofty portico, with an arch partaking of the form of the Gothic order, but differing in its proportions. Round the upper part of this are inscriptions in Arabic, done in black marble on the white ground.

Previous to viewing the grand chamber where the cenotaphs of the emperor and his queen are placed, it is usual to descend by a trap-door, situated in the entrance, into a gradually sloping passage, which conducts to the graves of the royal dead. The vault is lined with marble, and the pavement is of the same material. In the centre is the grave of the queen, for whom this mausoleum was solely intended; and the emperor's design was to have erected a similar edifice on the opposite bank of the Jumna, which river washes the foot of the Taje Mahal, and has a breadth of five or six hundred yards. The magnificent monarch did not mean to rest here; he meditated the joining the two mausoleums by a marble bridge, ornamented in the same splendid manner. Civil wars, caused by the rebellion of his four sons, suspended and finally put an end to these magnificent projects; and after a variety of sufferings, this unfortunate prince died in his prison in the fort of Agra, where he was held captive for seven years by his son Aurungzebe, then reigning emperor of Hindoostan.

Returning to the light of day, we entered the centre chamber. Description must here fail, nor can imagination figure any thing so solemnly grand, so stilly beautiful, as the scene thus suddenly presented to the view. Every tongue is mute, every sense lost in admiration. There are no gaudy, glaring decorations to arrest the vulgar eye; no glittering gold or silver to mark the riches of India's monarch. There is an awe, a feeling of deep reverence for the sacred spot on which we tread; an involuntary pause, a breathless suspension, and a recollection of, and recurrence to, events long past, which this scene conjures up in the breast of all who witness it for the first time.

Imagine a vaulted dome, of considerable height, of the most elegant and light Gothic architecture, all composed of the finest and the whitest marble; its form octagonal. In the centre stands a screen of the same, wrought into the most lovely patterns in fret-work, shewing a freedom of design and extreme minuteness of execution, unequalled in this or perhaps any other country. The form of this screen corresponds with that of the apartment, an octagon with four larger and four lesser faces. At each angle are two pilasters, on which the most beautiful running patterns of various flowers, true to nature, rise from the base of this screen, while a broad and rich border of the same surrounds the upper part. There are two arched door-ways in this screen opposite to each other, and over the top of which is a rich pattern of a stone perfectly resembling the purest matt gold. An entablature of the richest pattern surrounds the upper part of the screen; and in a border of pomegranate-flowers, which runs the whole length of it, every full-blown flower contains no less than sixty-one pieces of various coloured stones, according to the different shades required, and joined with such exactness and extreme nicety, that with a sharp-pointed penknife no seam can be distinguished. Within this screen are the two cenotaphs, on which the sculptor and mosaic artist have lavished all their skill. These are blocks of marble, and apparently one stone, ten feet in length by six broad. Below and above this are larger slabs, forming the pediment and cornice. A rich and large pattern is on the four faces of the cenotaphs, the two differing from each other; and the upper tablet on the queen's tomb has a cluster of flowers, arranged in the most elegant and free style of design; while that of the emperor is surmounted by the ***kullum daun,*** the distinguishing sign for a man, the woman not having this ornament. This screen had gates of silver in open filigree-work, which were carried off by some of the invaders of India. This tomb is not altogether the work or design of artists of Hindoostan: I have seen a list of the names of all the master-masons, sculptors, and artizans: the greater part are from Persia, Cabul, and some even from Constantinople, or Turkey, called by the Indians ***Roum.***

Some traces of similar inlaying and mosaic are met with at Dehli and in the palace at Agra; but the art is now lost, if it ever existed, among the Hindoostannies; and this tends to confirm the idea that it was the work of foreign artists.

The main part of this splendid edifice has fortunately been respected by all the invaders of Hindoostan, its great beauty being probably its protection. It is as pure and perfect as the day it was finished; and with common care, in the equal climate in which it is situated, it may last for centuries.

With the description of this wonder of the world, the Tour of the author closes. He is well aware that some errors may possibly be found in it; but these are almost inseparable from a work written, as this was, while moving rapidly through a country in which the subjects worthy of notice are so numerous and so widely scattered, that some, too many indeed, must be unavoidably passed unnoticed and unseen. As to the views, they are faithful copies from nature, in which no alterations have been made.

THE END.

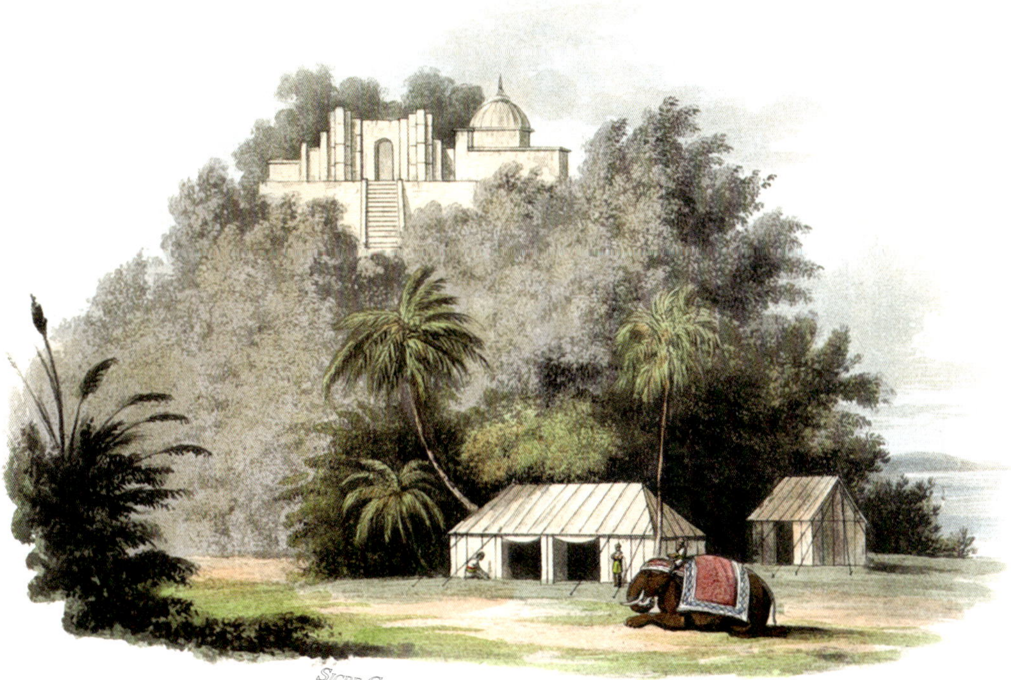

Sicre Gully Pass, between Bengal and Bahar.